PRAISE FOR *HOW BLACK HISTORY CAN SAVE YOUR LIFE*

"Spectacular! I've been following Brother Ernest Crim and his phenomenal posts for years, educating the community about Black history and events that happened in our country on topics that I never knew about or even considered before! After reading the pages of this book I can honestly say he's continued his legacy of excellence through education! Not only will the information he provided build you up and reinforce your understanding of self in a world designed to break you down, but his words will also broaden your understanding of your past, present, and future. Not to mention, it can truly save your life!"

—**Mo'Nique**, Academy Award-winning actress, comedian, executive producer, and bestselling author

"In *How Black History Can Save Your Life*, Ernest Crim III takes readers on a journey through his life, blending personal stories with untold lessons from Black history. With great insight and wisdom, Crim offers practical tools to navigate tough conversations about race and identity, inspiring hope and meaningful change. This book is a powerful guide to using history's lessons to thrive today."

—**Kimberly Latrice Jones**, *New York Times* bestselling author of *I'm Not Dying With You Tonight*

"Ernest Crim's story is both urgent and indispensable. To overlook his story is to ignore a fundamental reality of our society—one that, if left unaddressed, threatens not just some, but all of us."

—**Joy DeGruy**, author of *Post Traumatic Slave Syndrome*

"It is a very personal, readable, and accessible tool for my ever-evolving awakening to the other America, where a walk in the park with your wife on a perfect summer afternoon can turn ugly in an instant. I have grandsons who will grow up perceived as Black; this feels like required reading for me. Their journey will likely parallel Ernest's journey, but if we get our head out of the sand, it will be a softer ride. Check it out."

—**Larry Andersen**, producer of PBS documentary *Divided We Fall*

"*How Black History Can Save Your Life* by Ernest Crim III is a must-read for anyone needing a guidepost on how to navigate and awaken to their true power. Every Black child in America and parent should have this book as a staple in their home library! It is a powerful coming of age (auto) biography of the deep-seated hatred Black people face in America! Nothing is wrong with Black people... Something happened to Black people! *Ase.*"

—**Philippe Matthews**, host of *The Philippe Matthews Show*

"Most books of this type, I think, tend to either follow the cerebral or left-brain path of analysis and factual consideration, or the right-brain trail that focuses on the feelings and emotional content involved. As improbable as it might seem, Ernest finds a way to incorporate both sides without either detracting from the message carried by the other. In fact, he manages to have them complement and strengthen each other. As I began to read, I was prepared for a litany of the usual suspects and a set of arguments which are significant but ordinary. But Ernest found a way to constantly surprise and intrigue me."

—**Michael Rakowsky**, House of Delegate member at The People

HOW
BLACK
HISTORY
CAN SAVE YOUR LIFE

HOW BLACK HISTORY CAN SAVE YOUR LIFE

From the Talk to George Floyd,
Everything You Need to Know to
Deescalate a Racist Situation

ERNEST CRIM III, MA

MIAMI

Copyright © 2025 by Ernest Crim III.
Published by Mango Publishing, a division of Mango Publishing Group, Inc.

Cover Design: Elina Diaz
Cover Photo/Illustration: stock.adobe.com/OlgaTsikarishvili
Layout & Design: Elina Diaz

Mango is an active supporter of authors' rights to free speech and artistic expression in their books. The purpose of copyright is to encourage authors to produce exceptional works that enrich our culture and our open society.

Uploading or distributing photos, scans or any content from this book without prior permission is theft of the author's intellectual property. Please honor the author's work as you would your own. Thank you in advance for respecting our author's rights.

For permission requests, please contact the publisher at:
Mango Publishing Group
5966 South Dixie Highway, Suite 300
Miami, FL 33143
info@mango.bz

For special orders, quantity sales, course adoptions and corporate sales, please email the publisher at sales@mango.bz. For trade and wholesale sales, please contact Ingram Publisher Services at customer.service@ingramcontent.com or +1.800.509.4887.

How Black History Can Save Your Life: From the Talk to George Floyd, Everything You Need to Know to Deescalate a Racist Situation

Library of Congress Cataloging-in-Publication number: 2024949709
ISBN: (print) 978-1-68481-732-0, (ebook) 978-1-68481-733-7
BISAC category code: HIS056000 HISTORY / African American & Black

For those ancestors who are nameless to my memory, but alive through me, who last lived on the continent of Africa before being forced, against their will, to a place that intended on using them as chattel; and for my descendants who will carry the baton. Let this be your guide…

TABLE OF CONTENTS

Preface, 2024   13

Introduction   20

Part I   23

Chapter 1...**when I was told I was bad**   24

Chapter 2...**when I wanted my friends to sleep over**   35

Chapter 3...**when I wanted breakfast**   41

Chapter 4...**when I was on my way to the White House**   48

Chapter 5...**when he was told to go back**   56

Chapter 6...**when I was cute for a Black guy**   71

Part II   84

Chapter 7...**when I was acting white**   85

Chapter 8...**when I was driving while Black**   105

Chapter 9...**when Aaron taught me**   121

Chapter 10...**when I was first called nigger**   128

Chapter 11...**when Ghetto Bros and Big Booty Hoes partied**   140

Chapter 12...**when he changed his name from Gerald to Abdul**   152

Chapter 13...**when Jena 6 happened**   162

Chapter 14...**when Tupac was wrong**   173

Part III 197

Chapter 15…**when I noticed white-on-Black crime** 198

Chapter 16…**when it kept happening again, and again, and again** 217

Chapter 17…**when the hate was inherited** 249

Chapter 18…**when we had another Red Summer** 272

Chapter 19…**when I was faced with a hate crime** 283

Epilogue 297

Acknowledgments 304

About the Author 305

Works Cited 306

PREFACE, 2024

When I first published *Black History Saved My Life: How My Viral Hate Crime Led to an Awakening* (an earlier edition of this book) toward the end February of 2020, I had no idea what awaited us soon after, with the world shutting down due to the COVID-19 outbreak, or three months later, after George Floyd was murdered by a Minneapolis police officer, which subsequently ignited the largest civil rights demonstrations in world history.

I had actually finished writing this book at the end of 2018, but I didn't do anything with it for most of 2019. That year would consist of me teaching, speaking, and procrastinating. I also decided, on a whim, to run for city council in Joliet as a write-in candidate.

I was, as my students would say, "doing too much." And I didn't know what to do next. As someone who was set on self-publishing, I was confused about my next steps, but I knew for sure I had accomplished the most difficult part of publishing, and that's writing a manuscript. 2019 came and nearly went, and by the fourth quarter I had resolved that I needed to get this book out, not just for myself, but for my kids, my descendants, and for the world. I truly believed then, like I do now, that the information within this book was that transformative. I say this because you will be learning Black history from a first-person perspective, as I grappled with the legacy of racism, anti-Blackness, and the rich legacy of African history I descend from, as I grappled with the reality of facing a hate crime that subsequently went viral. This adds a new layer, because as a former public school history teacher of twelve years, I can tell you with the utmost certainty that history curriculums across America are not only Eurocentric and from an American exceptionalist perspective, they are also boring and taught in chronological order. Our kids don't often see how the past connects to their lives. This book addresses that and makes the reader feel as if history is alive, because it is. This book will force you to reflect on your own life at the ages of the various experiences I detail, and make you see it through a racial lens. It will feel personal to you because it is—and because it should be.

When I noticed a college friend had published a book, I reached out to her to see if she could help me. Jonnita Condra made this process easier than I anticipated. After meeting with her in October 2019, and receiving a self-publishing action plan, I was ready to go and became more motivated to get this book out right away. As fate would have it, February was coming up, and it felt right to publish it during Black History Month. There were some mishaps and errors along the way, but I'll never forget the feeling of finally seeing it on Amazon for the first time in February 2020, before exiting the car on a Saturday for a Black History Month event in Bolingbrook.

Now that the book was approved and scheduled to be released later that month, I had to figure out how to notify the public. Some of you reading this might know me from social media, television, or a speaking engagement. As of 2024, I have nearly one million followers across my social media accounts and my content reaches roughly four million people each month. However, when I published the book, my reach was nowhere near what it is now. At that time of publication, my biggest following was on Facebook, with roughly 7,000 followers. Of those followers, I would reckon that nearly 90 percent were from Joliet and Chicago, and they were likely aware of me due to my reputation as an educator, my grassroots activism, or the viral hate crime video. My Instagram was hovering around 3,000 followers. That means my total reach was roughly 10,000. I didn't care, though. I didn't have a marketing budget, team, or publisher to help, but I had passion, purpose, determination, and a message that needed to be heard by the world.

Preface, 2024

When COVID-19 happened, the world stopped, and virtual learning commenced. It was then that I was faced with hate again. In April of 2020, two months after I published my book, while meeting with my Black Student Union club virtually, we were Zoom-bombed by racist trolls who infiltrated our meeting and began to type "NAIL NIGGERS TO THE CROSS" repeatedly in the chat. What's more, they also shared their screen and displayed pornography. Yeah, I was the target of a hate crime yet again. Unlike the one my wife and I had encountered four years before, this time it was virtual, with my colleagues and students. We were shaken and traumatized. Like my previous experience, this got the attention of CBS's Chicago affiliate as well. None of us knew at the moment, but we would all be collectively impacted by another racist incident a little more than a month later.

The video of George Floyd being murdered by police officer Derek Chauvin on May 25, 2020, sent shockwaves through the world. Many of us had seen this type of grotesque imagery before, but this heinous lynching was different for a variety of reasons. Firstly, it appeared at a time when everyone was locked down, working virtually, and mostly sitting around scrolling on social media. Unlike the previously recorded lynchings I had seen online, this one happened with a captive audience that reached outside of the Black community, to other concerned people who had previously advocated for similar social and political issues. There was no going back to work the next day and "forgetting" it for eight hours. We all had to sit with this and decide what to do next. We also had the unfortunate reality of having a supposed "leader" in Donald Trump—a crazed, maniacal, sociopathic convicted felon of a president whose very presence led to the rise of hate crimes like the ones I encountered. Although he said that he felt "very bad" after seeing the video, and issued a statement that claimed he was sympathetic, I do not believe that he disapproved of the callous behavior of Derek Chauvin. If he did, he would not currently advocate for giving police officers full immunity.

Like many people around the world, I took to the streets with my fellow comrades in Joliet and protested, for what seemed like every day that summer. Not only were we concerned about Floyd's murder, but we had Ahmaud Arbery and Breonna Taylor's murders on our minds as well. The collective consciousness of people appeared to be at its apex.

As we have mostly gone back to our "regular" lives since then, that time serves as a constant reminder to me about what we can accomplish when we are not ensnared by the responsibilities, commitments, preoccupations, and meaningless tasks that are required for us to live and survive in a capitalist society.

In the moment of 2020, I began to ponder whether my own community had faced a similar tragedy. All politics is local, and as Dr. King once said, "a threat to justice anywhere, is a threat to justice everywhere." So, why would I assume that Joliet was immune to such behavior? Soon after, I became aware of Eric Lurry.

Brotha Lurry was a Black man in Joliet who had been arrested for drugs in January of 2020. While in custody in the back seat, he decided to swallow the drugs, presumably in an effort to destroy the evidence. In a video that was released that summer, while we were protesting for George Floyd, the officers were shown slapping him around, holding his nose, and placing a crowbar in his mouth to retrieve the drugs before he passed away. Where was the Narcan? It did not appear as if they were trying to save his life, or that they had any concern for his well-being. Rather, it appeared as if they were trying to retrieve evidence for an arrest. Unsurprisingly, none of the officers were ever held accountable. Needless to say, our protests during the summer of 2020 in Joliet became more personal. From there, my activism became more focused as I connected with fellow activists Alonzo Waheed, Karl Farrell, Tycee Bell, and Eric Lurry's wife Nicole, and joined a Chicago-based organization called Equity and Transformation.

By the end of 2020, many of us were relieved to know that Donald Trump wasn't going to be reelected, but by January of 2021, we realized that he would not go away easy, as some of his supporters attempted to violently take over the Capitol in DC with chants of "Hang Mike Pence" (Trump's vice president during his 2016–2020 term) as they stood outside with gallows. This situation was even more personal to me, considering that US Representative Bennie Thompson is my great-uncle (my grandmother's younger brother). Most might now know him as the chairman of the January 6 Committee, but on January 6, 2021, our family group chat was nervously awaiting a response text from our grandmother to be sure that he was safe. Had things gone slightly differently, he might not have been here with us today.

My book hadn't even been out for a year at this point, and I already felt overwhelmed seeing many of the same instances I wrote about repeating themselves cyclically. I grew frustrated because, despite all of these issues, I felt that there wasn't enough genuine urgency in our education system. Having learned from my failed run for city council, I knew the importance of focusing on and mastering one thing as a contribution to a team fighting for justice. As such, I decided to hone in on my passion for education even more. I had already been teaching from a liberatory perspective through anti-racist narratives and principles extracted from Black history. The only problem was, I was restricted because I was still a full-time public school teacher. Sure, I had the freedom to teach in this manner in my classroom, but having seen colleagues with Blue Lives Matter flags in their classrooms and having heard some of them spew historically conservative rhetoric (like claiming that the Civil War was about states' rights and not slavery), I wasn't content with my class being the only one that taught the truth. From my perspective, our students should be learning how to prevent more events like George Floyd's murder, Trump's ascension, and the January 6 riot, as well as how to build a system that serves all of humanity equitably. After my immediate supervisor sought to pacify my goal of restructuring our US history curriculum, I felt an urgency to leave the class to engage in public speaking, consulting, and engaging in advocacy full-time. I began to realize the limits of changing a system from within. I realized that what I was seeking was to reform an institution that truly needed a revolution. Our country's education system—much like our political, policing, and healthcare systems—is an institution that is content with the status quo and preparing our kids to continue a way of life that is failing and sinking right before our eyes. I had to go.

By late March of 2021, after a year of remote teaching, we had gone back to teaching in person. Around that time, I had been seeing the rise of TikTok. Before the shutdown, my students told me about it, and often showed me videos they found hilarious, but I didn't get how it worked or truly pay attention to it. However, as 2021 progressed, I saw more viral TikTok videos make their way to my Instagram feed, but I wasn't truly intrigued until I saw other history teachers (like Coach Curtis and Emily Glankler) using it as a tool to educate. It became practical to me then.

On March 25, 2021, I posted my first TikTok video. Because it was the anniversary of the day one of my favorite historical figures became an ancestor, I spoke about Ida B. Wells, with a video titled, "Ida B. Wells was a G!" Within a few days, this video had amassed nearly 10,000 views and had instantly become my most watched Black history video on any platform. I had been posting Black history and political content on Facebook and Instagram since August of 2016, but nothing I posted had caught on that fast, besides the video of my hate crime.

I was sold on the potential of using this app to teach, not only what I was teaching in my class, but also what I did not have the time to teach, for the purpose of helping liberate our minds and collective consciousness. I realized that I now had the potential to reach the millions of people I needed to in order to get this message out. Rather than just teaching thirty kids per period, or 120–150 per school year, I could travel around the country to speak to and teach hundreds of children across the country, or I could reach several thousand, or million, every time I made an educational post on an app originally created solely for the purpose of entertainment.

Within a few months, brands sent me items for free. By the end of 2021, I had my first brand deal. By July of 2022, I had enough followers and subsequent income from brand deals, speaking engagements, and book sales to walk away from my full-time job as a public school teacher and become a full-time public teacher of the world, author, content creator, activist, and promoter of social justice issues. Additionally, since creating content, writing this book, and resigning from my teaching job, I've been fortunate to speak to audiences across the world, from the UK to Harvard University, and I've even shared the stage with Colin Kaepernick. I've created content for companies like HBO, Hulu, Disney, Paramount, and the History Channel, and I have been featured on CNN, *The Washington Post*, ABC, WGN, PBS, CBS, and NBC. It is precisely because of this immense difference in reach that I felt it was appropriate to rerelease this book. I'm probably known more for my digital content than the content within this book, and I aim to change that. Those sixty- to 120-second videos are great, but they are only touching the surface.

I recall a friend once asking me what my plans were for my next book, shortly after releasing this one. I told him that I planned on promoting this one for the latter part of the decade because the information was that important, and I felt it needed significant care and attention to do it properly. I still feel that way. That's exactly why this new edition was done.

While this book mostly covers the racial experiences of my life from ages six through twenty-eight (1993–2016), it is my belief that lessons I've extracted from them are universal, and unfortunately still applicable to the moment in which you are reading it. The hate crime my wife and I experienced occurred in 2016, yet the FBI reported that, as of 2022, hate crimes are still on the rise, with Black people being targeted more than any other group. We have work to do, y'all. Not tomorrow, but now. And my hope is that this book gives you a better idea of your experiences, our experiences, and the role that you play on this collective journey to liberate us all.

INTRODUCTION

I was driving around aimlessly after I pulled out of the Farmers Insurance parking lot on Jefferson Avenue in Joliet, Illinois, in 2017. I had just called out of work because tears kept flowing. This was the true definition of a mental health day. Although it was about seven months after the hate crime that changed my life (in which my wife and I were called "nigger" several times and spat on by a white woman named Jessica Lynn Sanders on a video that subsequently was posted online and seen over twenty-five million times), my emotions were still in a whirlwind. Some days I was fine, and others I was not. This was one of those days.

I didn't feel protected. I didn't feel accepted. I didn't feel like being the token Black guy at work again. I didn't feel like being the one everyone depended on to rescue their Black male students. I didn't feel like experiencing the anxiety and stress of knowing everyone knew what had happened to me, yet weren't acknowledging the hurt and pain I endured daily since the incident. I didn't feel like being viewed as "the angry Black man" or "too Black" because I demanded equity for all children, especially those Black kids with whom I share similar experiences.

I was tired.

I drove into a random parking lot on Larkin Avenue, went to Google, and searched for "Black therapist in Joliet" and scrolled. I had only used my health insurance to meet with medical doctors, so I was completely lost in this instance. Eventually, I spoke to a Black therapist, who listened to me, but confirmed that she couldn't meet with me in person because she only took PPO insurance. I drove home and cried again. By now it was 10:00

a.m. and I was lost. Then it hit me. Why not do what I did throughout college as a rapper?

Why not write about how I was feeling? I grabbed my notebook as my last refuge and began to pour my heart out to relieve myself of the frustration and hurt I felt. Only this time, the words didn't rhyme, but they flowed rhythmically to the tempo of my soul.

As I continued writing, month after month, and then transferring the content to my laptop, I began to reflect on my life's experiences, and it was then that I realized that the hate crime that my wife and I were the targets of on July 30, 2016 (that would eventually shock the world and go viral, amassing over twenty-five million views) wasn't just a singular act. I realized I had been dealing with racism my whole life. Every racist blow I endured made me stronger, though. Each incident led me down a path of self-discovery and knowledge that would empower me.

What started off as my first therapy session quickly turned into my first book. I wrote this book to make sense of my life. I wrote this book because there are millions of people suffering, who have had similar experiences, and don't realize that there are others out there who have dealt with the same thing. I wrote this because our history in America is often erroneously sectioned off into three periods—slavery, Jim Crow, and the Civil Rights era—with the presupposition that everything was solved through the activism of the '50s and '60s. I wrote this because writing and Black history saved my life. I hope that reading this saves your life as well.

"If you don't know who you are, anyone can name you, and if anyone can name you, you will answer to anything."

—African proverb

PART I

CHAPTER 1
...WHEN I WAS TOLD I WAS BAD

I stood there with the phone in my hand, trembling, with my left fist balled, teeth clenched, sweating profusely, trying to register what had just happened. I started off recording the woman's racist barrage of "niggers," but never did it occur to me that this would escalate to her spitting on my wife and me. I looked down to ensure the phone was still recording.

I looked to my left and noticed that my wife had a similar expression. Dejection, sorrow, and infuriation were worn like a mask on Halloween. I began to wonder if anyone would come to our aid. Then I realized that the cornhole game we had been in was situated away from the larger crowd. We were isolated. What should I do? If I reacted the way I wanted to, would anyone believe me? Would anyone support me? Would the security guards in the distance even come to our aid, or would they assume I was the one who had initiated such a heinous criminal act?

It was a perfect metaphor for life as a Black man and woman in America. A white woman harassed and assaulted us and no one came to help, and so it persisted. The only people in the vicinity were her two Black friends, who defended her "nigger" barrage, and a white female friend who stayed in the back, as if to symbolize that it wasn't her problem to deal with.

All of this because a Black person dared to pick up an errant bean bag that had been previously used by a racist white woman.

We had just wanted to enjoy ourselves before returning to work in a couple of weeks. We just wanted to play a game of cornhole before leaving to pick up our kids. We just wanted, for one day, to not have to be reminded that we live in a racist society.

I only had a split second to decide what to do. In that moment, it was clear that my wife and I were the victims of racism, but this was not the first or only time. Sometimes it was subtle, other times overt. As the woman spat at us, I was taken back to all the moments and all the decisions leading up to this one and I realized that I had first experienced racism, not at twenty-eight, but rather, at six years old.

***

"Hello?"

My mom answered the house phone with a cautious, code-switched tone, and the type of trepidation that emerged in an era before ubiquitous caller IDs.

"Hi, yes, Mrs. Crim?! It's Mrs. Sullivan again."

My mom—a Chicago public school educator of thirteen years at that point in 1993—let out a deep sigh and clenched her teeth, attempting to conceal her anger and frustration, but she had quite frankly reached her boiling point. Mrs. Sullivan, who was seemingly in her mid-30s to 40s, was a white woman, as were most of the teachers at Mount Greenwood Elementary at the time. She didn't seem to understand me, or care to.

"Yes, this is she," my mom responded.

"Mrs. Crim, Ernest was really bad again today. He just wouldn't sit still and he kept distracting his other classmates. I just don't know what to do at this po—"

"Mrs. Sullivan." My mom interrupted with a stern and direct tone. The code she had answered with had been broken.

"Since this school year started in September, you have called me on almost a regular basis, telling me how bad my son is. It is now November. So, look. I want to make this very clear, because I've tolerated this for as long as I can. My son *is not* bad. Yes, he has done some questionable things, but he is just a young active boy. He is *very* smart, and as an educator, I would expect you to understand that children, especially boys, are easily distracted when they are doing work that doesn't challenge them."

Mrs. Sullivan tried to interject and get in a word, but my mom wasn't having it.

"Don't call my house again telling me how bad my son is. Tell me the great work he's done. Tell me about his behavior, but don't you ever utter those words again about my child. You know what, when I get a moment, I'll bring you a copy of Dr. Jawanzaa Kunjufu's book, *Countering The Conspiracy to Destroy Black Boys.*"

"Uh… That won't be necessary. Thank you for your time. You have a good day," Mrs. Sullivan responded shyly and submissively.

"Goodbye."

My mom slammed the phone onto the receiver so hard, she almost unmounted it from the wall.

"Baby, you okay?" my dad said to my mom, concerned, as he sat down with a plate of food.

"Yeah. I'm fine now, but I'm gon' need another copy of this book." My mom sat down with Dr. Kunjufu's book, which she had ironically been reading at the time Mrs. Sullivan called.

Mrs. Sullivan never called our house again, and my mom followed up that conversation with a visit that resulted in her delivering Dr. Kunjufu's book, as well several 100-piece puzzles to keep me occupied when I finished my work. Who knows if Mrs. Sullivan ever read the book, but one thing is for sure, and that's that she never conspired to destroy this Black boy again, whether consciously or subconsciously.

The tenets of the book, published in 1985, were still as relevant as ever regarding my treatment by Mrs. Sullivan. Dr. Kunjufu plainly laid out how Black boys are often (not always) mislabeled as having ADHD, or needing special education, because of what's viewed as hyperactivity and misbehavior. According to Dr. Kunjufu, this misbehavior is often the result of Black boys not being challenged academically and intellectually, or having their differences misdiagnosed as deficiencies. As a result, educators can view a Black boy's preference for hands-on activities and kinesthetic learning as disruption and worthy of a discipline referral. Whereas a white boy might get the benefit of the doubt, the Black boy will not. Seriously, expecting a child of any race or age to sit still for six to seven hours a day is flawed pedagogy and an unrealistic expectation. Understandably, Black boys might prefer tasks that are more personally interesting, and usually without an authority figure's approval.

This veering off, which through a conscious and caring teacher's lens would be labeled as intellectual curiosity, is viewed as insubordination and misbehavior through a biased lens. Dr. Kunjufu also describes how Black boys are usually enthusiastic learners until they catch what he diagnoses as "Fourth Grade Syndrome" as they transition from primary to intermediate school. This can be caught sooner, or later, in educational settings, but Dr. Kunjufu's theory additionally states that as boys grow older, the need for a positive male influence grows. This is particularly true for young Black boys, who greatly benefit from a positive Black male role model. According to Dr. Kunjufu, Black boys' eagerness to learn greatly subsides as they continue to be taught primarily by white women, who comprise roughly 80 percent of public school teachers, and based on the results of our education system, it would appear that they are not conscious of the harm their actions have caused. This is not due to the teacher's race, however. Children will love and appreciate those who genuinely love and appreciate them the most, regardless of their ethnicity, race, or gender, but what has been observed is that Black male students lose trust in these teachers. For Black boys, the questions and natural proclivity to be engaged in class can have them transition from curiously asking, "What does that mean, teacher?" to vexingly asking, "What's the point?" Because what Black boys have noticed in classroom settings, especially while being taught by some white women, is that they are ridiculed for what is perceived as misbehavior more than they are praised for what they perceive as positive participation in their classroom.

The question remains: just why was I, a Black American child born in 1987 in a predominantly Black community on the far South Side, attending a school called Mount Greenwood, where I was mostly taught by white educators at a mostly white school, when prior to *Brown vs. Board of Education*, Black teachers were 35–50 percent of the teacher workforce in segregated states? Furthermore, why was this the case when countless studies reveal that Black children perform better academically, exhibit better problem-solving skills, are less likely to receive disciplinary infractions, and are more likely to go to college when taught by Black educators? In the context of Black boys having the lowest graduation rate of any demographic and being half of those expelled from preschool in 2021, it would appear that there is something more systemic at play.

It's important to establish that Africans always prioritized education in America, during enslavement, and immediately after. Education is such a cornerstone of our culture that it was made illegal, most infamously after the Stono Rebellion of 1739 where enslaved Africans united to revolt in South Carolina. The immediate aftermath led to the passage of the Negro Act of 1740, which penalized assembling, independent movement, growing food, economic independence, and reading and writing. There was an understanding that these Africans, if able to read and write in a common language (since they were captured from various ethnic groups and tribes that spoke different languages in Africa), would use the information they obtained to unite and likely assemble to incessantly revolt against a system that sought to enslave and disenfranchise them perpetually.

One couple that personifies this commitment to education and tutelage excellently is John Berry Meachum and his wife Mary Meachum. They were so committed to educating Black folks who were enslaved that when Missouri made it illegal to do so, they opened a floating freedom school on a steamboat that was nestled on the Mississippi River in 1847. An intentional usage of education for liberation by enslaved Africans necessitated the passage of law by a settler colonial state for the purpose of codifying and signaling to whites the need to punish Black folks. These constructed barriers have never historically defeated the spirit of determination and fortitude of Africans, however.

When chattel slavery was abolished in 1865, one of the first things we did as people, besides attempt to find family members who were sold away, was attempt to get an education so that we could learn how to read and write and be aware and knowledgeable. Booker T. Washington, the founder of Tuskegee University, a Historically Black College and University (HBCU), exemplifies this well as someone who was born enslaved and resolved to walk 500 miles to Hampton Normal Agricultural Institute in Virginia to receive an education.

Oftentimes, those who educated us were our fellow Black brethren who were fortunate enough to receive an education, as was the case with Carter G. Woodson, the father of Black History Month, who used his education, and ability to read and write, to read the newspaper to the elders in his community that he worked in coal mines with. Yes, in some cases, white co-conspirators joined in to assist with this process (such as Spelman College, which was founded in 1881 by two white teachers named Sophia B. Packard and Harriet E. Giles, who received support and funding from the infamous robber baron John D. Rockefeller).

Throughout the period of Jim Crow segregation, when we were explicitly barred from attending school with our white counterparts in the early- to mid-1900s, we educated our own out of both desire and necessity. However, something changed during our pursuit of educational equity in the 1940s and '50s. While some of our forefathers fought to have Black-led institutions integrated with the resources and tax money we paid and were owed, others desired white proximity, because there was an assumption that we'd have access to greater resources, while others desired it because, as the old saying goes, "they believed that white man's ice was colder." That is, some perceptibly concluded that by gaining proximity to whiteness, we were making progress as people. That argument maintains that it would be best to attend their schools, as opposed to maintaining or building our own through the equitable distribution of resources. We must remember that our scope of education, from ancient Kemet's Per-Ankh House of Life educational institutions to the "University" of Sankoré, and the architectural ingenuity of the people of Benin who once built a wall that some scholars claimed was four times larger than the Great Wall of China, before it was destroyed by the British, was never based on reliance on whiteness.

However, with the *Brown vs. Board of Education* Supreme Court decision, which ruled that segregated schools were unconstitutional, the priority became disrupting Black institutions, rather than funding them, and shipping Black children to disproportionately funded white schools, rather than equitable fund distribution or forcing white children to attend schools in Black neighborhoods. Likewise, this Supreme Court decision, having occurred prior to outlawing housing discrimination (with the Fair Housing Act of 1968) and the practice of redlining, was seemingly counterproductive, since children will almost always prefer to attend schools in their immediate communities. Resources continued to flow to white schools, and now, unlike any other time, so did our children and the educators. Prior to this decision in 1954, there were about 82,000 Black educators across the country, but by 1964 that number was nearly cut in half with about 44,000 remaining. 38,000 of those teachers, who were no longer in the field, had been systematically removed by white administrators who fired them, even though they were often more qualified.

This Supreme Court decision, although it had the best intentions, failed our educational institutions and children because it was carried out for the purpose of maintaining white supremacy, rather than centering humanity and the Black American community that had been at a systemic disadvantage for centuries. Likewise, it put our children in harm's way in the hope that white Americans in these intentionally segregated communities, by being forced to attend school with children whose parents they were actively lynching with immunity, and subjecting to inhumane levels of violence and systemic disenfranchisement, would have a change of heart, gain a love and appreciation for all of humanity regardless of melanin content, and understand the error of their ways. From my perspective, white Americans who lived in those communities who already had an appreciation for all of humanity did not need to be convinced by forced integration.

We lost many of our Black-led schools, premier administrators, and teachers during this process, including schools such as Howalton, which was founded by three Black women (June Howe-White, Doris Allen-Anderson, and Charlotte B. Stratton) in 1947 and lasted until 1986 (a year before I was born). Howalton was Chicago's oldest African

American private, nonsectarian school. This school received national recognition for its student-centered approach to pedagogy that led to the highest first-grade reading scores in the Chicago area in 1974 and 1975. However, the economic issues that plagued our community in the '80s, along with the need to charge tuition to remain open, caused Howalton to close its doors as Black folks opted to attend neighborhood schools, or white schools (public or private) that they were permitted to attend in growing numbers following the *Brown vs. Board of Education* decision.

For the public schools that remained open in our community, they largely remained disproportionately underfunded. And not just that; *Brown vs. Board of Education* didn't wave a magic wand. Following this decision, many political leaders, and white families, were resistant to Black children attending their schools, so it remained a battle that was fought in various districts across the country. For instance, twenty years later, in 1974, there was another Supreme Court decision that challenged and reinterpreted the *Brown* decision. This Supreme Court ruling, *Milliken vs. Bradley*, resolved that suburban school district interdistrict busing to schools outside of the city (Detroit) to resolve segregation was unconstitutional. Furthermore, city lines could not be redrawn for the purpose of addressing school segregation. In response to this decision, Justice Thurgood Marshall, who was instrumental in the *Brown vs. Board of Education* victory, stated, "The very evil that *Brown* was aimed at will not be cured, but will be perpetuated."

My mom and dad, who were born in 1957 and 1956 respectively, represent the impact and lack of implementation of *Brown vs. Board of Education* in Chicago. They attended underfunded Black schools on the South Side of Chicago (my dad, for instance, attended Wacker Elementary and Fernwood Elementary, whereas my mom attended Stagg Elementary), and for at least a few years, received instruction out of a trailer that was next to their school building. These trailers were labeled Willis Wagons after the superintendent of schools at the time, Benjamin Willis, who held the position from 1953–1966 and

...when I was told I was bad   33

was someone who, along with the nefarious Mayor Richard Daley, ordered the implementation of these trailers. These Willis Wagons were used by Black students due to overcrowding and the City of Chicago's refusal to build new facilities, fund them properly, or integrate them in white schools outside of their neighborhoods. Much like the failed implementation of *Brown vs. Board of Education* on a broader scale, these wagons were used for the maintenance of white superiority.

This act of political neglect culminated in Chicago's Freedom Day School Boycott protest on October 22, 1963, roughly eight years after *Brown vs. Board of Education*. With this protest, 250,000 mostly Black Chicago students and residents walked out and protested to demand an end to funding inequity and segregated schools. It would not be until January of 1968, however, that my elementary school (Mount Greenwood) would integrate. This was fourteen years after *Brown vs. Board of Education*'s mandate, and the white residents of Mount Greenwood didn't take it lightly. For instance, the eleven Black students who integrated the school my sister and I went on to attend twenty-something years later were met by protests, not by the students themselves, but by adults—the same adults who would teach their children to hold the same insidiously racist mindsets. White adults spray-painted "White Power" on the side of the school, held signs that read, "Mount Greenwood weather forecast: dark and stormy," threw objects at Black students as they arrived at the school, yelled, "Nigger, go back to your old schools," and assaulted white counter-protesters who stood in solidarity with those eleven Black students.

I didn't know Ms. Sullivan personally, or where she was born and raised, so I can't say for sure if she was a product of the very environment that she taught in. Was she a child who grew up in Mount Greenwood and witnessed these protests? I don't know. Were her actions an explicit act of racial bias and racism, or an inability to learn the varying learning styles of her male students? I don't know. But what I do know is that the treatment I was subjected to then was historically consistent with those white Americans who have historically undermined Black intelligence and ingenuity with pseudoscience, and those who have, whether consciously or unconsciously, conspired to destroy Black boys. But this Black boy could not be destroyed, because his village was too strong.

CHAPTER 2
...WHEN I WANTED MY FRIENDS TO SLEEP OVER

I was simply coloring Santa the same color as me. It only made sense, in my opinion. I had brown skin, so surely, he should too. "Santa's not Black, he's white!" Jerry said with a chuckle as we sat at the same table in Mrs. Sullivan's first-grade class.

With a scrunched face, I murmured loud enough for him to hear, "The Black Santa Claus delivers to Black kids and the white Santa Claus delivers to white kids." I had heard my dad play "Santa Claus, Go Straight to the Ghetto!" by James Brown enough times to know that Santa Claus did in fact look like me and delivered gifts to my neighborhood.

I didn't think anything of it at the time, though. I was only six years old, and Jerry and his twin brother Jake were two of my best friends. I didn't even know what racism was.

I had befriended them while attending the predominantly white (Irish) Mount Greenwood Elementary School on the southwest side of Chicago in the mid-1990s, which had a vastly different racial makeup than my all-Black West Pullman neighborhood on the far South Side of Chicago. Like typical boys at this age, we had a variety of common interests, including Power Rangers, comic books, and sports. In fact, what drew us to each other was our affinity for Ninja Turtles. Our friendship grew when we realized that our moms had the same first name, so naturally we found it amusing when we asked them for permission to have a weekend sleepover after school one breezy autumn afternoon in November 1994.

I waited eagerly in anticipation of that Friday sleepover. For the whole week, whenever we had leisure time in class, Jerry, Jake, and I would sit near each other and plan our evening of rambunctiousness. When the evening arrived, I barely remember kissing my mom goodbye, I was so excited.

We stayed up all night playing Sega Genesis and practicing a variety of death-defying wrestling moves that could seemingly only be concocted by Hulk Hogan, while being interrupted by their agitated mother several times. Our thrilling sleepover concluded with an early breakfast in their dimly-lit kitchen. Scrambled eggs, fluffy syrup-drenched pancakes, and crispy bacon—which tasted as if it was submerged in an ocean of grease before it was cooked—were abundant.

As I chewed my bacon, I glanced to my left and noticed Jake's peculiar proclivity of eating his bacon by indulging in the fat and discarding the rest in the trash.

"Huh? Man, what are you doing?!" I recall shouting with gleeful disgust.

After the sleepover, all we could talk about in school was how much fun we had. We were determined to create that magic again. But a few months later, Jake informed me that he and his brother were moving to Minnesota because their dad had received a job offer for more money. Shocked, we left the conversation with the agreement that one last sleepover—this time at my house—was necessary because we'd likely never see each other again.

I ran home eagerly that evening, after I got off the school bus, to greet my mom, who was visibly flustered after a long day of teaching. After a quick hug and kiss, I wasted no time divulging my request.

"Ma, I was wondering—" Before I could continue, she abruptly intervened.

"I know what you're going to ask, and the answer is *no!*" she exclaimed without hesitation.

"But, why!?" I boldly protested.

Up to that point in my life, I had normally taken my parents' instructions and orders without questioning them or pondering the motive behind them. Sure, when I was three, I asked "why" incessantly, but that was the result of my ever-evolving brain attempting to make sense of a changing world.

This time, however, was different. I felt as a child that I had the God-given right to spend time with my friends and have fun whenever I wanted. I felt this was an entitlement that every child had. I realized at that tender age that if I wanted results, I had better start with a question and keep digging down the rabbit hole until I hit the core. Due to the audacious nature and temperament of my question, I surely expected my mom to knock me into next week. However, the solemn response she gave me was not what I had expected.

"I just got off of the phone with Jake and Jerry's mom, Melody, and…"

"…and what, ma!?" I responded with haste, because I couldn't understand why that conversation didn't serve as a definitive gateway to another sleepover.

"Well, Ernie. Your friends' mom doesn't seem to think our neighborhood is safe enough or good enough for her sons to visit."

I didn't respond. I sat and looked at my mom with a perplexed expression; I expected her to elaborate. I was genuinely confused.

She knew I needed answers, so she calmly continued. "Ernie, if someone assumes that what you bring to the table is inferior because of your appearance, then you need not associate yourself with them."

I was seven, so I didn't understand what she meant through a racial lens at the time, but the broader point was understood.

Why was my neighborhood so different, though? It had everything to do with redlining. After slavery ended (or transitioned, as I like to say), my people began to migrate to the North in search of better economic opportunities. This Great Migration skyrocketed between the first and second world wars. There was only one problem—in the 1930s, the entire nation, regardless of race, was feeling the effects of the Great Depression, which had a deleterious impact on homeownership. President Franklin Delano Roosevelt sought to change this reality by starting the Federal Housing Administration to assist Americans in purchasing homes by providing them with loans. There was one glaring issue, though. These loans were only being allocated to white Americans.

As Roosevelt's New Deal spurred the growth of a burgeoning white middle class, Black Americans, already suffering from the effects of hundreds of years of uncompensated slave labor and trauma, were left to fend for themselves, as their white counterparts, who had historically benefited from Black subjugation, had once again become the beneficiaries of de facto affirmative action. For example, Levittown, which is regarded as America's first suburb, had a policy that explicitly barred the sale of its homes to Black people. This wasn't just an implicitly stated practice. Much like today, this was an actual clause in the lease agreement. According to this clause, homes could not "be used or occupied by any person other than members of the Caucasian race" (Lambert, 1997).

On the rare occasion when a Black family was able to purchase a home in a white neighborhood like Levittown (from a private owner selling it), they were threatened by vicious white mobs who hurled rocks in their windows, burned crosses, and waved Confederate flags in their yards, as was the case with Bill and Daisy Myers in 1957 in Pennsylvania (Oliver).

In most cases, my people could have had the same income and savings as a white person, but realtors would refuse to show them houses in certain neighborhoods, and the federal government would refuse to loan them the money needed to purchase a house they qualified for, due to a racist preconceived notion that we would bring the property value down.

My Black brothas and sistas were relegated to demarcated neighborhoods in inner cities that were highlighted in red on maps created by the federal government. Thus the term *redlining*. We were placed out of sight and out of mind, without the federal assistance we severely needed.

This belief that Black homeowners in a neighborhood would devalue property—held by many whites who had rarely if ever interacted with a Black person on a personal level—was likely fostered by exposure to pernicious and racist propaganda that perpetuated the myth of Black inferiority. Banks refused loans to Black folks so, in turn, most of us were only shown homes in these segregated redlined communities. Our options were either living in an apartment (which meant we weren't able to grow wealth through real estate), applying for public housing, or purchasing a home with the same cash that could have afforded us a similar loan to our white counterparts. It's worth noting that "a study of 108 US urban areas found that formerly redlined neighborhoods are on average 4.5 degrees Fahrenheit hotter than non-redlined neighborhoods," because there are fewer trees and green spaces, which were systematically removed through colonialism and the expansion of real estate development. This of course, further exacerbates the climate crisis that we all endure in this country and the world (Enterprise Community).

Still, we rose. Communities like Bronzeville in Chicago, Black Wall Street in Tulsa, and Harlem in NYC thrived despite the prejudicial treatment we received from federal and local governments. Additionally, many great entrepreneurs were birthed from this struggle. This includes Victor Green, who published the "Green Book"—a guidebook for Black folks who traveled on the interstate during the Jim Crow era. In other instances, the lack of bank loans in our redlined ghettos meant that we could only afford dilapidated housing, which decreased the likelihood that businesses would invest in our communities by establishing a brick-and-mortar location. There would then potentially be higher rates of unemployment, thus continuing the vicious cycle of poverty, conjoined with the degenerate practice of racism.

So, any negative impression of my neighborhood held in the mind of my friends' mother existed because politicians in our government conspired and succeeded in creating segregated communities that encouraged racism, social stratification, and white supremacy to persist.

Still, I had not known these facts regarding redlining at the tender age of seven. However, I knew something wasn't right, and it troubled me. My propensity to ask *why* was planted in the ground of this disappointment. The nonsensical handling of this situation by the twins' mom inspired me and led me down a path of self-discovery and reflection about the situation I had been born into.

CHAPTER 3
...WHEN I WANTED BREAKFAST

If you didn't grow up in an impoverished neighborhood that's classified as a food desert, then you have no idea how excruciating it is to see commercials that expose you to the palatable possibilities of American cuisine—especially when the only restaurant in your neighborhood within walking distance is a fried chicken establishment. As is the case with most fast-food establishments in the hood, the only food options offered are a surefire path to heart disease—fried chicken, catfish, gizzards, pizza puffs, French fries, and more, drenched in a savory pool of sauce. Other than that, we had food and liquor stores that sold candy, and a Walgreen's. If my friends and I were up for an adventure, we could set aside a day to walk to Calumet Park, the nearest suburb, to indulge in Dillinger's hot dogs, McDonald's, or Burger King.

I wanted more, though. I was a skinny kid with a large appetite, and I was very impressionable. So, when I saw commercials with enticing images of food that we didn't have, I wanted it. I had not realized at the time that my appetite (which had nothing to do with my actual level of hunger) and perceived need to have three square meals a day was also the product of colonialism and racism. See, when Europeans colonized America, they noticed that the indigenous people often ate in a less rigid manner, one not based on a timetable of having three scheduled meals a day. Those Europeans, of course, labeled this cultural custom as primitive and savage. Nowadays, it's labeled as intermittent fasting, and is one of the newest fads. Had I known about this different way of eating, I would've disregarded it. My manufactured appetite was rooted in me through round-the-clock commercials, and the fact remained that I felt I had to have Denny's expeditiously. Luckily, I had parents who had an appetite as large as mine, so we'd eat takeout quite often if my dad had decided that he wasn't going to create a masterpiece in the kitchen.

The year was 1995. I was eight years old, and it was a Saturday morning in December. All I could think about was food. Could you blame me? We were only a little more than a week removed from Thanksgiving, and Christmas dinner at my grandma's seemed so far away.

While channel surfing, I came across a food commercial that I had seen often. This time, however, I watched the commercial with a renewed interest, because I was growing sick of the norm and wanted something new. McDonald's, Burger King, and Wendy's were cool, I suppose, but Denny's was what I now wanted. I saw a luscious mountain of pancakes, drenched in syrup, surrounded by succulent sausage and fluffy, yellow scrambled eggs. I had been seduced and convinced that Denny's was what I needed in my life at that very moment. The commercial was only thirty seconds, but it felt as if I had been caught in a trance that lasted nearly thirty minutes.

"Ma! Dad!" I yelled from my room frantically, hoping to get their approval to visit the nearest Denny's. As I walked to the kitchen, I stopped by my older sister's room to fill her in, so that I could gain support and hopefully successfully lobby for an excursion to the suburbs.

"Yes, dear." My mom had been reading a book quietly in the kitchen before we had bombarded her, while my dad was preparing to sit down to eat a leftover hot dog with a side of Lay's potato chips. She pushed her glasses up, as she tilted her head upward to get a better view of both of us while he scooted past us before sitting.

…when I wanted breakfast 43

"Can we *please* go to Denny's? Pretty please with sugar on top?!" I was begging with all my might. I meant business.

My mom stared at us anxiously with her lips clenched together, frowned, and then glanced at my dad and shook her head.

I felt an uneasy feeling, the same one I had when I found out that I would no longer see Jake and Jerry. I anticipated the best, but prepared for the worst.

My dad put his hot dog back on his plate and calmly replied, "Denny's is kinda far, Ernieboy."

My mom, seeing that we weren't buying that explanation, provided a more thorough answer.

"It's too far, and we aren't going because they don't serve Black people."

As we stood in the kitchen hearing the responses of our parents, we still were confused. We hadn't heard about the Jim Crow era (yet), so we were confused and needed answers and our parents could tell.

My mom sighed and my dad looked flustered. I could tell he didn't want this information divulged to us.

"If we go to Denny's and they say there's a thirty-minute wait for a table, a white family that comes in after us will likely only have to wait five minutes. They serve white people before us. If they don't respect us, then they don't deserve our money."

"Oh…wow." Nikki responded for the both of us. I was too dumbfounded to know what to think or say.

First, my "best friends" were no longer my "best friends" because their mom wouldn't let them come to my neighborhood. Now, in an effort to escape my food desert community for what I assumed to be better cuisine, I was again denied an opportunity due to racism. Seriously? It was all too much for my eight-year-old brain to comprehend. For a long time after that day, I assumed my parents had made that story up. I assumed that it was an urban legend that they might have heard from their friends. I hoped I was right, but I was wrong. I recall teaching about the Jim Crow era during my first year as a US history teacher in 2011, trying to find ways to personalize the information I taught to help my students better relate to it. The thought that immediately came to mind while lesson planning was the interaction I had with my parents. Were these Denny's allegations true? I went to Google to find out, and this is what I discovered.

In May 1994, Denny's agreed to pay over $54 million to settle a racial discrimination lawsuit that was mainly based on allegations made in California. Over the years, Denny's had received complaints from over 3,000 Black customers in southern California, as well as 1,300 more from across the country. Customers had claimed that Denny's either refused to serve them or made them wait longer to be served, pay for their meals in advance, or pay to be seated, all while not demanding the same from white customers. Additionally, some managers stated that supervisors instructed them to close if too many Black customers patronized their business on certain days. There was even a case where a Denny's refused to serve a thirteen-year-old Black girl a customary free birthday meal that had become a staple of the national restaurant chain. Most notable, however, were the accusations made by six members of President Bill Clinton's Black US Secret Service detail in the '90s, who claimed that they waited for over an hour to receive service while their white counterparts were served comparatively promptly (Leeds).

My parents were right, to say the least. In my innocence, I had felt they might have been overreacting, but what I lived through, unbeknownst to myself, helped me realize that legislation alone wouldn't eradicate degenerate behavior. This was proof that Jim Crow's descendants were alive and well. Till this day, I still have not patronized a Denny's, and I never will. I'll boycott that poor excuse of a restaurant until the day I die, for the culture. And for good reason, too. They haven't changed at all.

Denny's seemingly has had the same problems since their payout. As recently as 2017, they were up to their old antics. Four Black men were asked to pay after ordering but before receiving their food, and were also forced to wait an exorbitant amount of time before being seated, even though, according to an eyewitness, the restaurant was nearly empty (Christian). In April 2018, a large group of Black folks went to a Denny's after church and were refused service by a white waitress because she claimed they were understaffed. Right afterwards, however, she proceeded to seat a group of whites who walked in.

It's just not Denny's, though. Waffle House, another prominent breakfast establishment, has had just as many issues, particularly in 2018. In April of that year, a white gunman entered a Tennessee Waffle House and opened fire, strategically targeting Black and Hispanic customers. He killed four of them. On the same day, in Alabama, a Black woman was aggressively tackled to the ground by a pair of officers as she sat down at a Waffle House table, allegedly because she had refused to leave after bringing in alcohol. Less than a week later, a Black customer recorded a video of herself being locked out of a Waffle House as they appeared to be serving only white patrons inside. As she knocked on the door and pleaded to enter, they ignored her. Lastly, in May 2018 in North Carolina, there was a viral video that showed a white "officer choking and slamming a twenty-year-old Black man who was at a Waffle House after taking his sixteen-year-old sister to her high school prom" (Murphy).

If you didn't know any better, you'd assume that white folks had a secret breakfast recipe that they were reluctant to share with us. I'd reckon that there are racists in every sector of society. The issue for us as Black folks is, of course every white person isn't racist, but how do we know? We are in survival mode every day as a method of protection against the possibility of encountering someone who thinks the worst of us. Furthermore, what's publicly accepted has evolved so much that, most times, a racist won't announce themselves by blatantly calling us "nigger," so we have to engage in a personal investigation that includes an analysis of body language, tonality, and the potential usage of euphemisms to protect ourselves proactively.

We become paranoid for our own survival. Is that employee following me around the store, or did he really plan on stocking items in this aisle? Is this clerk being rude as I check out of the store because I'm Black, or does she treat everyone this way? Does this coworker interact nervously with everyone who says hi to him, or is he fidgety and brief with me because I'm Black? We often ask these questions as a method of survival and maintaining sanity.

It is because of these experiences at places like Denny's and Waffle House that we know that these incidents aren't unfortunate coincidences. Rather, this behavior and treatment from racists is the norm for Black people in America. Social media has helped expose what was once limited to news blurbs, nightly newscasts, and discussions at social gatherings. My mom and dad introduced us to this unfortunate reality at a young age.

Now, compare these restaurants to one we did frequent throughout my childhood, Red Lobster, which has a history of disobeying the social norms from which it emerged. For example, Bill Darden, who founded Red Lobster in 1968, initially founded another lesser-known restaurant called The Green Frog thirty years earlier in Waycross, Georgia. The Green Frog had Black employees, but in accordance with Jim Crow customs at the time, did not allow them to patronize their restaurants. Although reports differ, it has been stated by several sources that Darden did eventually open his doors to Black patrons who were not required to

...when I wanted breakfast

sit in a racially segregated area of his restaurant. What's certain, however, is that when Darden opened Red Lobster in Lakeland, Florida, he gained a reputation for being inclusive just four years after the Civil Rights Act of 1964 banned discrimination in public places on the basis of race, color, religion, sex, or national origin, and during a time when some restaurants opted to close, rather than integrate. Through the 1970s, Red Lobster began to expand outside of Florida, and its reputation for hiring and serving Black folks without issue spread. Oh, and so did its reputation of serving Cheddar Bay Biscuits, which are arguably the best biscuits known to man. I didn't know this then, and neither did my parents, but we naturally gravitated to this institution, not just in our household, but amongst many in our community (including close friends and family).

Needless to say, on that day I begged to go to Denny's, my dad made us the best pancakes and sausage we ever had. What's more, we continued to visit Red Lobster and various Black-owned restaurants in our community, and I never asked for Denny's again.

CHAPTER 4
...WHEN I WAS ON MY WAY TO THE WHITE HOUSE

I was smart and earned good grades in school when I was younger, but I also loved to fight. My mom said this was because I had a tremendous amount of energy and intelligence that had not yet been channeled correctly. Considering how I turned out, I think she was correct.

My anger got me into trouble quite often while growing up. In fact, most of the "big homies" on my block predicted I'd be in jail if basketball didn't work out. They spoke it so often that it might have come to fruition if I hadn't had parents and grandparents who often spoke life into me.

I fought every chance I got in my neighborhood. If you looked at me the wrong way, I was throwing hands. If you pushed me too hard while playing basketball, I would jump on you. If you bothered my sister, I'd punch you in the jaw. Mind you, all of this occurred before I was ten. I mean, it's bad enough that I almost got kicked out of kindergarten, but the tomfoolery I was involved in during my fourth-grade year topped that or any other temperamental action of mine.

What would you do if someone took your most prized possessions as a child? See, it all started when my best friend, Jermaine, and I were racing our cars on the bus. How did we do that? Well, school buses have these small ridges on the floor in the aisle that happen to align with the width

...when I was on my way to the White House

of Hot Wheels cars. So, we'd place them on those ridges in the aisle and watch them proceed forward as the bus driver accelerated. The problem with this is, if the cars go too far, they might reach the bus driver's pedals, and consequently obstruct his ability to drive. Understandably, the bus driver demanded that we put up our toys. Jermaine listened. I didn't.

After another failed attempt at ceasing my delinquency, the bus driver— an overweight, short, brown-skinned man with circular glasses, a receding hairline, and a gray, slicked-back ponytail who favored Dr. Robotnik from the Sonic the Hedgehog series—proceeded to stop the bus, pull over, and put his hazards on. After quickly releasing his seatbelt, he made his way down the aisle sideways, waddling, as he tried to fit his physique down the narrow passageway. He eventually stopped at my seat and demanded my toys. All of them. I was crushed, but I obliged.

Within fifteen minutes, we approached my bus stop. As my sister began to walk toward the front, I followed behind, anticipating the retrieval of my toys. She stepped off and waited for me, but I didn't move. I stopped and sternly looked at the bus driver to my left. "I need my toys back!" I nervously snapped, my heart beating rapidly, at the visibly frustrated bus driver, who was visibly shocked at the remark.

"No! Not until I speak with your parents!" That was all I needed to hear. I immediately dropped my book bag and began to wail haymakers at the bus driver, as if I was in an MMA octagon. The harder I swung, the more my punches seemed to bounce off his body. I wasn't sure my attempt at retrieving my toys was going to work, but at least I had relieved my frustration. Right? Wrong!

Afterwards, I received a legendary spanking (which seems counterproductive in hindsight), and I was suspended from the bus for the rest of that semester, which greatly inconvenienced my parents. And, of course, I had to apologize to the bus driver. Honestly, I wish I knew his name so that I could apologize again. How ironic, though, that one of my biggest epiphanies in life would come during the same school year as this travesty. The yin and yang of life, I suppose.

For someone who was such a delinquent on the bus and in his neighborhood, it might surprise you to know that I was mostly obedient in elementary school, except for one fight and a few minor disciplinary issues leading up to my fourth-grade year.

As President's Day approached, my rebelliousness began to shift to academia. After my comrades and I sat down following the recitation of the daily pledge on the Monday before the holiday, we began a week-long lesson on America's Founding Fathers and presidents. Funny, at nine I didn't question the requirement to pledge and commit to a country that has never consistently shown my people justice, but I surely questioned that bus driver about my toys. Priorities.

George Washington could not tell a lie, Abraham Lincoln freed the slaves from bondage, and Woodrow Wilson gave women the right to vote were some of the lies I remember my fourth-grade instructor espousing repetitiously on this bitterly cold February day. As an inquisitive student, I recall often going on my own pursuits of inquiry separate from what the teacher required. This time was no different.

As I voraciously sifted through this textbook, a text that likely inspired James Loewen to write *Lies My Teacher Told Me*, I noticed a conspicuous absence of people like me. Where were the Black presidents? I grew up in an era during which Black comedians had erroneously anointed Bill Clinton the first Black president because of his marital infidelity, admission to smoking marijuana, and ability to play the saxophone. These tenets and characteristics are not synonymous with Black culture, despite what pop culture says. However, this destructive notion of artificial and stereotypical Blackness is not what I sought. I yearned to see someone, male or female, that I could presumably relate to due to their melanin content, which would likely mean we had similar life

...when I was on my way to the White House 51

experiences. I found no one. In fact, the only individuals who looked like me in this textbook were Dr. Martin Luther King, Jr., Frederick Douglass, and Harriet Tubman. Admirable activists indeed, but they never ascended to the office of the presidency. Why?

"Does anyone know the name of the president Martin Luther King is sitting with in this picture?" I didn't know that it was Lyndon B. Johnson, and I didn't care at that moment. I needed answers.

Sweat trickled down my face and my heart began to beat rapidly, similar to the way it did on that bus the previous semester, as I contemplated raising my hand to steer Mrs. Erin away from her initial question.

"Anyone!?" exclaimed Mrs. Erin dauntingly, as if she felt ignored the first time.

"Mrs."

"Yes, Ernest!" Mrs. Erin barked back.

"I wanted to know if I could be excused to go to the restroom?"

My nerves had eradicated the courage I had previously seemed to muster. But why? Was I afraid of the flack I assumed I would receive? Was I embarrassed to ask such a question related to my skin color at that tender age because I was a token (something I wouldn't fully realize until I sat in several college classes as the lone Black representative)?

Whatever the case, I avoided any awkward interaction that would have occurred because of my genuine curiosity until I got home. I was back on the bus that semester and had been noticeably withdrawn, in contrast to my usual gregariousness prior to my altercation with the driver. However, I was even more reserved during this bus ride home.

As we drove, raindrops slowly slid down the window, echoing the melancholy emotions I held internally. As I walked into the house with my sister, I immediately went downstairs and sought out my mom, who was feverishly typing a graduate school paper on our typewriter.

As I approached her, I walked past walls decorated with posters from a series Anheuser-Busch created in 1975 with twenty-three African American artists, based on research done by Dr. John Henrik Clarke, on prominent kings and queens from Africa. People like Mansa Musa, Shaka Zula, Queen Amina, Queen Nzinga, Akhenaton, Thutmose II, Hannibal, Sunni Ali, and Queen Nandi—all people I would come across later in my life as my interest in Black history prior to slavery peaked. I had no idea the impact the early exposure to these historical figures would have on me until I remembered their faces while conducting research, as if we were childhood friends. I theorize that this is just one of the many reasons why I have been able to maintain a positive mental image of myself and my Black sistas and brothas.

I was greeted with glee by my mother as she held what I soon found out was a Young Authors assignment packet that she had received from a parent-teacher conference the previous night.

"Ma, why haven't we had any Black presidents!?" I blurted out.

My mom's response was not what I expected, but like my experience with Jake and Jerry, it would have a profound impact on me as I continued to mature and conceptualize the world around me. What's more, it appeared my mom was expecting to be confronted with my curious plunge into America's complex and nuanced oppression-based political strata, based on her immediate response.

"Well, son, it's because they're waiting on you to grow up."

...when I was on my way to the White House

Sometimes you ask questions pessimistically, assuming you already know what the response will be. This was one of those times. However, I can honestly say that my mom's response shifted my paradigm. For as long as I could remember, my mom and dad always reiterated that I could accomplish anything if only I put my mind to it. I honestly believed them, especially after this response. It implanted a level of confidence I hadn't previously had or, quite frankly, needed. The naivete of not fully understanding systemic racism and the perils of institutional white supremacy worked to my benefit at this tender, ignorant age. Imagine how different my life would be if she'd spoken to me as if I was synonymous with the problem I'd caused last semester, as opposed to the potential she saw in me as her child.

"Really—"

Before I could fully respond, my mom interjected. "You know what, let's write a book about it! This year's Young Authors assignment is due in a couple months; let's get started now."

"Okay!" I responded with gleeful optimism.

I couldn't quite determine if my mom truly believed what she said, or if she was attempting to further protect me from the harsh reality of growing up as a Black male in 1990s in America under the leadership of our faux-Black president—a president who was responsible for the continued mass incarceration of Black people with the passage of the Violent Crime Control and Law Enforcement Act. This legislation codified the three-strikes rule into law, gave life sentences to repeat offenders, increased the presence of police in urban areas, and helped expand the death penalty in states like California, where the vast majority of those affected were Black. Additionally, the law increased funding for prisons, gave money to states which implemented tougher penalties for crime, and kept the crack and cocaine sentencing disparity at 100:1. This meant that those found with crack (which was normally found in Black neighborhoods), even if they weren't selling it, could get five years in prison for one gram, whereas you'd have to have 100 grams of powder cocaine to receive the same sentence. In the more than twenty years after the passing of this legislation, the prison population had more than doubled. Yet Bill Clinton was supposed to be a liberal Democrat.

Although she was a big fan of poet and rapper Tupac, my mother vehemently disagreed with his assertion that "even though it seems heaven-sent, we ain't ready to have a Black president." Hindsight is indeed 20/20. Many of us can probably think back to situations in our life that, unbeknownst to us, would emerge as defining moments. Life's journey is jovial, or long and tedious, depending on your perspective. After experiencing highs and lows, we often approach forks in the road, and our decision to choose either direction will impact our life for better or worse.

I can't help but wonder how different my life would be if my mom had not taken the time to mold my curious inquiry with responses entrenched in the optimism necessary to lead a generation of youth born in systemic oppression out from the depth of the ghetto and school-to-prison pipeline to Black excellence and opulence. The power of the tongue that parents possess over their children is profound. I honestly believed, as a child in the mid-'90s, thirty years removed from the Civil Rights era, and roughly ten years from the crack era, while entrenched in the War on Drugs and an American apartheid system, that I could become the president of the United States if I chose to.

As I grew older, I chose not to aspire to be the president. Do you understand the weight of that statement? A young Black boy in America, born in the '80s, *chose* not to run for president—not because he was a victim of his circumstances and not because "the white man" was going to systematically eliminate his opportunity, but because he simply did not want to.

I have ancestors who were born during a time when aspirations for freedom were a lifelong goal and a grand achievement. I have ancestors who believed that gaining the position of house slave was progress. I also have ancestors who believed that simply attaining a job as a "free" man was honorable. Now, due to the pain my ancestors endured and the freedom they fought for, I was able to exist in an era when becoming president was plausible. The fact that I felt I had a choice meant everything.

When news got out about this conversation, my family began to playfully bombard me with comments about my forthcoming presidency. My family fully supported the result of the inquisitive nature of the conversation I had with my mother. It was flattering. I even got to visit my great-uncle Congressman Bennie Thompson in Washington, DC, and tour his office over spring break that school year. It felt real to me.

I began to think deeply on this topic. If I could accomplish this immense task, then could I also go on to accomplish even greater things, and have an even bigger impact on society? Who was greater, George Washington or Martin Luther King, Jr.? Abraham Lincoln or Frederick Douglass? Thomas Jefferson or Harriet Tubman? Woodrow Wilson or Ida B. Wells? JFK or Malcolm X? The answers I would choose clearly revealed themselves as I got older. I had started the school year confirming, through my actions, the life of the "big homies," but I concluded the year with presidential aspirations because someone with more influence and impact spoke life and helped actualize it. Thanks, Mom.

CHAPTER 5
...WHEN HE WAS TOLD TO GO BACK

I was as focused as I had ever been academically in my sixth-grade year, but my main priority was the forthcoming basketball team tryouts. As I anxiously walked into school on a sunny September morning, sidetracked by my propensity to delve into daydreams of my future NBA career, I noticed something strange as I approached my assigned seat. I realized that my best friend Jermaine was no longer sitting next to me.

After noticing this absence, I hesitantly pulled up my sagging navy blue uniform pants, placed my textbooks and wilted folders softly on my desk, and took a seat in my red, tilted chair. I glanced over my shoulder and, much to my chagrin, saw that Jermaine had already arrived, but was sitting in what I assumed to be his new seat. I was visibly perturbed and confused. Likewise, Jermaine looked perplexed as he peered at me and shrugged his shoulders.

Suddenly, the bell rang, and we rose for the obligatory pledge. Afterwards, Mrs. Miller walked to the center of the class to begin the day's lesson. Concurrently, I noticed a dark-skinned Black boy, who was slightly shorter than me, approaching the newly vacated seat. It was apparent that he was new to the school because the school's Black population was so low that we all knew each other.

As we began our lesson, Mrs. Miller walked toward my desk with haste. Before I could extend a greeting, she calmly said: "Ernest hon, Kola is not just new to this school, he's also new to the country. He's from Nigeria. When Mrs. Pelter told me about Kola's transfer, I immediately thought of you. Can you do me a favor, hon? Please just look out for him and help him get accustomed to the school as much as you can?"

"Yeah, sure, Mrs. Miller. No problem."

What else could I say to such an impassioned plea, even if I was initially hesitant?

Naturally, I was curious about Kola's experience in Nigeria as compared to America. The American public school system does a horrendous job of teaching students about African history, and anything else that doesn't fit the traditional Eurocentric Western narrative, so you can probably imagine why a person who asked his mother about the lack of Black presidents as a nine-year-old would be intrigued by this random pairing.

What was the perception of Africa that had been ingrained in my mind in the late '90s? Unfortunately, I was conditioned to think of Africa in the same way as most Americans: I saw poverty and destitution, an abysmal failure of catastrophic proportions. Never mind that Africa has fifty-four countries which were formed during imperialism, hundreds of languages, and thousands of cultures—I was trained to associate all of Africa (which I interchangeably called a continent and country) with the indigence shown on television.

Ask any kid about Africa and they'll immediately reference the propagandistic Sally Struthers commercials that begged and pleaded for thirty cents a day to feed children with swollen bellies, suffering from malnutrition. "Couldn't they feed those kids with the budget they spent on the commercial?" I often pondered during my childhood.

Sadly, the children I teach largely have the same misconceptions. I didn't know then that Africa was the birthplace of humanity and civilization. I had not yet known that ancient Greek and Roman scholars went to Africa—specifically ancient Egypt—for knowledge, as was notably referenced by Hippocrates, the father of Western medicine. My adoration of Egyptian chancellor, architect, and physician Imhotep had not yet developed. He is now regarded as the world's first documented doctor, 2,000 years before Hippocrates. I didn't know that Europeans and Asians came from all over to study, not just in Egypt, but in the West African region of Mali at Timbuktu University. I had no idea Moors from Africa helped rescue Europe out of the Dark Ages, while also introducing cultural traditions and technological innovation that would later become staples of European society. I didn't know that the Dogon people of Mali were so intelligent that they had knowledge of stars and constellations, like Sirius B, thousands of years before Europeans invented the technology that would grant them that exposure (and allow their discovery of Sirius B in the mid-1800s). Lastly, I didn't know that the wealthiest man of all time was a king from Mali named Mansa Musa. Instead, when I saw Africa at this age, I saw starvation and poverty, one of the many deleterious effects of imperialism.

The divisiveness and self-hatred that this imagery created subconsciously, along with a negligent curriculum that only discussed Africa when mentioning slavery, HIV, or primitiveness, was profound. When meeting someone directly from the motherland, I was conditioned to see a stranger with whom I was not connected to as opposed to seeing a brotha or sista in the African Diaspora with whom I would have a deep connection that was forcibly disrupted hundreds of years ago. I had been conditioned, like many of my African American brothas and sistas, to have more pride in representing my hood, hometown, clique, gang, or social circle than my African side.

The distorted views we have toward our brethren are rooted in the psychologically divisive nature of slavery. Millions of Africans from different tribes and with different languages were placed on slave ships for an arduous one- to three-month journey. Because of the exorbitant death and suicide rate (scholars estimate 13 percent), sharks would often follow these ships in anticipation of another body being jettisoned. Those who survived this traumatizing journey under the decks of a disease-infested ship, where they were lodged into compartments that were six feet long and three feet high, were sold to the highest bidder once they arrived in America, split from their families, and forced to relinquish their mother tongue in favor of English (Editors of Encyclopedia Britannica). Furthermore, legislation and plantation culture reprimanded Africans who were set on practicing their indigenous tribal customs because there was a fear that this would encourage unity and create a breeding ground for insurrection, especially after the Haitian Revolution's reliance on African spirituality. Voodoo, for example, was used as the primary spiritual force to ignite that revolution. However, it's usually promoted as a spooky religion in the media, even though it's based on divine spirituality and ancestor reverence, and has not been weaponized to colonize.

Thus, violent beatings and lynchings were commonly used as a scare tactic, so much so that, within a few generations, many of these sacred customs were likely lost. If they weren't, they were intertwined with white American customs or surreptitiously preserved. For example, Negro spirituals often communicated escape routes, and Black Christian church services often contained remnants of African spirituality, such as the emphatic manner of preaching and ecstatic nature of praise and worship.

It goes without saying, internally, that Africans were often pitted against each other due to the erroneously perceived superiority associated with lighter skin or house (slave) duties. As a result, you'd see your brotha or sista as your enemy, as opposed to your comrade. Divide-and-conquer tactics on the plantation, similarly to how race was used to disrupt a class alliance between Blacks and whites during the colonial period, benefited the pernicious motive of slave owners who wanted to capitalize on free labor by any means.

Individuals placed in this unfortunate circumstance were often so set on survival that they'd gladly sacrifice their true nature and cultural practices for another day of life. Thus, when we see Africans who have had the privilege of remaining in their country (or tribal region), surviving the rapacious nature of European imperialism and colonialism, we see strangers who share our complexion as opposed to distant relatives. However, unbeknownst to many, our cultural connections have largely remained intact. Have you ever seen a Djoanigbe and Zaouli masking tradition dance and compared it to the footwork dance in Chicago? Have you ever noticed that we as Black folks place a high precedence on greetings and acknowledgment, whether through a head nod, a warm embrace, or through a handshake? That's because in many West African countries, like Ghana, the cultural tradition and expectation is to acknowledge those you encounter. According to author Kwama Gyekye:

> Greeting people one meets is an important element of enhancing human relations and in making people feel good about themselves. The greeting is considered a way of acknowledging the other person as a fellow human being, and a person may feel deeply hurt if you pass him by without greeting him. The failure to greet him would be regarded as a failure on your part to recognize that he shares your humanity.

And yes, remarking that someone is operating on CP (Colored People) Time is not merely a joke; it is the expectation in West African countries. However, there it is not called CP Time; it is referred to as "Africa Time," wherein arriving earlier than an hour after the start time is a rarity and jokingly referred to as following "European Time." There's the conundrum: we come from a culture where we have been passed down traits, such as arriving "fashionably late," that are celebrated in

Africa, yet frowned upon in American and Western culture (Ghana Cultural Etiquette).

Besides the previous positive cultural commonalities we shared, Kola and I also shared historical trauma; not through slavery, but rather through colonialism and mental conditioning. For example, the issue of colorism assumes that lighter-skinned Blacks are prettier, smarter, and higher in a fictional societal hierarchy. That is related to Nigeria's addiction to skin-bleaching cream. In many ways, we have adopted the ways of our oppressors, so much so that we have in some ways reapplied the chains that were long ago released.

Although I was clueless at the time, these connections were present subconsciously when I met Kola at the age of eleven.

"Wassup, man?" I muttered inaudibly to Kola while our classmates were being loud and rambunctious in anticipation of our lunchbreak.

"Wassup…" Kola replied sheepishly.

Our friendship was off to an awkward start. I wasn't quite sure what to talk to him about. Was he a basketball fanatic like myself? Did he have Jay-Z's *Vol. 2… Hard Knock Life* in constant rotation as well? I hadn't the slightest clue what Nigerian culture was like. Furthermore, I didn't know how to strike up a conversation to disrupt the awkward silence that lasted only a few seconds but seemed like an eternity. The clock ticked.

"So, what's it like going to school with all of these white people?"

"They're cool, man," I responded with a rapturous laugh.

Kola's audacious follow-up question, as hilariously awkward as it was, led to a great friendship, though it was a short-lived one due to unforeseen circumstances.

As lunch began and I sought out my friends, Kola continued his comedic onslaught.

"Yeah, I got this scratch above my eye when I got attacked by a lion! I threw a spear at it and missed, and he charged at me and scratched me *hard!*"

We all sat there in silence for a few moments, because we didn't know if he was serious. Besides the promulgated caricatures we have been exposed to about African life in relation to disease and poverty, we also believed the myth that safari life was intertwined with urban life. We didn't know, for example, that in the fifty-four unique countries in Africa, there were hundreds of flourishing cities with prodigious skylines and urban epicenters that rivaled New York City and Chicago.

For example, Kola's hometown, Lagos, has a population of over twenty million people, and its country, Nigeria, is on pace to surpass France and the UK in economic production and people by 2050 (Voice of America News). Furthermore, Nigeria is home to five billionaires (Aliko Dangote, Mike Adenuga, Femi Otedola, Folorunsho Alakija, and Abdul Samad Rabiu) who amassed their fortunes in the food, oil, and fashion industries, whereas all of America only has four Black billionaires (Oprah Winfrey, Michael Jordan, Jay-Z, and Robert Smith), three of whom amassed their fortunes primarily through entertainment (Nsehe).

Kola's slight chuckle after his tale of the lion scratch assured us he was joking, or so it seemed.

Getting to know someone who looked like me but had an experience that was completely different than mine was eye-opening. I found it interesting, for instance, that soccer (or football as the rest of the world knows it) was Kola's favorite sport. As an ignorant and oblivious American, I didn't know that soccer was also the world's most popular sport. As such, I took the crown when we played basketball in physical education, but when we battled in soccer it was embarrassingly one-sided.

Our mutual love for sports was only eclipsed by our genuine appreciation for hip-hop. He sang the praises of Nigerian rap groups like The Remedies and Trybesman, while I heralded Jay-Z, Nas, Tupac, Biggie, and DMX as rap's kings. Unfortunately, streaming and file sharing services didn't exist yet, so I couldn't gauge whether his favorites rivaled mine unless he let me borrow a CD or cassette tape.

As our friendship grew, so did my curiosity. I recall asking Kola about his bus route once, assuming that he took a bus back to an all-Black neighborhood like every other Black person I knew that attended Mount Greenwood. However, I was astonished to learn that he didn't take the bus, because he lived in the Mount Greenwood community, a segregated neighborhood where 95 percent of the population was white.

"Yo, Kola! What's your number? You should hang out with me and Jermaine this summer, man."

When I exchanged numbers with Kola on the last day of school, I anticipated that our friendship would have the chance to grow. I also thought he'd help me improve my soccer skills. Before the ubiquitous nature of social media and smartphone group messages, the only way you could stay connected with your friends was through a phone call or arranged meeting.

I recall making a mental note to contact Kola several times throughout the summer, and I'm sure it was the same on his end, but I was constantly sidetracked. The allure of the scorching hot summer day without having the responsibility of homework was tempting. Plus, I didn't particularly like talking on the phone. My days consisted of basketball, basketball, basketball, bike rides, video game competitions, and conversations with friends on the porch until my hunger pangs needed tending to.

It was also comforting to spend time with my close childhood friends, with whom I shared cultural and racial experiences due to our common heritage and residence in a secluded neighborhood, which was a byproduct of America's apartheid system.

Time passed swiftly that summer without me realizing that the first day of school was soon approaching. I didn't realize it was the middle of August until my dad picked my sister and me up for our weekly visit on a dreary Wednesday.

"Where do y'all wanna go to get your school shoes?"

"Champs at Evergreen Plaza is cool with me," I responded, after pondering my options.

My sister nodded in agreement.

As we walked toward Champs at Evergreen Plaza, I tried to keep Kola on my mind so I would remember to call him when I got home. That would've been the perfect time for a quick text, but Steve Jobs was apparently behind schedule with the iPhone.

"What's the limit?" I asked hesitantly, expecting the worst.

My dad shocked me when he said that I could grab two pairs of shoes, as long as they qualified under Champs Sports's two for $90 special.

I was elated. My gear would remain in excellent condition this year because of this. Otherwise, I'd be caught in a conundrum of trying my best to preserve my new shoes in a crowded high school, full of teenagers who couldn't care less about the condition of your sneakers. At least now I could rotate.

"$5 if y'all can tell me who this is!" My dad exclaimed from the front of the car, as he turned the volume knob to the right and shrugged his shoulders vivaciously to the beat.

On car rides with my dad, we often played impromptu "Name That Tune" games as we listened to his favorite radio station, V103, which played R&B and soul music, affectionately called dusties (older music from his childhood, or the Motown era, that was so old you had to literally blow the dust off it). What I wouldn't do to have access to Siri or Shazam during those rides. I had no idea at the time that I was receiving a crash course in Black music history that I would not appreciate until later in life. Now, Earth Wind & Fire is arguably my favorite group and Stevie Wonder is one of my favorite singers. Back then, however, they were just multiple-choice selections for me as my dad tried his best to get us to guess the correct artist while wagering $1, $5, $10, and sometimes even $20, if he deemed the song to be at a premium level of difficulty.

What I cherish about those moments the most, as I play the same game with my own children and teach history lessons packed with a contextual framing of what inspired the artist to make the song, is the difference in tone, subject matter, frequency, and purpose of the music that was created during those eras.

For instance, Marvin Gaye's "What's Going On?" or "Inner City Blues," through his melodic reverberations, taught me so much about how many in the Black community viewed the Vietnam War, Civil Rights-era racism, and the conditions of our neighborhoods most impacted by structural racism and structural violence. Stevie Wonder's "Birthday" taught me how effortlessly one could remix a timeless American classic that was created nearly a century earlier by Louisville, Kentucky's Hill sisters (who were in fact inspired by Black music and Negro spirituals) for the purpose of furthering a political movement. Yes, when Stevie beautifully belted, "Happy birthday to you!" in his 1980 song, he did so in memory of Dr. Martin Luther King, Jr. as a way to advocate for a national holiday in his honor.

And Earth, Wind & Fire encouraged us to reach our fullest potential, regardless of our background and upbringing, while melodically singing, "You're a shining star, no matter who you are, shining bright to see, who you can truly be!" They also spoke to the potential that we all inherently have and can manifest as human beings, if we remember our deepest desires and wants and persistently work toward manifesting them in the physical realm for the purpose of the greater good, with lyrics like:

Every man has a place

In his heart, there's a space

And the world can't erase his fantasies

Take a ride in the sky

On our ship, Fantasy.

Not only did they provide a soundtrack for encouragement, love, and manifestation, they also provided esoteric visuals to lead us down a path of knowledge, wisdom, African history, and Afrofuturism. For example, many of their covers include ancient Kemetic/Egyptian pyramids that remind you of Giza, monuments that are reminiscent of Ramses II guarding entry into a tomb, and hieroglyphics like the ankh, which is shaped like a cross with a loop at the top and represents life, and Wadjet or the Eye of Horus, which comes from the myth of Horus, who had his eye gouged out in a battle with his uncle Set and was later healed by Thoth. The Egyptians believed that the eye protected against evil and reflected it back onto the evil-doer. Hindsight is 20/20, as they say, however, because in that moment I was clueless.

"Uhhh, Al Green!" I yelled. "Marvin Gaye!" my sister followed.

"Noooope! Maze featuring Frankie Beverly," my dad responded, ecstatic that he'd defeated us once again.

Upon arriving home, I fell asleep instantly, but when I arose the next morning, one glance at my shoes reminded me that I needed to call Kola.

After peering into my mom's room to see if she was on the phone, I went back to my room to give Kola a call.

"Ernest, wassup?"

Kola's demeanor seemed drastically different from what I remember on the last day of school in June. His tone was stoic and despondent.

"Whatup Kola? How ya been? You wanna play some basketball or soccer this weekend?"

"Man, that would be cool if I wasn't moving," he responded sheepishly.

"Wait…what? Whatchu talking 'bout, man?"

I was in disbelief. I'd barely known Kola for one school year and now he was moving. It felt like the experience I had with Jerry and Jake when I was in second grade. What type of parent would subject their child to such a thing, especially after just moving from a foreign country? My concerns seemed legitimate at the time, but they were undeniably selfish.

"We're moving to Hazel Crest. This neighborhood is crazy, and these white people are racist!"

Kola's demeanor hadn't budged since we began conversing. Either he was a great actor, or he was serious. I started to realize that it was the latter.

"Racist? What happened?" I interjected before Kola continued:

"They've been harassing us. They've been spray-painting 'Leave niggers', 'White Power', and 'Go back to Africa niggers' on our garage since May. We painted over it the first couple times and we told police, but they ain't doing nothing. My mom is scared… We're all scared. We never dealt with stuff like this in Nigeria." (Donovan)

I was perturbed as I heard Kola divulge the details of this hate crime where the culprit would never be brought to justice. I was upset and very surprised. Up to this point in my life, I had never faced something so racially venomous, so I couldn't quite relate. This was confirmation to me, though, that some of my white friends' parents didn't really want us there. Instead, they tolerated us as much as they could, lest we had the fortitude to ignore the obvious redlining that created these segregated neighborhoods and decide to move next door.

We were acceptable to those who practiced white supremacy until we outwardly expressed our inherent equality. That's when they felt obligated to denigrate and demote us back down America's racially-stratified society—a society that's set on terrorizing Blacks perpetually, especially when they escape the trenches of white oppression and subjugation, such as what happened in Tulsa when Black Wall Street was burned down many years ago.

This was my first introduction to the explicit nature of Mount Greenwood's racism, but it wouldn't be the last. My first time visiting the neighborhood since graduating came in 2016, when I spoke at a rally following the unjustified shooting death of a Black man named Joshua Beal by a police officer, as he was driving through the area in a funeral procession. The racist vitriol astonished me because I had never personally witnessed such behavior from those in the community, outside of what I heard from Kola. Between the racist chants, the Trump signs, and Blue Lives Matter flags, I felt like I was in an alternative universe where I was able to see the true colors of the environment some of my white friends were raised in.

Upon further inspection and conversation with some whites who were against the racism in their community on that November day in 2016, I could see that the police shooting and racist graffiti my Nigerian friend had experienced were the norm. In fact, since his experience in 1999, there had been at least five similarly reported incidents, which included racist graffiti and flyers being placed on cars. More recently, in July of 2019, the same thing occurred, prompting outrage from some white residents who opted to display "Hate Has No Home in the Nineteenth Ward" posters in their windows to show their solidarity (Sutter).

Their hate isn't just symbolic, though; it is systemic. Unlike any other Chicago jurisdiction in 2016, nearly 70 percent of registered voters voted for the harbinger of hate, Donald Trump (Malooley). Additionally, 40 percent of voters in two Mount Greenwood precincts voted for known Nazi and white supremacist Art Jones in the 2018 congressional election (Dudek). In terms of the conspicuous segregation that is pervasive in the community, a public meeting was called in April of 2019 by the Southwest Chicago Diversity Collaborative and Chicago Lawyers' Committee for Civil Rights to discuss a report by the Chicago Commission on Human Relations that describes Mount Greenwood as one of six communities in Chicago that still blatantly practice housing discrimination and redlining (Moran).

The report stated that African Americans received the most blatant discrimination: "The report's findings include evidence of outright discrimination, differential treatment, and different levels of customer service for prospective tenants searching for housing in Mount Greenwood—both on the basis of race and a person's source of income" (Moran).

All of this twenty years after Kola's family was chased out of the neighborhood. We like to think that time heals all wounds, but that's optimistically assuming that the perpetrator that caused said wound doesn't revert to the same behavior. As such, it seems as if America's race problem is permissibly cyclical. Who, besides the perpetual victims, would truly opt to end oppression at the expense of their privileges?

Kola's situation would reveal itself to be one grievance among a lengthy list of examples of racism and discrimination in this community, most notably beginning with the violently racist protest to keep Black students out of Mount Greenwood Elementary in 1968.

No matter how different I assumed Kola was when I first met him, he and I had something in common that holds true for all Black people, regardless of our nationalities or cultures—in the eyes of whites who practice racism, we'd never be anything more than niggers. It was our responsibility, however, to not internalize that, and understand that their perception of us was more of a reflection of them, than us.

CHAPTER 6
...WHEN I WAS CUTE FOR A BLACK GUY

The yearbook. From middle school through high school, it remained a vital component of end-of-the-year festivities. I wasn't sure if this archetype was subconsciously ingrained in my mind due to my penchant for excessively watching shows like *Saved by the Bell*, *Fresh Prince*, and other sitcoms spewing a narrative consistent with a teenage life dedicated to justifying the importance of seeking popularity by conformity and adapting to Eurocentric cultural and aesthetic values, or if it was a routine that I had created to counter my increasingly bashful personality. In other words, having my close female friends sign my yearbook would allow me to see if the girls I thought were attractive and friendly had the same sentiments toward me. If I approached them and boldly pursued a relationship, as I rarely did unless challenged, I would have to deal with the likelihood that I would be rejected, and I knew my fragile ego and meek personality couldn't handle that.

In fifth grade, the yearbook anticipation was no different. "Ernest!" As my name was called mid-June of my fifth-grade year by Ms. Falk in alphabetical order, I approached her desk with eager anticipation.

After hastily grabbing my yearbook, I proceeded to sit back down and scroll vigorously, looking to find my picture and any other candid photos taken by those students and staff members on the yearbook committee.

"All right, class. Did everyone get their book?"

Ms. Falk's question was overshadowed by the mutter and chatter that occurs when a class of eleven-year-olds are excited in anticipation of the school year concluding. The dispersal of the yearbook was the de facto gesture that symbolized that summer break was nearly here. Additionally, Ms. Falk's capriciously negligent attitude toward our youthful defiance, which wasn't typical of her, emblematized her allegiance to the whimsical nature of summer break.

"Feel free to take this time."

Ms. Falk's voice was drowned out by my table section peers who were exchanging their books for signatures.

"Ernest, can you sign my book next?" asked my tablemate Nicole over the faint sound of Ms. Falk's voice.

As I agreed to sign Nicole's book, I gave her mine and watched as my book went into rotation.

In 1998, before social media applications like Facebook, this was analogous to receiving thirty simultaneous notifications that your Facebook wall was written on. After impatiently waiting, I finally received my yearbook back from one of the prettiest girls in school, a white girl named Mary, who I assumed had added her signature and comment last.

Mary was a girl who had been in Mount Greenwood since first grade, like me; however, we didn't have classes together until fourth grade. It was at that time that she caught my eye. That crush would only grow during our fifth-grade year, since we had the same class again. We were only "cool," though, in the same way all fifth-graders are cool with each other because you're not teenagers yet and haven't begun to dislike your peers for insignificant reasons. In fact, I had a cordial relationship with nearly everyone in my grade.

As I began to peruse my yearbook, quickly reading the comments left by friends, my mind was clouded with thoughts about Mary as I approached the last page. What did she say? Did she leave her phone number? Was she attracted to me, too?

There it was, on the last page, tucked in the lower right corner. I recognized her signature, which began with a huge "M," from having graded her papers so much when Ms. Falk prompted us to switch with our peers.

I read the comment slowly. "Hey, Ernest. I hope you have a great summer! You're cute for a Black guy."

I was honestly confused. I didn't know if I should take it as a compliment or a flippant denunciation of my racial categorization in America. Beside the fact that I was still largely ignorant of the different layers of racism, I was still aware of the fact that I was Black. I was also aware of the fact that I was not a part of the privileged class in America because I was Black. To solve this mystery, I decided to do what any ten-year-old would do when caught in such a precarious predicament: I consulted my confidant Jermaine, who had been my best friend since first grade.

"Maaaan, this is your chance. I'd go up to her and see what that means, like, so we could possibly go out, right!?" Jermaine exclaimed with a subtle grin after I showed him the comment.

I fell into a stupor for the rest of the day. I refused to take heed of Jermaine's advice because, once the astonishment subsided, my temperament shifted toward a feeling of resentment and contempt for Mary and what she now represented. I was ten years old and enduring an existential crisis.

In one sense, I felt flattered because she obviously found me attractive. However, her seemingly innocuous yet disparaging comment caused an internal conflict at my tender age. A simple crush (or love for others) is something that should not be defined by a racial categorization—a social construct that was originally meant to divide others and create a permanent lower class. And, having been overexposed to Eurocentric standards of beauty my entire life, I unfortunately valued her opinion. My self-image as a young Black boy evolved tremendously due to this episode.

As we stood in 1998, unbeknownst to us, we were just thirty years removed from a Supreme Court case, *Loving vs. Virginia*, which forbade states and jurisdictions to create laws against miscegenation or interracial relationships and marriages. Additionally, this incident took place thirty years after the first Black student integrated Mount Greenwood, and fourteen years after the *Brown vs. Board of Education* Supreme Court decision was supposed to integrate schools nationwide.

It goes without saying that tens of thousands of Black men had been lynched by white terrorists who claimed to be protecting white womanhood from the perceived promiscuous and barbaric nature of Black men. The perception that Black men and boys couldn't control themselves around white women, to the point where they'd rape them at any given moment, was the false narrative that has proliferated for hundreds of years in America and was made famous with *The Birth of a Nation* (Brook).

These imbeciles were threatened by Black patriarchy and genetic annihilation. One only needs to mention the infamous name of Emmett Till to conjure the reality of the previous statement.

I don't believe Mary was malicious or consciously racist. I believe she was subconsciously and implicitly biased in the same way most white people are if they don't have someone consciously intervene to teach them that they are not superior to anyone. Either that, or they would have to come to this epiphany on their own and educate themselves, like Jane Elliott or Tim Wise—two prominent white anti-racist educators who are known for challenging their community's racial biases. As we currently stand, American society, through commercialization and government propaganda and judicial rulings, produces a superiority complex in whites and an inferiority complex in Blacks.

When we were born, both Mary and I became victims of a nation that anoints and rewards whiteness. Her victimization granted her lavish privileges, though. Mine did not. She was born into a physical realm and existence in which her skin color granted her certain societal privileges that came as a result of some of the worst crimes known to mankind. As such, whiteness and the phenotypical traits that come with that social construct were the norm to her. My victimhood was associated with being born into an existence that sought to greatly punish, in perpetuity and without logical reasoning, those with melanin content and West African physical features. This meant that at this juncture in history, in America, Blackness was associated with otherness, despondency, and deviance.

My conversations with Mary were limited, before and after that comment, and never typically evolved past cordiality. I never even sought an explanation, as Jermaine had attempted to compel me to do. I felt no reason to. It wasn't my duty to plead for acceptance from her or any other white person. However, I often ponder and reflect on the root of her comment. Was she explicitly or implicitly taught this? From my vantage point, she may have made that statement because she genuinely viewed Black people as unattractive, ugly, and repulsive, and was shocked to find me attractive. I could be wrong. It's quite possible that she feared the social expulsion and denigration she'd receive from friends and family for dating someone Black.

Whatever the case, I'll never know the answers to these questions at this juncture in my life. However, what I do realize and know now as a Black person is that our worth as Black folks cannot be defined or viewed through the lens of people whose goal has been to subjugate us generationally. As a minority group in this country, we have lost twice before the game starts if we internalize the malicious images that have been propagated through the vast media of all types that they control.

"Ernie, don't bring no white girl home," my mother exclaimed after coming across another story about a Black male celebrity divorcing his Black wife for a partner who lacked melanin.

"Why ma? Okay, what if she…"

My mom's statement cast her as a curmudgeon who was against interracial relationships, but her sentiments were based, not in contempt for white women, but in a childhood and historical experience where she personally witnessed and experienced Black women being overlooked, abused, and portrayed as undesirable to every racial group of men, including Black men, in a society which incessantly promotes Eurocentric beauty standards as the norm and prototype. From her vantage point, if a man loves his mother and exalts her like the queen she is, then he ought to want to bring home someone who resembles her.

Likewise, my sister Nikki will tell you that, while growing up in Chicago during the '90s, it seemed as though whenever she came across male athletes or celebrities in the media, they were almost always wed to a white woman, as if to say Black women weren't sufficient for marriage. Furthermore, as an adult, she had experiences at places of employment where Black male managers catered to white women, granting them privileges she couldn't garner, even with her seniority.

My wife also had a similar experience attending a predominantly white high school in the early 2000s. She recalls her Black male counterparts joking with white guys at the school about how unattractive Black women were, proclaiming that they'd never date them. She even got into a dispute with a group of guys who joked that she resembled Sheneneh, a fictional character in Martin Lawrence's sitcom who was created and played in drag by Martin himself. She was often ridiculed for the way that she spoke, and recalls how she and Black female friends noticed the adoration their Black male peers had for the white girls in their class and the attention they gave to them. The tension between the Black male and female community was so tense at the school that my wife opted to attend prom with someone from outside of the school, due to her Black male counterparts' fawning desire to exclusively date white girls.

According to the Pew Research Center, "In 2015, 17 percent of all US newlyweds had a spouse of a different race or ethnicity, marking more than a fivefold increase since 1967, when 3 percent of newlyweds were intermarried." Additionally, even though it might appear that Black men marry outside of their race more than any other group, US-born Asian and Hispanic newlyweds are more likely to do so than any other group, with a rate of 46 percent and 39 percent for newlyweds, respectively. Within the white American community, men and women tend to marry outside of their race at a rate similar to those who are Hispanic or Latinx. Among Asians, women are far more likely to marry outside of their race then men (36 percent to 21 percent). As for the personal experiences my mom, sister, and wife have had, the statistics validate them. According to this source, "Among Blacks, intermarriage is twice as prevalent for male newlyweds as it is for their female counterparts. While about one fourth of recently married Black men (24 percent) have a spouse of a different race or ethnicity, this share is 12 percent among recently married Black women."

Even though this is more prevalent in the Hispanic and Asian American communities, the historical context isn't the same, and neither are the circumstances that have produced this statistical difference. Black women are often portrayed negatively to the world, which is particularly damaging to a group that is demographically less than ten percent of the American population. Media conglomerates such as Viacom profit off the denigration of Black women, for example. Growing up, I'd see scantily clad Black women on BET, VH1, or MTV gyrating next to rappers who demeaned them while throwing cash, pouring champagne, and swiping credit cards through their butt cheeks. This would be fine, of course, if it was the women's choice, but rarely did I see a Black woman who was similar to the regal ones who helped raise me. Nowadays, the only difference is that music videos are rarely shown on television. The pernicious images and stereotypes remain, however.

Shows such as *Love & Hip Hop* and *Basketball Wives* show our Black sistas and brothas exploiting themselves and bringing these stereotypes to life for profit and to continue a legacy of racism and white supremacy.

If you turn off the television and choose to listen to commercialized rap music, it's quite possible you'll come across a rapper who holds similar sentiments toward Black women. For example, platinum rapper and producer Yung Berg once said:

> I'm kinda racist… I don't like dark butts… You know how some women prefer light skin men or dark skin men. It's rare that I do dark butts—that's what I call dark-skinned women… I [don't date women] darker than me. I love the pool test. If you can jump in the pool exactly like you are and you don't come out looking better than you looked before going in the pool—then that's not a good look. Any woman that uses brown gel to set down her baby hair is not poppin'! (Bossip)

Additionally, another platinum rapper, Kodak Black, exclaims:

> It's just not my preference to deal with a dark-skinned woman. I'm already dark. I like light-skinned women. Dark-skin women

> are more difficult. I like light-skin women. They are more
> sensitive. (Jackson)

These sentiments weren't birthed by Black men and women, though. There are deep historical roots to the hatred that is shown toward Black women in America, dating back to slavery and the Jim Crow era, of course. Since ownership of humans was legal during slavery, it should come as no surprise that raping Black women (and at times Black men) was commonplace and permissible. In fact, twelve of the first sixteen presidents owned slaves and likely engaged in this type of inhumane debauchery. Most notably, Thomas Jefferson was known to repeatedly rape a teenage enslaved African that he owned named Sally Hemings. Although several kids came as a result of this relationship, Jefferson constantly denied her and his Black offspring during his lifetime.

To continue the persistence of this vile pestilence of a belief over the course of history, the media back then was used, as it is today, to further propagate the myth of Black female inferiority. They did this by the propagation of grotesque stereotypes. Black women were viewed as nothing more than child-bearing mammies whose only purpose was to be overweight and tend to household duties (especially as the "help" for white families), sexualized Jezebels who yearned for sexual pleasure from their white masters despite the fact that they were often violently raped and viciously beaten, or the Sapphire who is often personified by depicting our queens as "angry Black women"(as if they don't have a reason to be mad at how they're often treated).

Never is it taught or shown, however, that Black women have historically had to boldly speak up and fend for themselves and their children in the face of white supremacy as their families were torn apart during and after slavery. How else would you expect someone to react to the constant systemic decimation and obliteration of their family structure, even after slavery, with the Black Codes, Jim Crow-era policies, and the ongoing War on Drugs?

Based on the factual history of Black women, the stereotypes shown should be more consistent with Queen Hatshepsut of Ancient Kemet (Egypt), whose reign led to a period of economic prosperity. Or Queen Nzinga of Angola and Queen Nannie of the Maroons of Jamaica, who showed the warrior spirit present in Black women when it came to resisting European oppression and slavery. Lest I forget our most notable Black American queen, Harriet Tubman, whose altruistic approach to activism afforded many enslaved Blacks freedom, whether through her Underground Railroad routes or her service in the Civil War as a spy.

Black women historically have often been portrayed as angry, bitter, hyper-sexualized, promiscuous, and irrationally defiant, as opposed to beautiful, intelligent, wise, resilient, supportive, captivating, strong, courageous, and innovative. Notice, too, that none of the prevalent historical stereotypes profess the notion that Black women—the mothers of all mankind—are suitable for marriage or committed relationships. That distinction is usually reserved for white women.

The blatant disregard for accurate representation of Black women has served to justify the abusive brutality they are faced with in America. With so many Americans living in segregated communities still, exposure to other cultures often comes from the media. So, it should come as no surprise that the following incidents occurred.

In 2014, Marlene Pinnick was pulled over and punched in the face more than ten times by an officer while he straddled her on the side of a highway as if he were a UFC fighter (Moshtaghian). Cherish Thomas was viciously body-slammed on the concrete on the side of a highway for recording a traffic stop in Rio Vista, California (Washington). Katie McCray was beaten like a rabid wild animal in a DeKalb County, Georgia, liquor store for shoplifting. The baton beatings caused her to "sustain a laceration on her leg and multiple contusions on her arms and legs" (Burke). In Atlanta, Georgia, Maggie Thomas was pulled from her car during a traffic stop (while already parked), body-slammed, tased, and punched in the face repeatedly in front of her four-year-old daughter for allegedly not having insurance (B. Edwards). In Joliet, Illinois, Konika Morrow was violently tackled and swung around like a rag doll on the curb and grass for attempting to counsel her nephew who was being detained for riding a dirt bike. She was later admitted to the hospital with a swollen face, sprained knee, and several scratches on her arm (Ferak).

With the exception of the first case, all of the aforementioned incidents occurred in 2019. These assaults by officers just don't happen to the same degree to white women, who are a higher percentage of the female population in this country than any other racial group (US Department of Health and Human Services). With that said, I completely understand why my mother felt the way she did, especially considering the time period in which she was born (1957).

Although she alluded to Black women being disrespected and often overlooked, I didn't quite get it because my scope of reality was so limited. In my neighborhood, I was often the youngest one, so there weren't many girls my age I could "date." As far as I am concerned, love is love, and I don't think that can be restrained to someone's "racial" background. With that said, I firmly believe that Black women are the most beautiful, intelligent, innovative, inspiring, captivating, nurturing, and resilient women on this planet. Conversely, my personal experiences, reflections, aspirations, and cultural practices mean that I am at my best personally when I am with a Black woman—a sista. That's precisely why I married my wife.

As a young man, however, I was just trying to figure out life. At Mount Greenwood, I "dated" two Black girls for a short period of time; however, there was one sista named Denise that I always had my eye on who had been dating the same guy for as long as I could remember, so I didn't stand a shot. I hadn't grown out of my shy stage when it came to approaching girls, so I had a variety of crushes that never materialized due to my own inhibitions. During my eighth-grade year, this same girl

I had a crush on, Denise, helped orchestrate the shortest "relationship" I ever had with another girl I had a crush on who was white. This girl was also named Mary (quite ironically, not connected to the previous situation).

We had been friends who a while, and through Denise's cajoling, I was able to find out that she liked me as well. After a few days of passing notes through Denise, Mary and I were dating. What I didn't account for, however, was that even though we liked each other, our cultural differences, and family dynamics, would serve as a barrier to any substantial relationship being formed. When we spoke on the phone, there were awkward silences, and our pop culture references were limited to what was most germane to white American culture. For example, we could speak about Adam Sandler's movies with ease, but she was clueless about Ice Cube's classic *Friday*. This, more than anything, reflected the expectation of acquiescence to white spaces that Black people are expected to endure, an expectation that is nonexistent for most white people. Our relationship would end soon after, in a span of about three days, when I was informed, not by Mary but by Denise, that we needed to cease dating and talking to each other over the phone because her dad did not approve of her dating a Black boy.

Although I'm certain a real relationship would've never lasted, it was embarrassing and infuriating that I was told that it could no longer exist due to our race, rather than our cultural differences. From the time I started at Mount Greenwood at age six, to the time I graduated eight years later in 2001, my white friends and I grew apart from each other, and this situation, which occurred shortly before graduation, personified that growing gap. It wasn't our choice, however. Society told us that we would have to eventually go different ways, because we had different roles to play in this social structure. Whereas I would be going back to the Black side of Chicago for high school, my white friends, male and female, would mostly remain in their neighborhoods and sink further into the socialization that regarded their race and culture as norm and superior, while I would now be tasked with the responsibility of rejecting the socialization that told me and my Black friends that we were inferior in every capacity.

I tried to keep in touch with my white friends after graduating, but it was difficult, especially in an era devoid of smart phones and social media. I even took the bus to Mount Greenwood to see a close friend named Nick, on a half-day in high school. That didn't last, however, because it became too burdensome. We would go on to mostly establish segregated social circles, not because we wanted to be, but because society had established a design that predetermined that this would be the inevitable course, in order to continue to perpetuate the myth of race, and its companion, white supremacy, or racism.

PART II

CHAPTER 7

...WHEN I WAS ACTING WHITE

Even though I had survived the Y2K scare of New Year's Eve 1999—when the world grappled with its possible end due to a paranoia that all computers would simultaneously malfunction—my uncertainty resided in another aspect of life: high school.

The inevitable next step in my life was causing more anxiety than I could handle at thirteen years old. While my white friends were immersed in what I've coined "Catholic School Hysteria" or CSH, I wasn't sure what high school I would be attending. I was often lost in the discussion that emerged between white friends during lunch as they discussed the possibility of attending Catholic schools in the area such as St. Rita, Brother Rice, or Marist. Inadvertently, my Black friends and I would cower during such discussions, since we already knew our parents couldn't afford to send us to those schools.

Besides that, these schools were more than 90 percent white, and it was paramount at this point in my life that I find an environment that was more inclusive racially and socially. I couldn't help but be reminded of Kola's experience as I weighed my decisions. "Go back to Africa, nigger!" replayed repeatedly in my head.

If these friends weren't caught in CSH, they were discussing the newly constructed Chicago High School of Agricultural Science (CH-SAS) which had immensely more resources than my neighborhood school. Johnson High School, the school I would have to attend, was failing, and its population dissipated yearly as more and more Black residents opted to send their children outside of the neighborhood for a better opportunity in their academic careers.

In my hood, my friends discussed Johnson High School as if it was a prison. You had to fight to survive because daily physical confrontations were inevitable. If you didn't get into an altercation on campus, you'd surely get jumped at the bus stop on the way home. How much of this was fact or fiction? I had no idea, but as a naïve eighth-grader, I rarely heard anything positive about high school, particularly Johnson High School, unless it centered on the freedom you'd have during lunch and the girls.

My mom, a lifelong Chicago Public Schools educator, was conflicted about Johnson High School because of its reputation. She was concerned about the school's report card and the dismal percentage of students who were college-ready by graduation. Although I didn't know what I was going to study in college at the time, I knew I was going because my parents had ingrained it in my head from childhood. The only thing more important than my hoop dreams was college enrollment.

My generation was taught that college was paramount for success, so if a school's report card didn't measure up, parents would do anything to ensure their child had a better opportunity academically. In fact, many of my neighborhood friends found ways to attend more attractive schools in the south suburbs.

You know what's funny? I've never heard of white residents in Chicago sending their children to suburban schools for a better education. Maybe that was because, under Richard Daley (and Rahm Emanuel), tax money was constantly used toward providing fantabulous facilities and supplies for schools located near downtown and the north side. Unsurprisingly, these are the locations where most of the city's white residents live, outside of Mount Greenwood on the southwest side.

Schools like Jones College Prep, Northside College Prep, and Payton College Prep continued to thrive while schools on the far South Side in my neighborhood were deemed failures. I wasn't sure if that stigma was because of their academic record or because of their downtrodden and decrepit buildings. Symbolism at its finest.

My eventual choice for high school, Morgan Park, represented a duality. This is because Morgan Park had a reputation around the city as a "good" school, and it was. However, it was more nuanced than people knew, especially when I started in 2001. There was an element of prestige and high academic standards, especially with their honors classes and IB program, which admitted middle schoolers in seventh and eighth grade with an opportunity to graduate high school early. What wasn't often advertised about Morgan Park in the early 2000s was its dichotomy. There were just as many students at Morgan Park who had unfortunately adapted to an environment that was predicated on survival, while immersed in redlined neighborhoods that lacked adequate resources, basic necessities, and access to educational institutions like museums and libraries.

Because of this, I had just as many peers who had been deleteriously impacted by their redlined communities as peers who strived to be admitted to a top college. Fortunately, though, I was able to evade the desire to acquiesce to the temptation of living that was predicated on survival and the entrapments that were intentionally designed by the architects of redlining. I saw the money my comrades in the street had, but I feared my parents' wrath more than any officer or prison. Although we weren't rich, we had access to everything we needed, and imaginative parents who gave us educational experiences that weren't as easily accessible in our neighborhoods. That made a tremendous difference in the lives of me and my sister.

I stepped foot on the campus of Morgan Park after Labor Day in 2001 confused and feeling culturally inept. Although I was a born and bred Chicago South Sider and had been fully immersed in Black culture my entire life, I had attended a white school for eight years, so I was ignorant of what it meant to assimilate to a Black school. At Morgan Park High School, I was no longer the token, so at the time I assumed I wouldn't encounter racism again. That's before I realized that the demographics and perpetually impoverished condition of the neighborhood in which I lived and attended school was the result of institutional racism.

Morgan Park was essentially a microcosm of the Black experience, as it exhibited the challenges that existed when one attempted to climb the social ranks while remaining true to one's cultural identity. Geographically, the school represented this duality in its location of 111th and Vincennes. On one side, there was the bourgeois element of Beverly, which ironically led to my old school, Mount Greenwood. On the other side, which led to my home, was the hood. That side of the street had liquor stores, fast-food restaurants, and fried chicken spots galore, whereas the Beverly side contained coffee shops, bookstores, and yoga centers. One part of you wanted to remain true to your roots, while the other part was innately curious about life on the bourgeois side of town.

I didn't realize it at the time, but the aesthetic of the Morgan Park neighborhood was as intentional as our enslavement, Jim Crow apartheid, and subsequent redlining. Morgan Park, which was on the far South Side of Chicago, began as a suburb, until it was eventually annexed in 1914. The Black population in Morgan Park grew tremendously following WWI, as they migrated from the South during the Great Migration, and from various other parts of the city for more secure employment (particularly as a Pullman porter). While this was happening, racially dividing lines of segregation were being drawn at the same spot where I noticed a stark difference in resource allocation. Morgan Park's white community primarily lived to the west of the de facto dividing line of Vincennes Avenue, and to the east was Morgan Park's Black community.

The white community protested to create and maintain this status quo, and that intolerance unsurprisingly made its way into the classroom. Black students who attended Morgan Park High School in the 1920s under these conditions complained about being unfairly graded by white teachers. Additionally, they were excluded from certain extracurricular activities, segregated during graduation, and regularly encountered racism at football games. The cheerleading squad is said to have chanted "Nigger, nigger, pull the trigger" toward Black students. This behavior was never punished within the school. This isn't hard to conceptualize when you consider that the principal during this time, William Schoch, often referred to Morgan Park's Black students as "blackies." Led by their parents, white students at the school even objected to a successful protest by the Black community that overturned a decision to send Black freshman to a local elementary to counter overcrowding. It is on this foundation that I attended my first Black public school. With a historical foundation like that, and without any intentional remediation or repair for the students and community, it is clear that my high school was only Black in population. The institution that maintained it and that contributed to its emergence was unequivocally white supremacist (*Schools of Our Own: Chicago's Golden Age of Black Private Education* by Worthi Kamili Hayes, 55–56).

It wasn't too long after starting at Morgan Park that I found my community, and we bonded quickly, much like my forefathers did when they moved from the South. That included Anthony, who was a tall, skinny (formerly overweight), brown-skinned, gregarious dude who was about 6'4" and loved baseball, laughing, and girls. He also favored Sean Carter (Jay-Z), so he was often teased with a diamond hand gesture and shouts of "Hova! Hova!" and "Jigga!" We started high school the same year Jay dropped his magnum opus, *Blueprint*, so imagine the jokes Anthony heard.

Ben, another close friend of mine, was average in height, at about 5'9", stocky, dark-skinned, and jovial, with a penchant for using profanity. Now, we say he favors James Harden, but from 2001–2005 we'd call him "Black ass" and "tar baby" as he hurled insults back at Anthony and me about our noticeably African features (big nose and lips) and my apparent "swole neck." No one was hurt emotionally, though, as it was the norm. We just laughed at each other. Some would refer to this as "the dozens," but our generation aptly called it "heating" or "roasting" because once the jokes were dispersed consecutively in a barrage, you felt like you were in the hot seat. Not being prepared to respond accordingly in a humorous manner was utterly embarrassing.

Unbeknownst to us, our berating and degrading jokes were a catharsis rooted in the oral tradition of West Africa, where it was used to strengthen bonds amongst neighboring tribes. This tradition was later transplanted to America during slavery where it was bastardized (Wald). This lighthearted game poked fun at the least desirable enslaved Africans who were often sold to other plantations in groups of dozens, due to the physical torture they endured for disobedience. Being sold in dozens, at the lowest rate possible, was such an embarrassment that the victims had to protect their pride by being able to verbally retort to detractors with the most hilariously vile insults, usually directed toward the opponent's mother, without losing their cool. Inevitably, "the dozens" served as a coping mechanism for a group of people who were physically and psychologically berated and "roasted" by whites daily. It allowed enslaved Blacks to express frustration in a jovial, nonphysical manner toward their brethren, a frustration that wasn't allowed to be directed toward the people who were the true cause of their woes without the fear of death (Saloy).

Essentially, what this meant was that enslaved Blacks ridiculed other enslaved Blacks for not being valued as a highly profitable asset by their owners when placed on the auction block. It seems as if that would be celebrated, especially considering that most of these enslaved Blacks were devalued for disobedience, which presumably meant their defiance was likely an attempt at gaining freedom or an assertion of equality.

Although this game is a personification of the ingenuity of the African oral tradition, its American-centered jokes tended to reflect the self-hatred many Blacks were indoctrinated with as a means of social control. Infamously, this intraracial conflict was best espoused in the fictional Willie Lynch letter:

> Don't forget you must pitch the old Black male vs. the young Black male, and the young Black male against the old Black male. You must use the dark skin slaves vs. the light skin slaves, and the light skin slaves vs. the dark skin slaves. You must use the female vs. the male. And the male vs. the female. You must also have your white servants and overseers distrust all Blacks. It is necessary that your slaves trust and depend on us. They must love, respect and trust only us. (The Final Call)

Jokes denigrating dark complexions, wide noses, and thick lips—all African features—were pervasive as we unknowingly mocked and ridiculed the natural beauty that God had blessed us with. We thought these were just jokes. We had no idea how sick this pestilence was that had been bestowed upon us by our forefathers. So, the hatred we expressed was simply an outward expression of our internalized trauma.

Subconsciously, through our overtly espoused hatred for African features, we unknowingly expressed a love and appreciation for Eurocentric features, which were simply an adaptation of the migration patterns of Africans who opted for a colder climate. It's simple biology that I was never taught in high school.

We're all from Africa, but due to our rich melanin content, we were more closely related to the original woman than the few white students at Morgan Park, whose ancestral lineage was more closely tied to those who migrated from Africa to the colder climate of Europe thousands of years ago. There's pride now in knowing my melanin content connects me to the original woman, but that pride didn't exist then. Essentially, my comrades and I expressed an unfaltering disgust and repugnant view of our long-deceased mother. Hatred, racism, and self-hatred are learned.

As I assimilated to the culture of Morgan Park High School, I attempted to force myself to care about my attire. I often sheepishly coaxed my parents into buying me name-brand clothes when back-to-school shopping came around. I tried to convince them to buy me a pair of Jordans or two, but the best I could do was get the $100 Jumpman shoes. Honestly, I didn't care about the Platinum FUBU, Rocawear, or Sean John I wore. I didn't care about the new Jordans I never got either. I only truly cared about acquiescing to the popular trends in our culture—which were ultimately established by hip-hop artists and the white oligarchs who owned the labels they were signed to—as a means of blending in and avoiding the wrath of a student on a roasting rant. My skills were average at best; even still, you never wanted to put yourself in a position to be an easy target. Your proverbial "roasting" gun had to remain loaded while you were concurrently draping yourself with bulletproof armor (your clothing "gear"). If not, you'd likely hear these words as someone in Division (a common period similar to homeroom) crept up behind you loudly uttering, "If you don't get yo' Payless Shoe shopping ass outta here!" I recognize that type of frugality as intelligent now. In fact, I've purchased some dress shoes from Payless as an adult. However, you wouldn't want to be caught dead with a pair of shoes from there at my high school. This new desire for consumerism was not compatible with my personality and nature, but I went along with it. However, I always felt something was off. I knew I was meant for something greater while I was draped in these expensive clothes because I innately question things constantly.

Academically, I wanted to excel and maintain anything ranging from a 3.5–4.0 GPA so I could get into my college of choice. I had no idea what having a 3.5 exactly meant yet, but I figured it was good since a 4.0 was the standard of excellence. I was competitive, and not just while playing basketball. By the time I had graduated from Morgan Park four years later, I had accrued a transcript that was full of honors-level courses and an attempt at an AP course that failed due to a scheduling conflict with my work-study job. However, my high school career didn't start this way.

By far the toughest class I had in high school (excluding chemistry, because it never made sense to me) was my freshman year world history course taught by the energetic Ms. Donovan.

It became apparent immediately that Ms. Donovan, regardless of her vivacious and gregarious spirit, held high expectations and was strict in the implementation of them. However, there seemed to be only a few students in the class, myself included, who were prepared to attempt to meet those standards.

One thing that continuously shocked me, as I endured this arduous process, was the fact that many of my classmates seemed to have an apathetic view toward competing academically, at least in this class. This became especially apparent on exam days, when our review sheets were due. Ms. Donovan would give us small review sheets prior to the exams that detailed various topics that we discussed throughout the most recent unit on a half-sheet of paper.

I recall, on a dreary autumn day in October, navigating and scurrying through the vast school hallways like a fullback searching for an offensive lineman-created hole as we transitioned from seventh to eighth period in anticipation of Ms. Donovan's most recent exam on ancient Greece (ironically, we'd start our world history course with Europe, as opposed to Africa, which is the origin of mankind and human civilization). Fully equipped with a massive black Jansport book bag, which was hanging sloppily off my shoulder, I finally reached Ms. Donovan's class. I was the second student in the class. Second only to a cute girl named Tamika, who I quietly competed with for the highest grade in the course.

At this point in the school year, I had a high C average in the class, so this exam was pivotal for me. If I didn't perform well, I would have the stain of a C in a report card full of As.

Soon after I arrived, the rest of the class followed and hesitantly seated themselves before the bell rang. As I reached into my messy book bag to pull out an equally crumbled-up review sheet, I noticed student after student whispering and chatting discreetly. It piqued my curiosity because the conversation seemed to quickly disseminate across the room as Ms. Donovan remained outside to greet each student with a high five.

In no time, I was wrapped up in the furious chatter when I was tapped on the shoulder by a tall and lanky student named Mitchell. "Yo, E, you do your homework, jo?"

Before I could decipher what this conversation might lead to, I hesitantly and naively responded and assured Mitchell that I did in fact complete it.

"Bet! You mind if I see it real quick, jo?" Mitchell quickly responded.

I reluctantly obliged, and as I looked around the class, I noticed that about half of the students were also frantically copying review sheets provided by myself, Tamika, and a few other students who had completed their work. In other words, the students who had the highest averages provided answers to those who were barely passing the course. Although I loved being an asset to anyone in need of assistance, that situation didn't sit well with me, especially since the individuals in that class who requested my assistance weren't friends of mine.

As the bell rang, Ms. Donovan began talking in her usual boisterous tone, requesting we pass up the homework. I unenthusiastically did so, as I could not shake the feeling of being used—something that I resent. There was no time for this prolonged reflection, however, because I was intently focused on passing this exam with an A so that I could at least get a B in the course in time for report cards.

In my household, for as long as I could remember, my parents and grandparents consistently promoted the benefits of academic success in terms of providing a guaranteed pathway to success as an adult.

My maternal grandmother, Ollie Mae, was so serious about the promotion of academic excellence that she essentially bribed me and my sister for every A and B we got on our report cards while in high school. She was so stringent that we were required to read books and magazines at her house before we watched TV, something that I frowned upon because I absolutely detested reading books at that age. Now, I often employ the same tactic with my children. How's that for irony?

To make matters worse, she didn't have cable on her gargantuan-sized television, so when we completed the tedious task of reading and providing a report for whatever book or magazine (usually *Jet*) that she had available, it behooved us to continue out of sheer boredom and lack of tangible options. The only other choice was to watch the local news channels broadcast the same propaganda every hour cyclically. Although it was frustrating to us in our adolescence, I now have a better grasp of my maternal grandmother's reasoning as a Black woman from the South.

Ollie Mae Knight was a sharecropper from a small town in Mississippi called Bolton in the 1930s and '40s as America was still recovering from the Great Depression. Having dealt with economic turmoil and overt racism throughout her life, she decided to relocate to Jackson, Michigan, and ultimately Chicago, after meeting and marrying my grandfather, James Knight. After having three beautiful daughters and divorcing when she was in her 40s, my grandmother enrolled in college and eventually graduated with a master's degree in social work. She then became the vice president, and later president, of a social service agency in Chicago that afforded her the opportunity to aid those afflicted by drug abuse. She also got to travel the world, earning a hefty annual salary.

Education literally granted her a better life and more opportunities, and she wanted nothing more than for her grandchildren to take advantage of the same opportunities she had been afforded. So, the payola we received was deeply rooted in the red soil of Bolton, Mississippi. This was one of the reasons that homework and high academic standards were expected, but my father's indelible impression would serve to be just as impactful.

My father's perspective on education was quite unique and vastly different from my maternal grandmother's. As a highly intelligent man who was the model for consistency (he worked for one company his entire career), I could tell that he wanted me to take a different route and create a new legacy for Crim men, since he did not have a college degree.

While I might've seen my grandmother once a month, I saw my father weekly. After my parents divorced, it had been arranged that he would pick us up from school every Wednesday, and we'd also spend the night twice a month. When my sister went away to college my freshman year, those car rides to my dad's house became a solo venture. As a younger child, those rides were usually jovial. However, as I approached middle school and high school, those conversations were more nuanced and rooted in academic achievement.

I distinctly remember not wanting to attain a C on any assignment because I dreaded having to reveal the details to my father on that twenty-minute ride to his house. Like clockwork, whenever my dad picked me up on the corner of Monterey Avenue off 111th street, in front of Morgan Park, he'd greet me with a hug and a kiss. This quickly transitioned to a question about my grades.

"What did you get on your test, Ern?" he'd ask sternly and methodically, while maintaining a steady focus on the road.

What irritated me the most about this question was it was almost as if he'd had a prior conversation with my teachers or eavesdropped on their teachers' lounge diatribes. How else would he know about my exams? This was even more irksome when you consider that I went to high school during a time when you couldn't access your overall grades online. We were at the mercy of our teacher's green gradebook. So, he'd have no way of accessing my grades unless he called my teachers or asked me, as he did weekly. Putting the pressure on me, however, caused me to be accountable. Also, in hindsight, I know that he was able to simply conclude that I would likely have at least one weekly assessment in one of my seven classes, but back then, it felt as if he was in cahoots with my instructors. Even if I did not have an assignment that could be deemed a summative assessment, he'd continue to badger me with questions until I revealed some sort of quantitative data related to the assignment.

I deemed myself to be precocious, especially during my freshman year, so most times this interaction was quite pleasant because I'd simply be relaying to my father that I received an A or B. However, when I received a grade lower than that, I resented the question and tried to avoid it at all costs. "How about those Bulls?!"

My diversion tactics hardly ever worked. If I wasn't interrogated in the car, I'd surely be confronted with that question when we arrived at his home. What's more, whenever I got a B or C, he'd always pressure me to strategize what I could do to attain an A on the next assessment.

The process was a trivial annoyance, but it caused me to raise my expectations. Additionally, from an historical perspective, that academic apathy wasn't in alignment with who we were historically as Africans. Black Americans directly descend from those who lived in west and central Africa, and have always prioritized education and teaching the youth as a matter of cultural capital. The empires that many of us descend from, which consisted of the Benin, Songhai, Zimbabwe, Ghana, and Mali empires, to name a few, contained great learning centers and educators, like griots, who kept our stories, customs, and traditions alive.

The Mali and Songhai empires, for instance, contained a large city called Timbuktu, which emerged as a lucrative trade center and center of Islamic culture and scholarship in the fifth century. Timbuktu was also the home of one of the most well-known educational institutions in the world at the time. This institution, the Sankoré Madrasa or University of Sankoré (using contemporary language), was a mosque and learning center that was established in the thirteenth century. From the thirteenth century, through its peak in the sixteenth century, which also corresponds with the origins of the transatlantic slave trade, these Africans wrote as many as 500,000 texts, according to some estimates, on a variety of topics ranging from art, mathematics, science, and astronomy to human rights, poetry, medicine, philosophy, and religion (the Quran). These texts were used as the foundation for the instruction, facilitation, and teaching that occurred at the roughly 180 Koranic schools at the University of Sankoré, which had about 25,000 students (which is on par with many large state universities in the US today). It should be no surprise, then, that the educators in this region were Black (West African, to be exact). That was the norm. Because these peoples weren't yet impacted by systemic racism and colonialism, there was no inferiority complex that associated Blackness with ignorance or assumed that educational attainment was not synonymous with West African culture.

It's hard to fathom an environment where 100 percent of the educators and students are of African descent and not being targeted by outside forces due to the high level of educational success and attainment, or being systemically robbed of resources like many Black-led schools and HBCUs. On the contrary, to be Black then was to be viewed as someone who was expected to reach great heights educationally, because you were all that existed for thousands of miles. This wasn't just germane to

West Africa, however, as it is stated that curious students traveled from various other parts of Africa, as well as Asia and Europe, to learn from the scholars at this fine institution.

One scholar, who was likely Sankoré's most well-known educator, was Ahmad Baba (1556–1627). Baba was a prolific writer who authored more than forty books during his time, and because of his commitment to Islam was viewed as the reviver of the religion (the Mujjadid) during his time. His work was so revered that his legacy lives on with the aptly named Ahmed Baba Institute, which is the only public library in Timbuktu, Mali, and contains over 18,000 manuscripts.

This is just a glimpse of our commitment to education as West African people. Even beyond that, the most famous African civilization, ancient Kemet (Egypt), set the standard for education, not just in Africa, but in the world, several thousand years ago. These Africans created educational systems and institutions, like the temple at Waset (which is regarded as the world's first university) and Per-Ankh ("House of Life") learning centers. These institutions allowed the dissemination of knowledge and eventually led to the creation of such marvels and edifices as the Great Sphinx of Giza, obelisks, Abu Simbel, pyramids, and various other architectural marvels whose production still confuses Western scholars.

This ancient society laid the foundation for many of our arts, sciences, mathematics, and wisdom. For instance, the oldest book in the world, *The Maxims of Ptahhotep*, was produced around 2375 BC by Ptahhotep, who is said to have produced the book for his son. Additionally, Imhotep, the famed and revered polymath (multi-genius) whose mathematical and architectural knowledge was responsible for the construction of the Step Pyramid of Djoser around 2630 BC is also viewed as the first medical doctor in recorded history. In fact, his foundational medicinal knowledge inspired Hippocrates 2,200 years later, through his medical manuals that would later be renamed the Edwin Smith Papyrus.

Realizing this made the accepting mediocrity unacceptable, as it would be a shameful representation of my upbringing, the tutelage and wisdom I was afforded, and the sacrifices of my parents, grandparents, and ancestors I never had the opportunity to meet. Because of this, I couldn't fathom perpetually missing homework assignments, especially in preparation for an exam. How would I be able to explain the lackluster grade I would likely receive to my dad, due to negligent preparation? How would my grandmother react? I didn't have a job at this point in my life, so a low grade would have a deleterious impact on my finances, amongst other things. When I handed Mitchell my homework that day, I felt as if I had disrespected the hard work I put forth. Furthermore, it felt disrespectful to the wisdom that I had been fortunate enough to receive.

It wouldn't become apparent to me until I was moved to honors classes the following year that the culture in the classes I had my freshman year was not conducive to embracing the standards of academic excellence that I expected. I was told in that class by my peers that a commitment to academics was "acting white." In my honors classes, I was never the smartest person, statistically, and when I forgot my homework, I was always in the minority. In those classes we competed and strove to get higher class rankings. Showing effort and continuously striving to achieve excellence in those classes was the norm; however, in the courses I took my freshman year, it was a rarity. Again, the duality of Morgan Park. The nuance of the Black experience.

It seemed to me that an ostentatious appearance (access to the latest clothing lines and Jordan shoes), persona, and access to highly-coveted material items granted you popularity and respect amongst your peers, as opposed to the flaunting of your academic skills and success. In hindsight, this ideal is an American problem, too. Kim Kardashian gets paid more than your local teacher, for example. That's a problem.

This mindset and notion that academic achievement is "acting white" is a viewpoint that is deeply entrenched in our community, with roots reaching back to slavery, and at one point served as a defense mechanism for survival. How disquieting that such a malevolent pestilence continues to have a grasp on our children.

During slavery, it was illegal for enslaved Africans to be taught how to read and write in English. In fact, you would be punished by a public beating, castration, staking to the ground, or worst of all, death, amongst other things. Likewise, whites who were caught teaching enslaved Africans how to read could be punished by receiving a fine or jail time. Imagine the effect this abrasive approach to education had on Blacks, even when they gained "freedom" following the Civil War.

The seeds of destruction and educational malaise and disregard were planted during slavery. The government's failure to provide adequate remediation or reparation during and after the Reconstruction period led many Black communities to search for equality while fully immersed in an educational, economic, and political deficit, without the necessary aid to cure the ailment. However, the intrinsic motivation and persistence of "free" Blacks after slavery, like Mary McLeod Bethune, W. E. B. DuBois, and Booker T. Washington ensured that education remained a paramount fixture in the Black community.

Why the haste, though? What was so powerful about education from the perspective of the slave owner? Look no further than abolitionists and revolutionaries such as Nat Turner, Frederick Douglass, and Paul Cuffee, who used the English language to gain exposure and act on the concept of liberation theology from the Bible, and various other texts. The Bible was also the book that was used to justify the enslavement of Africans. This type of pernicious intent was successful with many, except for the sagacious enslaved African who discovered the various tales of liberation and freedom in the Bible. Knowledge was and is power, so those enslaved Africans who learned how to read were an imminent threat to the racist and capitalistic white supremacist power structure in America. Frederick Douglass said it best:

"Education means emancipation. It means light and liberty. It means the uplifting of the soul of man into the glorious light of truth, the light by which men can only be made free."

Africans who were enslaved in America were illiterate in English when they arrived here, but not because they lacked the intellectual capacity. Rather, they were illiterate in English because, prior to slavery and colonialism, the language served no purpose in their native land. For example, American heroes such as Harriet Tubman and Sojourner Truth were illiterate, but intelligent enough to know they were regal beings who did not deserve the inhumane treatment to which slaves were subjected.

At present, there are at least 1,500 languages and dialects spoken in Africa (Matshego). This is an immense number indeed, but imagine what it used to be before the rapacious and avaricious nature of European imperialism and colonialism. English and French now serve as two of the most dominant languages in the African continent. Before imperialism and colonization, languages that were spoken in western Africa, such as Igbo, Somali, Fulani, Swahili, Yoruba, Wolof, and Arabic, stem from the same east African (ancient Kemet/Egyptian) root as all European languages, which is Medu Neter. Ancient Greeks spoke Latin which has roots in the ancient Egyptian dialect of Medu Neter. Not only did ancient Greek philosophers such as Hippocrates, Pythagoras, Plato, Homer, Socrates, and Aristotle come to Africa (Egypt)—the epicenter of knowledge thousands of years ago—to learn the foundations for mathematics, philosophy, astronomy, architecture, medicine, spirituality, and literature as created by such African scholars as Imhotep, Akhenaten, Ptahhotep, Amenemhat, Merikare, Duauf, and Amenhotep, they also learned the basic tenets of the Medu Neter, which they would use as the foundation for Latin (Asante).

The Western father of medicine, Hippocrates, learned extensively from Imhotep in Africa and even "borrowed" his common phrase, "Let food be thy medicine and let medicine be thy food." In terms of Medu

Neter's roots in Latin, the best example would be to dissect the word "philosopher," which translates to lover of wisdom. The affix *phil* means "lover," whereas the suffix *sophia* translates to wisdom. This paradigm and concept of "loving wisdom" comes from the Medu Neter word *seba* or *sebo* which mean "the wise" (Asante).

Latin, which borrowed its foundational principles from Medu Neter, then gave birth to the Germanic languages, which include English, the same language that was used as a phrenic weapon during slavery by being prohibited to the enslaved African community—the same language that was used to degrade an entire "race" of people. The same language that we currently lack fluency in, due to past and current oppression, and that was used to degrade our very existence and hide the impressive achievements of our ancestors. The weaponization of this language, which led to the creation of a pathology of educational nihilism in certain segments of the Black community, was essentially foundationally created by our distant relatives (Asante).

Africa's impact on the intellectual development of Europe did not cease with the conquering of ancient Egypt around 300 BC by Alexander the Great. If we fast forward to the 700s, we are able to witness Europe, in the midst of the Dark Ages, experience a reemergence of intellectual gravitas due, yet again, to the influence of Africa.

It has been well-documented that Europe, at this time, was plagued not just with health concerns, but with an illiteracy rate as high as 99 percent in some regions. Over the course of 700 years, African Moors provided pathways to education, literacy, and adequate health by establishing schools, universities (like the world's first great university, Timbuktu, in the West African kingdom of Mali), sewage systems, and even hospitals. Conveniently, Christopher Columbus's voyage and subsequent plundering of the "new world" (a world visited by Africans and Asians for millennia prior) and enslavement of those with melanin took place soon after the Moors were displaced from Spain, in 1492 (Sertima).

As I expressed shock and whimsical bewilderment with the lack of academic concern from some of my peers, I was completely unaware of the historical context that preceded this train of thought. The nihilism some of us had then, and still have, toward education is not innate or indigenous to our culture; it was created and manufactured to systemically destroy our very being, to further ravage the world and deplete it of its vital resources for capital.

The current advancements that have been made philosophically, intellectually, and dialectically in the present day are owed to an intellectual foundation that was laid by Africans of varied descents, whose appearance mirrored that of myself and my classmates. For example, without Henry Sampson, there'd be no cell phone. Without Dr. Mark Dean, we wouldn't have the personal computer. Without Lewis Latimer, we wouldn't have a light bulb. Without Dr. Shirley Jackson, we wouldn't have the caller ID or technology for "call waiting." Additionally, without Marie Van Brittan Brown, we wouldn't have the home security system. And of course, without Dr. Katherine Johnson, we wouldn't have made it to the moon (ironically, the first Black woman in space, Mae Jemison, is also an alumna of my high school). The people who descend from this level of genius are the same people who are viewed as intellectually inferior in America. These are the same people who sometimes brandish intellectualism as "acting white." Wow.

CHAPTER 8
...WHEN I WAS DRIVING WHILE BLACK

November 7, 2003 was a day I'll never forget. I had finally turned sixteen and was now old enough to get my driver's license. My anticipation was unparalleled because I had a late birthday throughout my academic career. Now, in my thirties, it's great, because I'm younger than my friends, but as adolescents we were all racing to become adults, as if we could change our positioning in this "race." Older age was associated with maturity, independence, and manhood, despite our remaining fully dependent on the income of our parents.

Unlike my friends who turned sixteen during their sophomore year, I had to endure a frustrating and grueling summer as I drove around with them, equipped with only my six-month-old permit. We had fun, of course, but the fact that I had to still get dropped off and picked up frustrated me. Sure, I could've driven my mom's car alone with my permit, like many of my friends did before obtaining their license, but my momma wasn't going. In other words, she was a stickler for following the rules as it pertained to driving because of the stigma that came with driving while Black, a concept I didn't fully understand until I began driving alone. Even though I was aware of Rodney King, I was too young to comprehend and fathom the magnitude of such a polarizing event and court case.

On November 7, I woke up bright and early, with an anticipation that hadn't been felt since the Christmas mornings when I still believed in Santa Claus. As I wiped the sleep from my eyes, I immediately jumped out of my bed, nearly tripping, to locate my mom, who was already up on her computer, working. "Maaaa! What time are we going!?"

I pestered my mom as if I was the parent with an agenda of things to accomplish that day. "As soon as you get dressed, honey, because they close early."

The lines were excruciatingly long, and the employees were as impatient as the customers, but that didn't bother me because I had a goal and agenda that centered on freedom. It was all a blur. As I eventually sat down in my chair and gave the photographer my paperwork, I gave the camera the biggest Kool-Aid smile I could muster.

"Oh, it's your birthday, huh?" the lady at the DMV said with a slight smirk.

"Yep!" I replied out of the corner of my mouth in order to maintain my posture and smile. I felt she'd snap the picture at any moment, and I didn't want to be caught off guard.

"Ernest Crim!" When my name was yelled to signify my license was ready, I hopped up eagerly, grabbed my new license, and walked to the car with my mom and sister, feeling such a jubilance that I became immune to the dreary, bitter fall morning where the temperature barely crept above thirty-five degrees.

The drive home was refreshing, but I wouldn't be fully satisfied until I was driving without my mom or sister in the car. Later that evening, I planned on picking up my friends and driving to the mall with the sole purpose of stuntin', talking to girls, window shopping, and immersing myself in a moment of unadulterated freedom and liberty that the Founding Fathers would envy.

Although I was excited, I could tell that my mom was in a state of deep thought and reflection. "Make sure you call your dad back before you head out tonight, Ern."

I nodded in agreement, assuming she saw me, as I darted through a yellow light with 50 Cent's "In Da Club" bumping blaringly through my mom's red Ford Explorer speakers. "Slow down, boy!"

No matter how fast or slow you drive with your mom in the car, she's always going to lecture you, because in her mind you're always surpassing the speed limit by at least twenty m.p.h. I tend to think it also had an ounce of symbolism behind it, as she was likely reflecting on her youngest child approaching adulthood. That chant of "slow down" rang ominously as an order to halt, or at least slow, the inevitable progression toward college.

I returned my dad's call with a sense of pride as soon I got home. I felt like I was nearing adulthood, and who better to share this joy with than my dad, the man who taught me how to drive on the expressway and somehow remained calm and patient as I accidentally bumped a car while driving with him on my permit.

"Happy birthday, baby boy!"

Before I could reply with "thank you," he immediately interjected with a level of seriousness I had not heard from him since my parents were still married and I was being scolded for senselessly fighting someone who looked at me the wrong way.

"It's very important that, as you begin to drive alone without me and your ma, you stay alert and stay aware. Okay? As a well-mannered, intelligent young man, you have to understand DWB."

Before my dad could continue, I solemnly asked, "What's DWB, Dad?"

As he explained the phenomenon aptly titled "driving while Black" to me, I began to harken back to the images I had seen of Rodney King being viciously beaten in the early '90s when I was five years old. Although most of what I remember came from satirical shows like *In Living Color* mocking King's "Can't we all just get along?" comments, the images suddenly became crystal clear in my memory.

Before I got off the phone, my dad reminded me of the importance of remaining calm, following the officers' orders, and not riding with friends who might be involved in gangs or drug activities. Most importantly, he told me to avoid riding in a car full of friends under eighteen, because as young Black males we'd surely be the targets of officers.

Ridiculous, I thought. I'm sure my white friends didn't get this lecturing from their parents. Why should I avoid riding around with a car full of my friends if that's what we wanted to do? Why should my teenage years involve evasive respectable driving practices due to a fear of racist belligerence from local police officers?

I didn't quite understand what my dad meant by that statement then, but I would certainly find out very soon.

Spring break couldn't come fast enough during my junior year. As anyone can tell you, junior year tends to be the most stressful for those making plans for postsecondary education. The stress of keeping your grades up while taking honors courses and preparing for and taking college entrance exams like the SAT or the ACT that determine your future is taxing. It goes without saying that you also have to balance an extracurricular activity schedule (for some this also includes work). Without a doubt, it's the most important year of your high school career. So, I was crawling my way to spring break with eager anticipation.

"Yo E, you tryna hoop?"

When I received that call and question from Anthony on Monday morning, it was no doubt in his mind or my mind that I was on board. Besides playing NBA 2K or Madden, hooping was always a priority.

After receiving confirmation from my mom, I packed my Nike basketball shoes, malodorous shorts, and Gatorade and waited patiently for Anthony to come and pick me up at noon. We then drove back to his house to meet Ben, Darnell, and Derrick. The only thing that mattered to us that day was hooping.

As we departed, we engaged in our usual tomfoolery. The windows were down and, as we cruised down Stony Island to the University of Chicago, Anthony aggressively increased the volume of our favorite Three 6 Mafia, Lil' Jon, Jay-Z, and Dipset songs to ignorant levels to ensure that our neighbors on the road were aware that these five teenagers were unabashedly on spring break and enjoying every second of it.

We stayed for over five hours as we played nearly every person who came to the gymnasium at the University of Chicago that day.

"Catch it, E!" Ben exclaimed loudly as he threw me an alley-oop off the backboard before we got dressed in the locker room.

I wasn't anticipating it, but I quickly turned, ran, jumped and threw it down with tenacity one last time. I jumped so high that when I landed, I had to catch myself by strategically placing my hands on the ground to prevent my knees from slapping the freshly waxed hardwood floor.

That high would metaphorically represent a foil to the antithetical low that awaited us as we departed the premises.

As we crowded into Anthony's Chevy Lumina, Jay-Z's *The Black Album* commenced loudly, but not loud enough to drown out our raucous chants and proclamations of who had the better outing. Although we came together, we only played a few games on the same team, which meant we often guarded each other. Ben would always make the most outlandish claim to rile up everyone in the vicinity.

"Ain't none of y'all fucking wit' me. I Kobe'd all y'all bitches!" Ben said emphatically as we drove down Harper Avenue. For those unaware, only the greats can have their name turned into a verb equating to basketball domination over a competitor.

As we continued to drive and banter, I noticed a car in the rear view, a Pontiac Grand Prix to be exact. This keen observation wouldn't be so conspicuous had the car not seemingly shadowed the last three turns we made. It was likely that this car was on the same path we were on, but in Chicago you can never be too careful or suspicious.

We weren't even through "Dust Your Shoulder Off" when our debates abruptly ceased due to the interruption of loud sirens as we drove down Lake Park Avenue. We hoped they were from a passing ambulance, but unfortunately that would not be the case. My intuition was correct. I guess I wasn't paranoid after all.

"Oh shit," Al said, understandably nervous, as we all were. From my knowledge, we were going the speed limit, and we all had our seat belts on, which admittedly was a rarity. So, what could be the issue? We were loud, yes, but that's not a crime, and he couldn't tell that from following us, so what was the problem? The only other obvious factor: our car was full of five young Black men between the ages of sixteen and eighteen.

That was it, and that was all the Chicago Police Department needed to pull us over.

I clenched the armrest intently and dug my fingernails into the tan leather design as Anthony turned the music down and slowly pulled his car to the right side of the street in a state of utter disbelief. The car that pulled us over was the Pontiac Grand Prix I had spotted, so we had been stopped by undercover cops. How long had they been following us? Did they have covert information on someone in the car?

An unspoken acknowledgment of befuddlement, shock, and awe descended on us immediately. None of us had ever been pulled over before, yet we knew to remain quiet and obedient to the cops' requests as they approached the car slowly. All I could think of was how my dad warned me about riding in a car with four other brothas my age. I should've listened. Why did I have to play by different rules simply because of the color of my skin, though?

Regardless of my anger and contempt, I had to face reality. The fact remained that we were beholden to the cops' requests, even though we all proclaimed innocence prior to their arrival. This was seven years before Oscar Grant's videotaped murder in Oakland, and roughly ten years before the amalgamation and barrage of videos of police murdering Black men would flood the internet. What's more, camera phones had just been introduced and were a rarity, so the likelihood that we'd have any sympathy or support from the public outside of our community if something occurred was minuscule. We hadn't conceptualized the probability of being murdered in police custody. Those stories weren't reported as such, even though we now know they occurred as regularly as they do now, but the possibility of being brutally beaten rested on our subconscious due to the proliferation of the Rodney King video.

As the cops approached the car in plain clothes, we anxiously braced ourselves in anticipation of the worst.

Anthony gave the officer on his side his driver's license and registration while stuttering a combination of inaudible words. The officer, as usual, went back to his car for nearly fifteen minutes before returning. As we sat in the car, no one said a word.

"Step out of the car, gentlemen."

Although we didn't realize it then, we didn't have to comply with this order unless he had a valid answer after being asked, "Are we being detained?"

It's my theory that the immoral people who don the uniform of a police officer salivate at the thought of coming across a Black person who's ignorant of the law. This allows them to take full advantage of them without recourse or punishment. It's not illegal unless it's reported, right?

Why weren't we more informed as new drivers? Why wasn't there a portion of the driver's education course/test on the rights and liberties you have as a driver? This is especially important for Black and brown children, who are pulled over disproportionately more than their white counterparts. Without proper education regarding matters of racism and discrimination, targets of such abuse become perpetual victims trapped in an endless cycle devoid of preventive and empowering knowledge that could prepare them for the inevitable traps set by those whose motives are rooted in bigotry and avariciousness.

As we sheepishly got out of the car, we were explicitly scolded and loudly instructed to sit on the curb.

We sat on that curb for what seemed like an entire day, but it was more like thirty minutes, as they remained in their car and did whatever it is cops do during that period where you're forced to wait. It was like the anticipation a couple must have had on *Maury* as he held the envelope containing their paternity results.

One officer, a tall white man with freckles in light blue jeans and a tucked Nike shirt, motioned back and instructed each of us to stand one by one, as he thrust us onto the trunk of the car with our arms spread and searched us aggressively.

The other officer, a tall, light-skinned, bald Black guy, began to vigorously search through our belongings in Anthony's car like he had misplaced something in his bedroom and was determined to find it. One by one, our bags ended up on the grass, thankfully away from the busy traffic on the street.

"What we do, though!?" Ben said softly but loud enough for us all to hear.

It was a fair question, but obviously it infuriated these cops. It must've felt like a blow to their pride.

"Shut the fuck up!" the white officer interjected immediately.

In no time, the officer found his way toward Ben and began vigorously patting him down for what seemed like an eternity. He then told us to sit down on the curb as Ben was forced to stand by the hood of the car with his arms and legs spread for an extended time as if he was going to be arrested.

We all sat, mute. This had been a life-changing experience for all of us and it wasn't over yet. We felt the pressure transition from all five of us to Ben, solely because of his question. Could it also be Ben was visibly darker than all of us? My theory was that his pigment led to the more aggressive nature in which he was approached, even before his question. The brutality darker Blacks have been faced with throughout history in America is unparalleled. Our darker-skinned brothas are often portrayed as animalistic, whereas lighter Black folks are sometimes given the benefit of the doubt due to their closer ties to Eurocentric standards of beauty. Historically, lighter enslaved Blacks were sometimes afforded house slave duties. They'd still be oppressed, but they were convinced to believe their condition was better than their field slave brethren because they weren't picking cotton (Bennett). It's an ingenious tactic in divisiveness that worked and continues to work. The irony in this whole situation is, dark-skinned Blacks have a richer melanin content and are more closely related to the original man and woman who all originated in Africa. Why else would they try to keep us down so much, unless they knew our potential?

After three hours of our being erroneously detained, the officers returned our licenses and let us go free. Before departing, though, Anthony mustered the courage to ask the officers why we had been stopped. They simply replied that we fit the profile of a group of robbery suspects in the Hyde Park area of Chicago and got back in their car and departed. We didn't have criminal records, but we were born suspects. As young Black men who lived (and currently still live) under a system of white supremacy and oppression, it was important to understand that we are always potentially suspects.

Furthermore, Black men and women, as residents of a police state, can have their status questioned at any moment without recourse or valid reasoning. Claiming we fit the profile, whether true or not, can be used as an excuse to detain five young Black men who fit the young Black thug profile that the media proliferates daily through various avenues ranging from the news to TV shows to movies.

It was reminiscent of the Fugitive Slave Act of 1850 that allowed escaped and free Blacks to be sold into slavery regardless of their prior status. Often, this became an avaricious pursuit of money as free Blacks, like Solomon Northup (whose story was told in the movie *12 Years a Slave*), were arrested and sold for profit.

It should come as no surprise to you, then, that the primary goal of the first police forces in the United States was to protect property and not the well-being of the citizens. The first publicly funded police force in the northern states (Boston) was hired to protect the commercial interest of entrepreneurs as their goods were being transported to prevent the likelihood of theft. This was in the 1830s, and slavery (but not racism) had been abolished completely in what would become the Union (the northern region of the United States). However, in the South, the property was African people. Whereas in the North property could potentially be stolen, the problem that racist capitalists encountered in the South was the potentiality of their property running away in search of freedom, liberty, and the pursuit of happiness. This desire to maintain a system of agriculture-based slavery led to the creation of slave catchers in the early 1700s in southern states like South Carolina. These officers would patrol regions, stopping and frisking unaccompanied Africans who weren't in the presence of their slave owners, badgering them to show proof that they were free or given permission to leave their plantation (Waxman).

This is also eerily reminiscent of New York's failed stop-and-frisk policy in the 2010s that profiled young Black and Latino men to check for weapons or intent for criminal activity. This policy had a 10 percent success rate as it continued the normalization of the profiling of young Black and brown men. Additionally, it is also comparable to Arizona's SB 1070 anti-immigration law in 2010 that allowed police officers to detain Latino men if they suspected that they were "illegal" undocumented immigrants. They could demand that they show them proper US identification or be arrested, regardless of their citizenship status (Stop and Frisk Data).

The purpose of policing as it relates to Black folks has always been tumultuous because it has been vested in maintaining the status quo for capitalist whites and protecting their property and investments. So, it should come as no surprise to us that Blacks in America have constantly had a contentious relationship with a police force that has barely evolved and progressed in its purpose since its inception. It should be no surprise why we were stopped on this fateful spring day, then. These officers assumed that we, five young innocent Black men, had damaged and stolen property and in America, property, especially property that is owned by whites, takes the highest precedence, based on judicial decisions over the course of American history. (This all goes without saying, of course, that there are some officers working within the police force who are advocates for change and are committed to revolutionizing the stigma associated with policing Black communities.)

It was only through the grace of God and sheer luck that we weren't taken to jail, where our fate could've been like sixteen-year-old Kalief Browder's, who was wrongfully jailed at Rikers Island over an alleged book bag theft. The trauma of his time in jail, especially the excessive beatings and overexposure to solitary confinement, eventually led him to commit suicide upon his release (Gonnerman). Had any of us had a blemish on our record, we could've had a similar experience. We could have just as easily been framed if these officers wanted to take this breach of the law a step further.

The ride home began awkwardly, as one could imagine, but we regained steam as we realized how lucky we were. We immediately began to laugh at how obvious it was that Ben was singled out and treated worse than any of us due to an honest inquiry. We laughed at the trauma this caused, but inside we were all shook. I hadn't even been driving with my license for a year when I became accustomed to the reality of perceived Black criminality in America. Simply for existing.

My only recourse was my anointed regality. I knew I wasn't what those cops claimed I was because my parents had instilled a knowledge of myself and my history in me from an early age. I was told from a young age that I was the descendant of regal geniuses who established the foundation for all civilizations. I was told that I was smart. I was told that I was going to college, no matter what. And I was told that I could be the first Black president if I wanted to, during a time when a potential Obama presidency was unheard of. I knew these things about myself from my parents and family, so these cops' assertion that I was something else was comical, ludicrous, and asinine. How would I have reacted if I had not been anointed positively as a child? I probably would have believed their lies and adopted it as my truth.

Whether good or bad, I was taught that I had to excel at a higher level than whites in America because being born Black in America meant you started in a deficit. Because of that, much of adolescence is proverbially spent on probation, trying to expunge one's record. The biggest irony is, Blacks are always perceived to be criminals when they have in fact been the victims and targets of the biggest human rights violations and criminal activity in American history (outside of our indigenous brethren) by the very whites who demonize them.

Being a Black man in America is a continuous paradoxical struggle that entails a desire to live one's own purpose and self-defined image while constantly being bombarded by and confined to the hazardous narrative that has created you in the mold of the most dangerous entity in America. That is precisely why it is imperative that parents, teachers, pastors, and mentors intercede in our children's lives early on to proclaim and profess their prophetic regality and prepare them for the inevitability of those set on tearing them down racially, due to their own insecurities and false generational teachings.

As you can probably imagine, my mother was irate. But her tears overshadowed any fury that was felt. Understandably so. After explaining what happened, she grabbed me and gave me a bear hug for what seemed like a longer time than the cops had detained us on the side of the road in Hyde Park.

My dad wasn't shocked, and was a lot calmer than my mom. His calm demeanor put me at ease and gave me hope, which might explain my present demeanor when enduring tumultuous life experiences. However, they both agreed that something needed to be done.

My parents' support was pivotal because they didn't condemn me. They provided emotional support and reminded me that I didn't deserve this treatment. However, they also reminded me that white society rarely sees the regality that they do when viewing me and my sister. I was showered with love, as I had always been, and reminded of the importance of self-love, especially as a Black man in America. Most importantly, I was told that I had a duty to ensure that this behavior wouldn't continue.

After I finished talking to my dad on the phone, I checked on my mom, who was still wiping away her tears. She seemed to be taking it worse than I was, maybe because she had grown up in the '60s in Chicago, a city that Dr. King described as more hateful, vitriolic, and venomous than Mississippi (Bernstein). Maybe because she began to realize that things hadn't gotten much better since the time when she wasn't "permitted" to cross Western Avenue in Chicago in the '70s because white kids would chase her and her sisters and throw rocks while yelling "nigger." Maybe because she campaigned for Harold Washington in the '80s while pregnant with me, hoping for a better day, only to be disappointed when he suddenly passed away in questionable circumstances after he had a heart attack at City Hall. Maybe because Jimmy Knight, her father and my grandfather, had equipped her with the spirit of a fighter. A man who told her that the only gang she belonged to was the "Knight Gang" during an era when Chicago street gangs were on the rise. A man who taught her to defend her young sisters at any cost.

Whatever it was, my mom wasn't going to take this lying down, and she made sure that I didn't accept it as the norm either. She was not satisfied with what happened, even though I was safe.

"C'mon, Ern."

We immediately went to the car, and she began driving with a ferocity that would surely attract another group of bigoted cops. Although I had no idea where we were going, I had a hunch, and it was correct. We pulled up to the police station that was located next to my high school. I already knew what was going to happen next.

"C'mon, we're gonna report this!"

My mom didn't tolerate disrespect of her children. Whenever it occurred, especially from a person in authority who had obviously taken advantage of us, she was ready to fight, and Dr. King's approach wasn't her preferred method. However, she was extremely intelligent, so she was tactical in how she approached things. She realized that this was a matter that needed to be resolved the appropriate way.

We went to file a police report on the police. Correction, I did it. She made sure that I took the leadership role, although maintaining her silence would seemingly require a muzzle.

As I approached the front desk with obvious trepidation, I wasn't sure what to do or say. "Can I help you?" a female officer calmly asked.

"Yes, I'd like to file a police report...against two cops," I said with my lip quivering and heart beating tumultuously.

The officer gave me a stern look for what seemed like an eternity before asking for a general overview of what occurred.

I felt that this was a joke to her. I can't prove it, but the strange looks and condescending tone that followed signified that she only continued to fill it out as a matter of protocol, not because they would fervently seek out these officers and investigate the matter. If we're honest, these situations of abuse of authority by the police happen way too often. We're overexposed to it now due to cell phones and body cameras, but can you imagine what we would've seen had there been this type of technology in the 1960s or any earlier period in American history?

I knew in my heart that nothing would get done. In fact, reporting abusive police is seemingly counterproductive, but what other avenues exist? Back then I'd be mum with an answer, but now I understand the hierarchy that exists in government, especially city governments, and social media is a great way to expose corruption to hold people accountable.

Tragic situations never reveal their meanings to us at that exact moment. However, if we persist on a virtuous path throughout our lives, its meaning will be revealed as a life lesson with the purpose of preparing us for something greater. The process my mother had me go through, although seemingly pointless at that time, was powerful and a subtle foreshadowing for what I would endure twelve years later at the Chicago Margarita Fest with my wife. It let me know that I had a voice. It let me know that I had a civic responsibility to hold those in power accountable, no matter what their title.

Although those officers escaped without punishment, my tenacity when facing injustice increased with my parents' support.

The unfortunate part of this story is it was far from the last time I received malicious and discriminatory treatment from officers.

CHAPTER 9
...WHEN AARON TAUGHT ME

I thought I was going to be a platinum rapper. The problem was, a million other Black boys had the same aspirations, with more skill, tutelage, and desire. Pursuing rap and poetry as a hobby was one of the most significant stages in my life because it served as a turning point and coming of age for my life's trajectory.

Up to this point in my life, I had been a kid whose life consisted of basketball, academics, my friends, and my high school girlfriend. I followed a straight path and had not veered off that road. I loved hip-hop, and still do, because of the duality and outlet it provided me with. Sometimes it served as an escape from the harsh realities of life with the rambunctious, boisterous nature of acts like Three 6 Mafia and Lil' Jon. Other times, it served as a counselor, teacher, and confidant through the poetic and therapeutic messages conveyed through the rhymes of oratorical rap geniuses like Joe Budden, Nasir Jones (Nas), Tupac, Royce da 5'9", and Jay-Z.

Regardless of my infatuation with the art form, one thing I never considered doing was rhyming and putting a pen to the pad myself. I had convinced myself that my voice was too deep and baritone. It had

sounded like a combination of Dr. Dre's voice mixed with that of I-20 (a rapper who was once Ludacris's protégé). Furthermore, I was shy, and rappers must perform to gain exposure and proliferate their message for capital. Had I not taken this plunge, though, I never would have become a teacher and public speaker.

The summer before I began my studies at U of I would challenge my self-doubt. Not long after I graduated from high school, I found myself driving my '97 Pontiac Grand Am to one of my best friends' houses in Matteson for our de facto weekly meetup.

"Ernie!"

Mark, Aaron's stepdad, greeted me at the door, as he always had, with a jovial spirit. I always felt like I was at home whenever I went to Aaron's house. Not only was he was one of my closest friends, his mom and stepdad were like another set of parents to me, which explains why I affectionately called his mom "Mom Two." Our bond had grown over the years since meeting them at church, and I had been all but adopted into their family after taking a trip to Disney World with them at eleven. I entered the door and hugged his stepdad Mark as we cracked jokes about each other, erupting in laughter so loud that we drowned out the voice of Aaron's mother, who approached me for a warm embrace.

When I scurried upstairs, Aaron's door was closed, with the sound of loud banter emanating from the room. I knocked loudly and flung the door open because, as his best friend, I was obligated to be rude. There was no telling what I'd see. Most times, he'd be sitting in the middle of his bed meditating, something I had never seen a Black person do before him, much less a teenager.

"What are you doing?" I responded with a slight chuckle.

I had encountered Aaron yelling into his new Apple Macbook, but for what reason?

...when Aaron taught me

123

"Yeah..."

He proceeded to press play.

"I don't know what a 'Hollaback Girl' is, but Gwen Stefani, you can have my kids."

What played was the beat to the Pharrell Williams-produced "Hollaback Girl." But this wasn't Stefani's song. Aaron was rapping over the beat himself. I was expecting to come over and play a game of basketball in his driveway, or NBA 2K5 on his Xbox, so imagine my surprise and utter shock when I encountered this scene without warning.

I laughed hysterically, but as the song continued, I had to admit that his effortless flow and witty punchlines were actually pretty good.

"Dude... That's tight."

He simply nodded in agreement.

I immediately followed up my comment with an inquiry into how he had done this.

"Check it out, man. I did it on this program called GarageBand."

Aaron picked up his laptop to show me what he had been working on and how he had started rapping earlier in the week, since GarageBand and a built-in mic had come with his Macbook. I couldn't let him have all the fun himself, so I had to give it a try.

"What other beats do you have?" I exclaimed eagerly.

"Not many, but download whatever you want!" Aaron clicked on Limewire at the bottom of the page and handed me his laptop.

The first song I thought of was Beanie Sigel's "Feel it in the Air," because of the mellow vibe that would complement my voice and lead to introspection. I then began to write my first rap, which wasn't as difficult as I thought. I had some issues with the alignment of the bars, but besides that it felt natural and cathartic. As I wrote, I harkened back to a writing assignment I had some years before, in elementary school, where we were commissioned to write a poem. I recall it being effortless to me. This was no different.

"Ugh, I feel it in the air, with nothing to spare, I take a route that is rare, not known as debonair, something else, don't compare, with visions of running Chi city like the mayor."

As I left Aaron's house later, I asked him to email me a copy of the song I recorded. I couldn't wait to burn it to a disc and hear myself in my car. I departed that night not knowing that my life would be changed for the better. I would soon embark on a journey that entailed filling several notebooks with rhymes and an attempt to find a mic with good quality on a tight budget.

Besides rapping, Aaron's own reflections and experiences with race would have a profound impact on me and my evolving racial socialization. As an ardent follower of Malcolm X who attended a white Catholic high school, Aaron had an experience I could not relate to. I recall him telling stories of his punching a white kid who called him nigger for refusing to move during class. In another instance, Aaron was perturbed with the lack of an African American history course at his school, so as a sophomore he successfully petitioned in support of its addition by amassing hundreds of signatures and submitting them to the school board. He thought nothing of the accomplishment, whereas I was enthralled by his ability to ferociously commit himself to a seemingly insurmountable task, especially considering the demographic of the school.

Nothing, however, would impact me as much as the revelation he shared with me one day, as a junior, when he came over to my house and proclaimed that white people were mutants. Perplexed, I asked him to repeat himself, in case he misspoke.

"Yeah, nigga, they're mutants."

He walked to the corner of my room, took a seat, scooted toward my computer screen, pushed his glasses up his nose, and showed me the article in *The Washington Post* (Weiss). I was befuddled, because the only understanding I ever had of mutants was the kind Professor Xavier protected. However, after perusing the article, I gained a deeper understanding.

Europeans weren't mutants in the X-Men sense. Rather, their biological traits, which included pale skin and straight hair amongst other things, were a biological genetic adaptation to the colder climate nomadic Africans encountered as they sought refuge out of Africa. Their genes had to mutate out of necessity, in order to survive. The African, being the original man, flourished with dark pigmented melanin and coarse hair which was compatible with the hot climate of east (or west) Africa.

This was basic biology. However, this basic biology wasn't taught in school, at least not in my high school. It's almost as if the education system sought to continue the myth of white superiority and Black inferiority. Including basic truths like this would cause a racist to self-implode and possibly see the humanity in every person. These truths could possibly also cause a Black boy from the South Side of Chicago to have pride in his indigenous nature to every continent on this planet. We are everything. We are one.

Aaron would also reintroduce me to Malcolm X. I always tell people I grew up in a Malcolm X household. What I mean is, my mom was partial to the combative mindset that Malcolm X had, as opposed to the rhetoric of Dr. Martin Luther King, Jr. We appreciated them both, but Malcolm X's story was more relatable.

Aaron had inadvertently reintroduced me to many of the Black scholars that my mom taught me about as a child. I wasn't ready for all of it at the time, but I took a liking to Malcolm X. After intently studying Malcolm's X's philosophy and reading his autobiography, I quickly placed this visionary leader on my Mount Rushmore list of historical figures.

Malcolm had a story that most inner-city youths could relate to, having immersed himself in the street life and getting arrested at a young age due to a lack of direction. He would later find out who he was in prison when he converted to Islam before his release. He then committed his life to the Black cause during the Civil Rights era and continued to evolve, later understanding how imperative it was to realize that not all our white brothas and sistas were committed to white supremacy. He also discovered the importance of creating bonds with Blacks he disagreed with previously, like Dr. King, with whom he formed a relationship with before he was assassinated (Blake).

Malcolm caused me to question the perception I had of myself as a Black man in America. He taught me to love myself. He was a Black nationalistic accountability partner that sought to unite us as Black folks together first, before seeking acceptance from others. He also wanted the government to be held accountable. Much like Dr. King, he received the brunt of his criticism from the government (the FBI) when he sought international allies for our cause.

Whenever I hear a student despairingly remark about their dark skin, broad nose, big lips, or coarse hair, I immediately respond with:

> Who taught you to hate yourself? Who taught you to hate the texture of your hair? Who taught you to hate the color of your skin? To such an extent you bleach, to get like the white man.

> Who taught you to hate the shape of your nose and the shape of your lips? Who taught you to hate yourself from the top of your head to the soles of your feet? Who taught you to hate your own kind? Who taught you to hate the race that you belong to so much so that you don't want to be around each other? No. Before you come asking Mr. Muhammad does he teach hate, you should ask yourself who taught you to hate being what God made you! (X)

Whether he knew it or not, Aaron's reintroduction of Malcolm into my life would be just as impactful as introducing me to rapping.

Aaron was a year younger than me and regularly received lower grades than I did in school. In fact, he eventually dropped out of high school, but it wasn't because he did not have the intelligence, obviously. He made a choice. That choice eventually led him down a path of self-destruction and death at the tender age of twenty-nine. I often wonder what would have happened if he had used his ingenuity and inquisitiveness to serve his anointed purpose. Nevertheless, our friendship and his scholarship had a profound impact on my life and paradigmatic evolution. I wouldn't be the person and educator I am today if we had not crossed paths.

It's deeper than rap.

CHAPTER 10
...WHEN I WAS FIRST CALLED NIGGER

I honestly never had a dream college. That seems counterintuitive for someone who knew that he was going to college since he was in elementary school, but it was a reality. I went through the motions so much in high school that, had my college choice been predetermined for me, I would've gone along with it as if it was the norm. The only legit college visit I participated in was when I attended the University of Illinois Urbana-Champaign for a basketball camp with Aaron during my sophomore year.

I entered my senior year with a mediocre twenty-one on the ACT, having to make the most important decision of my life. I planned on taking the exam again while simultaneously applying to a school for early admission because it would increase the likelihood that I would be admitted. I didn't know what school to choose. These decisions are much easier when you are continuing a legacy, but being the first male in my family equipped with making this daunting decision meant I was also the first one in my family who had a real choice in the matter.

My mom chose her school out of convenience. She went to the University of Illinois Chicago, partly because she wanted to be able to assist her mom, who had recently divorced my grandfather. My sister, as intelligent as she was, didn't have a dream school either. She attended Tougaloo (a historically Black college) in Mississippi initially. However, that didn't last long. Nikki only stayed for one year because of an issue with her roommate. She transferred to Northern Illinois University for the remainder of her undergrad career. It was the perfect choice for her because it was a good school, but also because it allowed her the opportunity to come home weekly, since it was only sixty minutes away.

Her choices gave me a lot to ponder, because even though I didn't realize it at the time, my older sister served as a great role model for me. Throughout our childhood, she constantly bombarded me with her hip-hop choices and tendency to critique food and opt for healthier choices. I hated it at the time, but then I became someone who loved Nas, who I previously thought was boring, and I now eat a plant-based diet. You never know when the seeds someone planted in you will begin to sprout. So, as before, her choices would have a profound impact on me.

I decided that I wanted to stay close to home, but not too close. I passed on attending an HBCU, although in hindsight I wish I had considered going. My mindset at the time was vastly different. Having grown up in an all-Black neighborhood and nearing my senior year at an all-Black high school, I felt I needed a change of scenery. I recall several voices in my ear telling me that attending a PWI (predominately white institution) would immerse me in a society that was similar to the "real world" I would encounter upon graduation. As you'll find out later, this was accurate.

After weighing my options, I decided I wanted to apply to the top public school in the state: the University of Illinois Urbana-Champaign. Although I wasn't aware of my alma mater's academic prestige at the time, I was intrigued with their athletic prowess in basketball—this coming from a guy who barely played a year of high school basketball and walked out of varsity tryouts due to exhaustion (we ran suicides the entire time and I wasn't having it). Regardless, I loved the fact that the school size was the equivalent of a small town, and I liked the prospect of being able to walk on as a basketball player if I trained hard enough. Sure enough, after applying early, I was admitted in October of 2004. Luckily enough for me, I was admitted to the only school I applied for.

The following summer, in August of 2005, I began my freshman year at the University of Illinois Urbana-Champaign and my life would never be the same.

When I moved in on the Wednesday before classes started, I was immediately immersed in what it meant to attend a PWI as a Black student. As I walked toward my Pennsylvania Avenue Residence Hall room, I noticed my roommate, a friend from high school, was already there with an older Black gentleman dressed in an Iota Phi Theta shirt and durag, who appeared to be a relative or upperclassman.

"Whatup Greg!?"

"Whatup E?!"

We greeted each other with a handshake and warm embrace that reflected our excitement. Before we could continue, Greg's friend abrasively interrupted.

"You don't wanna wear dat shirt here, dawg."

"Who, me? What's wrong wit' it?" I interjected with bewilderment as I stood with a droopy and wrinkled gray and navy blue U of I baseball shirt with the Chief mascot at the center.

"There's been a lot of controversy over our mascot, Chief Illiniwek, man. Basically, a white dude dresses up as an Indian who does a bogus-ass ceremonial dance. It's a minstrel show. A lotta Black and Hispanic students have been trying to get rid of it lately, so tread lightly… You might get strange looks."

I was stunned. Not because I disagreed, but because of my naivete surrounding the matter. At this age, a mascot was just a mascot to me, but through my narrow point of view and life experiences I was able to realize how sheltered my educational experience had been, especially as it pertained to the true history of oppressed people in America, my folks included.

To most, Native Americans were just a group of people who barely existed anymore because their immune systems couldn't handle the diseases that came from exposure to Europeans. However, this couldn't be further from the truth.

A group of people who at one time numbered in the several millions on this continent were now less than one percent of the current inhabitants due to a mass genocide by European plunderers such as Christopher Columbus, Hernan Cortes, Andrew Jackson, and various other presidents. From Columbus and his crew raping, pillaging, slaughtering, and dismembering natives in 1492 to the Wounded Knee Massacre in 1890 and the present-day systemic subversion of their culture and race through reservations, America, particularly racist ethnocentric whites who have had power, has never respected the indigenous people of this land (Roy).

When did I realize this? I'm not sure, but it wasn't in school, unsurprisingly. It just never made sense to me. Why did we celebrate a man every October who didn't truly discover anything? And why weren't we told what happened to the Native Taino people? Using common sense and critical thinking led me down a curious path that culminated with this conversation with my roommate's friend. Needless to say, I took the shirt off.

It wouldn't take much longer for me to be fully immersed in the racial politics of U of I (and America as a whole). In fact, my experience in college would be characterized and defined by a racial existential crisis and awakening centered around my race as it relates to living within a society that has been molded and shaped by the false belief in white supremacy.

Later that week, as I prepared for my first day of class, my roommate and I stumbled across an event that was being held by the Central Black Student Union on campus on the quad by Foellinger (the biggest lecture hall auditorium on campus). This event would consist of a candlelight vigil with the purpose of commemorating something called "Project 500." I wasn't aware of what that was at the time, but my roommate and I figured we'd go because it could be a great way to network with our fellow Black students, and some of our dorm buddies agreed to go as well.

As we approached the south end of the quad near Foellinger Auditorium, we noticed a medium-sized crowd was congregating. As we searched for familiar faces, I noticed a student passing out small candles to the attendees. Was this a vigil for a slain student? Did someone recently die on campus? I wasn't sure, but I would soon find out.

After the last candle was passed out and dusk fell over the campus, the program started. Now, we'd begin to see what we were here for.

"We stand on the shoulders of those…"

As we all huddled together with our candles, a light-skinned Black woman with bright red lipstick and neatly permed hair, wearing an all-black t-shirt, who appeared to be a graduate student, began speaking emphatically to the crowd.

"It is because of them that we exist here…"

It symbolically grew darker the more she talked. Before long, this small gathering was illuminated solely by the streetlights along the quad and, of course, our candles.

...when I was first called nigger

We eventually discovered that this program was in honor of the school's affirmative action program entitled Project 500, which began in the 1960s during the Civil Rights Movement.

During a period when the collective consciousness of Blacks and other oppressed people rose significantly as they became more aware of the congruence of maltreatment, Black students at U of I decided to carry the proverbial baton.

When Dr. King was assassinated in April of 1968, the African American student body decided that they needed immediate change. Faced with the reality of stagnant Black attendance rates, or the prospect of those numbers regressing, a conscious collective decided to protest.

When an institution of higher learning has a student population of over 30,000, you'd expect the racial demographic to mirror the general United States population. But this is America, or 'Merica as I like to say, and this country has been rife with hatred, racism, and discrimination since its founding. This of course means that every sector has been infiltrated with racism, covertly (systemic) and overtly. That's precisely why you need systems in place to hold people accountable so that they provide the equity that is promised in the Constitution. That is owed to all Americans, especially Blacks, because this country was built on our free slave labor. There is no American empire or wealth without my people's hard work; however, we're very often shut out of the banks, despite providing them with their wealth, metaphorically and literally speaking.

The fact that there were only 372 Black students out of 30,400 in 1968 was cause for concern. Especially considering that number equates to roughly 1 percent of the student population, whereas in America, African Americans were about 11 percent (Project 500 and the Struggle for Campus Diversity). The school year after King's assassination resulted in the most direct action. Furious with the school in September of 1968, students concerned with the Black population's treatment and low enrollment took to the same quad to protest at the Illini Union.

As a result of this resistance, 240 students were arrested. However, their efforts were not in vain. It is because of their persistent agitation during such a critical period in American history that we were able to attend this prestigious university. Shortly after their activism came a school policy called Project 500 which stated that the University of Illinois Urbana-Champaign had to admit at least 500 Black students per year to increase diversity and provide equity and justice to help resolve past and present (systemic) racism.

"The fight is not over, students! To you freshmen out there, I need you to realize that the enrollment of Black students has not improved! It's still 500 annually! That's not progress!"

Lakeisha, the speaker for this event, was the director of the Bruce D. Nesbitt Center (African American Cultural Center) and had been holding this event for some years to remind students of past sacrifices and current struggles.

Indeed, it was a wake-up call. Between being warned about my Chief shirt and this event, I had already begun to realize that my existence on this campus would likely be defined by my ability to grapple with the issue of race. It was apparent that it was a volatile issue on campus that needed further addressing. In what capacity, though? What was the race question for this generation?

As I began to walk back to campus with my roommate and an empty candle holder in hand, I couldn't help but be consumed with my thoughts and the words Lakeisha had uttered.

…when I was first called nigger   135

As if that wasn't enough, I soon realized that she was right when she stated that the fight was not over, and I found out why nearly two weeks later.

My first semester at college consisted of parties, parties, and more parties. Oh, and late nights playing basketball at the gym, or thrilling NBA 2K tournaments that temporarily ended friendships. By the end of the first semester, I was on academic probation. My social life was stellar, but my study habits weren't. However, regardless of my grades, I've always been quite inquisitive and curious about my surroundings. It's an attribute I've been blessed to maintain past my childhood. I couldn't help but notice some stark racial differences between Blacks and whites that didn't make sense to me. Being ignorant about Greek culture before starting college, I assumed that every fraternity and sorority had a house. As I walked around the campus during my first few days as a student, I was in awe of the fraternity and sorority houses I had encountered.

There were brown brick homes with pillars that resembled the White House. There were four-story homes across from some of the buildings I had classes in, with balconies and huge emblems to signify their fraternity or sorority. These weren't just homes; they were mansions right on our campus. It was an amazing sight to see.

As I learned more about campus life, I was made privy to the Black Greek organizations which have an illustrious history in the service and activist sector of the Black community, especially on college campuses across the country. Dr. Martin Luther King, Jr. was an Alpha, for instance. Furthermore, Langston Hughes was a Que Dawg (Omega Psi Phi), Ralph Abernathy was a Kappa (Kappa Alpha Psi), Bobby Rush was an Iota (Iota Phi Theta), George Washington Carver was a Sigma (Phi Beta Sigma), and my mentor, Jamil Johnson, was a part of Phi Rho Eta.

In the beginning, I was just concerned about their parties. So, imagine how giddy and excited I was to find out that one frat was going to have a party at their home at the conclusion of the first week back. I was hyped because, with the image of the white frat mansions I encountered, I felt assured that this would be a party to remember. What I encountered was not what I expected.

My friends and I attempted to find the house using the address we were given, but we quickly realized that we were in for a longer trek than anticipated. I assumed we'd be walking to a house that was on campus, or possibly a block or two or away. I was wrong. We began walking past every noticeable home in clear view to a nearby neighborhood of residential homes. Surely this was a mistake, right?

Upon finding the home, we realized that it was regular, normal house. There isn't anything wrong with that, but when you anticipate partying at a mansion you tend to be disappointed to find out that the location of a college party is not too different from the house you grew up in. But why? It hardly seemed fair to have such a prestigious campus with a variety of fraternities and sororities with such a stark contrast based on the ethnic group of the Greek organization.

I quickly realized that the same inequity that existed in the "real world" existed on college campuses, even at a top forty institution and the best public school in the state of Illinois. It wasn't simply a U of I problem, it was an American problem, exemplified at Urbana-Champaign through its Greek organizations.

As I thought about it more deeply, the symbolism was profound. The redlining that occurred in America and that I had experienced growing up on the South Side of Chicago also existed on campus. Due to systemic racism, white Greeks have benefited from an entire political structure that compensated them financially at a higher rate than Black Greeks. While white Greeks were amassing wealth from an alumni endowment, Blacks in America were trying to avoid the perils of Jim Crow, which included acts of terror and a malignant social stratification that had a

...when I was first called nigger

deleterious impact on Blacks for years after. While Black Greeks were fighting for admission to U of I, white Greeks added more zeroes to their bank accounts.

By the time Black students received legislation that sought to provide some form of equity on campus in terms of admission with Project 500 in 1968, whites likely had several mansions on campus. In short, our organizations had the same plight as Blacks in every integrated major city across the country. Our Black Greeks' purchase of any home is an accomplishment when you consider the perilous route they had to take and the late start they had in the proverbial "race."

Regardless of the size of the frat house, I had a great time. If college would afford me these types of parties, then I was surely at the right place. I spent most of the time propped in a corner against a wall next to the window in the living room, dancing with a fine sista, who grinded against my jeans constantly to the beat of D4L's "Laffy Taffy." We called it juking.

It didn't take much effort to enjoy myself. The place was packed. As Nelly's "Grillz" transitioned to Dem Franchize Boyz' "I Think They Like Me," I slid behind another girl and juked with her and got thrown back against the wall. As someone who can't dance, juking was always my preference at a party. I could appear to be dancing without doing any work at all besides grabbing my dance partner by the waist and holding her against my pelvis.

At around two in the morning, the lights flashed in the house and a loud voice announced to everyone that the party had concluded. In other words, we didn't have to go home, but we had to get out of there expeditiously.

Greg and I immediately made eye contact in the crowd and headed toward the exit together, grabbing our friends along the way so that we could all leave the same way we arrived. Although I surely enjoyed myself,

as a polymath, I couldn't help but continue to meditate on the stark
contrast between the white Greek houses and the Black Greek houses.
It bothered me, because it was further evidence of the racism that Black
students have been subjected to on campus.

With those thoughts on my mind, we began to walk back to our dorm
surrounded by a heavily intoxicated student body.

As we slowly walked down Green Street under the illumination of
streetlights and engaging in loud gregarious banter regarding the party
we had just left, we noticed the streets were full. Green Street was the
equivalent of the Strip in Las Vegas, except it was full of intoxicated
teenagers and young adults.

As we began to approach Walgreens, we noticed a loud woman
screaming, in a celebratory manner, indicating that she too was under
the influence. The weather was nice; some cars drove past with the
windows down blasting music to continue the party. One car stopped at
the red light adjacent to the block we were on, with the windows down,
playing "Damn" by the Young Bloodz loud enough for all to hear. We
all began to do a two-step while shouting "Ayyyy" due to our familiarity
with the song.

As the car sped off, we shared a laugh, especially as it pertained to the
screaming girl we had encountered before. However, we were abruptly
interrupted by a group of four white students in a green four-door car
headed south, presumably drunk as well. I looked right to ensure that
there wasn't a car approaching the stop sign, since I was at the front of
the crowd. As we crossed the street, I turned my head back left as the
streetlights illuminated and shined a spotlight on our group.

The green car slowly rolled down its window from the passenger side.
From the shadows of the car appeared a white female with blonde hair.
As her piercing eyes stared at us all, she yelled:

"Go back to the hood, niggers!"

And just like that, the group inside the car laughed, as the white woman rolled the window back up and they sped off.

What just happened?

My friends and I, shook, all stopped for a second and stood in disbelief as we talked amongst ourselves, attempting to connect the proverbial dots to complete this nefarious picture.

We were all intelligent enough to ascertain that racism still existed, obviously, but not to the degree where someone would feel comfortable abrasively shouting a racial epithet at you publicly, especially in 2005. As kids born some twenty years after the Civil Rights Movement concluded, we assumed racism was receding slowly due to Martin Luther King, Jr. and Malcolm X's efforts. Wounds heal progressively, so wouldn't the scar of unjustified hatred and vitriol that is so deeply rooted and embedded in the moral fabric of America begin to form a scab that heals us all as a nation to create an American utopia?

Not exactly.

We were flabbergasted. We had experienced all facets of American racism in the span of a few hours, from systemic to overt, and we had not even realized it. As the immediate shock subsided, however, we continued our trek back to our dorms silently, defenseless, numb to the pain and numb to the reality of how to properly navigate white America and survive unscathed. In short, we weren't racially socialized to this experience yet. This would be our first incident, but it surely wouldn't be our last.

CHAPTER 11
...WHEN GHETTO BROS AND BIG BOOTY HOES PARTIED

As an older millennial, I always feel something like a grandparent reminiscing on the "old days" while in my classroom discussing how social media used to be before Facebook colonized the internet. My students typically marvel and snicker as I nostalgically extrapolate on the evolution of social media from sites like MySpace, Tagged, and Black Planet to the current models, to which we are all currently addicted.

As a freshman at U of I in 2005, I was a part of Facebook's sophomore class, which still entailed exclusivity. During the first few years of Facebook, users had to have a college email to sign up, which makes sense considering Mark Zuckerberg and his comrades created the app while at Harvard, specifically for college students. Facebook became our main medium of connecting with our fellow college students. It also allowed us to stay abreast of events on campus.

During those archaic times, Facebook was devoid of spam, sponsored posts, meaningless notifications, status updates, live broadcasts, and the perils of "fake news." In fact, you weren't even able to upload photos from your phone, so you'd have to take a digital camera on every excursion and quickly upload them to your computer and Facebook upon arriving home, with a limit of ten pictures at a time. Imagine that!

One sunny autumn Saturday morning in mid-October leading up to Halloween, and not too far removed from the Green Street "nigger" incident, I logged onto Facebook on the gray Hewlett-Packard laptop on my desk in the corner of my cramped dorm room. As I scrolled down, I initially encountered the usual onslaught of party recap pictures from my Facebook friends, which made me envious because my college friends and I had opted for a night of basketball as opposed to our typical social outing. However, a few pictures caught my attention.

I noticed photo after photo resembling caricatures and stereotypes of African Americans, reposted by an upperclassman in a sorority. Although I didn't have the verbiage to properly communicate it at that moment, I had encountered my first experience with blackface and minstrel shows. I hadn't learned about minstrel shows and the demeaning nature of blackface from my honors United States history class in high school. Rather, I learned about them by way of the hip-hop group Little Brother, whose album *The Minstrel Show* was released in September of my freshman year.

Prior to purchasing that album, I had no idea what the shows entailed. After discovering their purpose, however, I began to feel as if they still existed. Considering that the white-owned BET began to propagate pernicious Black stereotypes in the mid-2000s, combined with the rumors that they refused to play one of Little Brother's videos because it was "too intelligent," I felt justified in this sentiment.

According to Encyclopedia Britannica: "Minstrel show, also called minstrelsy, an American theatrical form, popular from the early nineteenth to the early twentieth century, that was founded on the comic enactment of racial stereotypes. The tradition reached its zenith between 1850 and 1870."

The earliest minstrel shows were staged by white male minstrels (traveling musicians) who, with their faces painted black, caricatured the singing and dancing of slaves. Scholars usually distinguish this form of the tradition as blackface minstrelsy. The father of the blackface show was Thomas Dartmouth Rice, popularly known as "Jim Crow," an early African American impersonator whose performances created a vogue for the genre. The pioneer company, the Virginia Minstrels, a quartet headed by Daniel Decatur Emmett, first performed in 1843. Other noteworthy companies were Bryant's, Campbell's, and Haverly's, but the most important of the early companies was Christy Minstrels, who played on Broadway for nearly ten years; Stephen Foster wrote songs for this company.

The white faces I saw on Facebook that day, sloppily smeared with what seemed like black shoe polish, accompanied by red lipstick forcibly drawn in the manner of a smile, with their eyes bulging, haunted me. The images were parallel to what Little Brother had shown in their CD booklet, without the parodical nature.

As I scanned the rest of the images, I noticed that the white women were wearing gray sweatpants, equipped with a lumpy protruding derrière that seemed to be stuffed with someone's old gym sweatshirt or hoodie to mimic the curvaceous nature of Black women. Black women are beautiful, the most beautiful women on the face of the earth from my vantage point, so to mimic their God-given aesthetics, which some white women pay millions of dollars to attain (lips, tans, butt injections) was slightly comical in that it seemed to be rooted in jealousy more than anything.

The white men in the picture not only had blackface as well, but they wore white tank shirts, extremely baggy jeans, and their hats backward, seemingly to mimic the hip-hop fashion style many Black men wore at the time. To top it off, these men had forty-ounce malt liquor bottles duct-taped to their hands as if they'd spent an afternoon watching *Menace II Society*, *Boyz In Da Hood*, or *South Central*. It was the worst depiction of Blackness and Black masculinity I had encountered, and it came from teenagers and young adults who attended one of the best universities and institutions of higher learning in the nation. The irony.

Even more appalling was the name of this thematic party being held by the white fraternity: "Ghetto Bros and Big Booty Hoes."

Not long after I encountered this atrocity, I encountered another upon scrolling—the same day, no less. This time our Hispanic brothas and sistas were the targets.

This party, held by Zeta Beta Tau and Delta Delta Delta, exhibited similar behavior that was just as explicit in its provocatively racist nature and portrayal of stereotypes. It was aptly entitled "Tacos and Tequilas" which of course sounds like a great food choice at a Mexican restaurant until you realize the visual accompanying the party is less than favorable (Garennes).

There were swarms of white folks, based on the pictures from the event, in stereotypical Mexican attire. Nearly everyone I saw had similar clothing, unlike the Ghetto Bros party. The shameful attire included a sombrero and a conspicuous white tee shirt that was ripped. Initially, I was confused. "Why would the shirt be ripped?" I quietly pondered.

Upon scrolling down, I noticed the symbolism behind these shirts, as a few of the partygoers took a picture with their backs turned, arms raised, with both thumbs pointing downward at the derogatory word "wetbacks." This utterly repulsive phrase, which was sloppily written in with a black Sharpie, probably while these imbeciles were drunk, was wedged among a cascade of rips and tears which, like the front of the shirt, seemed strategic.

Then it hit me.

The rips and tears were supposed to mock Mexican migrants who attempt to migrate to America by crossing border walls or fences. Furthermore, the term "wetback" disrespectfully refers to Mexican migrants who swam to America during the 1920s. There were also groups of white students dressed as landscapers and as pregnant Mexican woman, further perpetuating stereotypes of Mexicans and undocumented immigrants (Garennes).

The biggest irony of it all is, non-Anglo whites (Italians, Germans, Eastern Europeans, for example) were once the newest group of migrants who faced discrimination and ridicule. How soon people forget that they were once what they now chastise and mock.

At that moment, I could no longer scroll. I slowly released my right index finger from my laptop mouse and sank into a deep state of anger, bewilderment, and confusion. How could something like this happen without punitive measures being taken to assure the student body this wouldn't happen again? Were the appropriate authorities even aware? If they weren't, I was going to make sure that they were.

I felt overtaken by a spirit of defiance as I was reminded, not just of the historical stories of rebellion I was told, but also of all the times my mom exhibited activism to combat similar circumstances when I was a child. From Denny's to the incidents with police officers I encountered as a child, she was always proactive.

The first step was to create a space to discuss these issues on the platform where I'd encountered them: Facebook. And thus I created my first group, entitled, "Students Against Negative Stereotypes" (a title that seems oxymoronic in hindsight, because stereotypes are inherently negative), which included the atrocious pictures that were the motivation for the group's creation along with an in-depth description of the contextual meaning of the stereotypes. I invited my entire friend list and watched the group amass nearly 1,000 students on campus by Monday morning, presumably because of the outrageous party.

As I walked around the quad the following Monday, I had an urgent desire to follow through with my activism so that the conversation did not remain trapped in the realm of social media. Much to my surprise, the upperclassmen did not waste any time. As I departed from my 11:00 a.m. class and walked toward the Union, which was at the end of the quad, I noticed a large crowd gathering around a group of Black and Hispanic students vociferously speaking on the very issue I had encountered on Saturday.

Until then, I had been concerned about being late for my 12:00 class on the other side of the Union in Lincoln Hall. I realized, however, that I couldn't let this moment pass. My English class would have to wait. I was completely captivated, not just by the speakers, but also by the crowd of concerned young adults who were presumably just as infuriated as I was. Although I was struggling academically at this point, my social consciousness and awareness were evolving, and I was in the perfect environment to nurture that growth.

As I readjusted my durag and the right strap of my cumbersome Jansport book bag, I frantically navigated the growing crowd to get a better view of the speakers.

"We will not tolerate racism at this institution!"

As I listened intently, I realized that the gathering was impromptu, which led me to believe that there would be a next step. And right before I could gather myself to leave, one of the speakers stated that the conversation would continue at the Hispanic Cultural House that night at 7:00 p.m.

The pictures clouded my thoughts for the remainder of the day, so much that I could hardly concentrate in any of my classes. Were my professors aware? If so, why didn't they mention it in class? Who exactly was in those pictures? Was it possible that they were in my class? It's not like I'd know for sure anyway, seeing as how I was almost always the only Black student in my college classes.

I wasted no time attending the joint meeting later that day, with several friends from my residence hall. We all wanted to know what the next step was. All being from redlined neighborhoods in or around Chicago, we were new to this form of racism. Furthermore, how would we get the results we desired? What results did we even seek to obtain?

In the family room area of the house was a group of about five Hispanic and Black leaders on campus from various fraternities, sororities, and student organizations. One of them, a brown-skinned Puerto Rican woman, began by recommending a march and demonstration that would take students around the campus, concluding at the chancellor's office, and demanding punitive action.

"Whatever we do, we gotta do it now," a tall dark-skinned male in Omega Psi Phi garb muttered.

"It's sad we only decide to do something when Hispanics are targeted. They been doing this to us for years now," whispered a Black female student to a nearby friend.

Overhearing that comment left me curious about the state of affairs for Black students on campus, but nevertheless I remained focused on the issue at hand.

The Puerto Rican upperclassman, Denise, who initially led the meeting, continued:

"Meet at noon Wednesday on the quad to march! We'll create a Facebook event too, so spread the word! Come with posters! We also need volunteers for a display we want to create once we return to the quad after marching. Any takers?"

My roommate Greg and I thought for a second, glanced toward each other and smirked as we both leaned against a squeaky brown wall and sheepishly raised our hands in unison.

"Why the hell not?" We seemed to telepathically communicate before raising our hands. This was our chance to be a part of something powerful and to help promote necessary change. Plus, we were two dudes from the South Side of Chicago. We were bred for this.

On Wednesday, I was anxious to participate, so it was hard to concentrate in class and maintain focus. After my 11:00 a.m. English class concluded, I refastened my blue New Balance shoes, pulled up my sagging jeans, readjusted my book bag, and made my way to the Union with haste. As soon as I stepped out of the English Hall and glanced to the left in the direction of the quad, I noticed a swelling crowd equipped with various picket signs. There was clamorous banter as the crowd waited impatiently for directions from Denise, who I viewed clenching the megaphone from the top of a stoop positioned in front of green bushes parallel to the quad.

I put my arm through the left book bag strap to balance the weight of my books and notebooks in anticipation of a long walk, and submerged myself in the crowd. Everyone began walking toward Green Street and onto Wright Street during the busiest time of the day on campus.

Although the megaphone wasn't used, we trekked down Wright Street with unity and solidarity. It was as if the Biblical Moses was present, the way the overcrowded street seemed to open as we made our way to the chancellor's office.

As we turned the corner and proceeded past the financial aid office, we were in direct proximity to the chancellor's office. It was then that our voices began to project rage, as we released the years of frustration from racial antagonism and being made a mockery of due to our melanin.

"No justice… *No peace*! No justice… *No peace*! No justice… *No peace*!"

We marched and chanted for what seemed like hours, but was more like thirty minutes. With each step and scream our rage grew, collectively and in unison. As our voices rose, I felt the power of unity emanating from our souls. Having dealt with racism and responding proactively with parental support on a personal level, I had never experienced something like this, and it was gratifying and addictive. Although I didn't have proof yet, I felt that we were making a difference that would ripple through the course of U of I history. The glaring and piercing eyes of students, who walked past confused and befuddled, only served as motivation to enrage them even more or educate them. You'd think we'd get tired, but as we stood in front of the chancellor's office protesting, we raised our posters and turned around, so every passing car and student could see the issue at hand.

After about an hour, we marched back to the quad, near the Union, for the next phase of the protest. This is where Greg and I would discover what we eagerly volunteered for while the spirit of rebellion radiated within us.

One of the leaders of the march, having spotted us on the way back to the quad, pulled us to the side and instructed us on what was to occur next.

Before we knew it, we were posted on the steps of the quad, chained together, holding posters which explained the root of certain harmful stereotypes. Additionally, I donned a pair of baggy pants, a long white shirt, a backwards-fitted hat and sunglasses, whereas Greg had on a raggedy tan suit with a blue dress shirt. The purpose was to show that we, as Blacks in America, were prisoners of the very stereotypes we try to escape, whether we wear formal wear or urban street apparel mimicking our favorite rappers and fulfilling their warped pernicious image of a thug or gangster.

I looked further down to my left and noticed four other people, one of them a Hispanic comrade about our age, standing in unity with us in similar garb in relation to the "Tacos and Tequila" party. We stood, linked in chains and shackles, sweating profusely on a mild warm autumn day while tightly clenching the poster boards; I felt an energy shift.

"Can you believe we're actually doing this, man?" I muttered to Greg softly.

Like a bashful caterpillar, I felt my shell slowly shedding. It was one thing for me to march, fully immersed in a crowd, capitulating to the majority. But it's a completely different experience when you're one of six people on display in caricature-themed attire for the campus to see at one of the busiest locations to make a political statement. Lest I forget, Black students were (and still are) only 5 percent of the campus population. With that said, this was a bold move. A move that was also exhilarating and a springboard to a life devoted to activism.

The feeling following the protest was euphoric. I felt I was a part of what my mom taught me about as a young child, as I was constantly surrounded by stories of Black excellence and success and encouraged to choose from our library when doing research projects for school. I didn't realize it at the time, but those years of racial socialization and tutelage implanted an awareness in my subconscious that would make it imperative that I continue to involve myself in resolving issues of injustice. I felt that I was making history.

Nearly a month after our protest, I stood on a bus stop on Green Street in the frigid, gloomy autumn weather with a leather jacket draping off me, patiently waiting for my transportation back to my dorm, when I noticed the latest edition of the *Daily Illini* in a newspaper box to the left of the bench.

I quickly took my hands out of my pocket to avoid the icy cold and grabbed the paper from the box, and noticed the glaring headline that read: "Two Greek Houses on UI Campus Face Sanctions" (Garennes).

I was overcome with a feeling of elation. I couldn't contain the grin that appeared on my face as I read the article a few times to make sure I had read it correctly. Our goal was accomplished. We made a difference by speaking out and letting our voice be heard on a mass scale, although, in perspective, I wish individual students were punished as well.

I was able to experience for the first time in my life the result of direct civic action in the form of a peaceful protest. And this experience brought together two historically disenfranchised groups for a common cause. This alliance, which is necessary to the dismantling of the implementation of white supremacist policies, followed in the long tradition of Black and brown unity most infamously made by Fred Hampton's Rainbow Coalition in the late 1960s, which united the Black Panthers with a Puerto Rican political group (Young Lords), a Mexican political group (Brown Berets), and a poor white political group (Young Patriots).

We certainly share commonalities, but let me be clear: it is my belief that Black folks who are descendants of Freedmen (those who were enslaved in America) must prioritize their/our issues as a community, as other communities do, before seeking to collaborate. I can't help you build your house if mine is falling apart.

As the bus approached and crept to a screeching halt in front of the Union Bookstore, I folded the paper neatly, put it in my book bag, boarded the bus, and grabbed a window seat. I reflected on a memorable experience, but as the ride continued, the feeling of contentment subsided. I was struck simultaneously with feelings of inquisitiveness and dissatisfaction.

"What else is out there?"

I was no longer satisfied with this symbolic victory. I needed more. I needed to find the root causes of these problems. Why did it keep occurring? Why did the school have to implement Project 500 to admit

Black students? Why was I the only Black student in nearly all of my classes during my first semester at U of I?

I began to realize that the racist parties were just the symptoms of a sickening disease that was ubiquitous in America, even at institutions that promoted liberalism, inquiry, and scholarship.

What was at the root of these parties? I would soon find out in the most unfortunate of ways.

CHAPTER 12

...WHEN HE CHANGED HIS NAME FROM GERALD TO ABDUL

After declaring undecided the previous semester and realizing I had a passion for (Black) history, I decided to take a step back, assess the broader view, and see if this new realm of thought was the direction I sought.

My first decision came when I signed up for African American Studies 100. This course, unlike the 101 class I took previously, dealt with social and historical issues and themes, as opposed to chronological and linear topics. This thematic course was shunned by everyone I had encountered. I was told that the class was difficult, overbearing, meticulous, and not worth the trouble. How could a class about your history and your ancestors be such a burden? It didn't register with me.

Upon entering class on the first day, on time, I immediately went to the front row. I made a commitment after speaking with Jamil several times and assuming the role of president of the Minority Leadership Group to be more proactive in my approach to excel academically. My first order of business was establishing relationships with my professors, regardless of the course.

This class was unlike any other I had experienced. As I walked in, I heard Dead Prez blaring from the speakers. This became a common theme as the professor played everything from Nina Simone to Curtis Mayfield and provoked a discussion about the identity of the artist, similar to what my dad had done with me and my sister during our rides back home.

Toward the front of the auditorium was a tall, slender, light-skinned, gray-haired, bald man with glasses, slowly nodding his head to the amplified sounds of Prez's "Hip Hop." I was shocked, but excited.

As the class began and his voice amplified, the professor, Abdul Alkalimat, expounded upon the course in an exhilarating, articulate, and passionate manner. From the beginning, I was hooked. Whereas Professor Lang introduced me to an overview of historical topics that fed my initial curiosity on the topic of African studies, Alkalimat cemented my inquiry by delving deeper on thematic issues such as the contrasting views of scholars and activists such as Dr. Martin Luther King, Jr., Malcolm X, Booker T. Washington, and W. E. B. DuBois. He lectured on the topics of religion and theology, socialism, pan-Africanism, colorism, and the exclusion of Black women from the feminist movement, to name a few. It goes without saying that he was the first professor I heard publicly state that race is a fictional social construct because all humans are from Africa, particularly Ethiopia, as the most recent evidence suggests. My paradigm shifted with every class and discussion session, and I loved it.

Although I still enjoyed partying every now and then, it was no longer the feature of my week. Besides spending time with my girlfriend Cassie, the only thing I anticipated more was Dr. Alkalimat's lectures. I had become a philomath, and it did not bother me one bit.

Beside expanding my paradigm with his pedagogical approach, he also inspired a work ethic and drive that I did not know existed within me. Part of my success in history courses, beside loving the content, came because I was able to explain myself thoroughly in papers and, more importantly, on tests. I realized through my tribulations with psychology that my erratic brand of thinking wasn't conducive to logical-mathematical intelligence-driven assessments and methods of teaching. Rather, I preferred philosophy and existentially-driven questions and assessments that allowed me to express my feelings and elaborate my thoughts.

In my previous psychology course, my grade was based on three multiple-choice assessments, some of which were pop quizzes. However, Dr. Alkalimat employed a completely different method that has impacted my own pedagogy, as well as the very method I used when writing this book. He did not assign one test throughout the entire semester. No, we did not have a midterm or final exam. Instead, Dr. Alkalimat made us write and write until we could not write anymore.

I recall the groans and smacked lips when he first introduced this methodology to us during the first class in 2006. Many had a strong disdain of this approach, but I preferred it.

Instead of reading to prepare for a multiple-choice exam, we read (often from his own online book, which was another transformative approach for that time) to write a paper. We had a two-page paper due every week on the topic he lectured about during class. There was no way around it. You couldn't cheat, because he'd find out you'd plagiarized. You couldn't guess because it was based on your own research, inquiry, thoughts and—quite frankly—grit.

Nothing molded me more as a college student than this process. Typically, like a traditional procrastinator, I'd wait until the last minute to do these short papers. However, the difference with this process was, I procrastinated because I looked forward to completing the task because I loved the subject so much, so I opted to complete my other class work prior to Sunday so I could give the topic of the week optimum focus and attention.

...when he changed his name from Gerald to Abdul

Imagine me now going in the direction of a history major with a girlfriend who was a mathematics and education major. Our Sunday dates were intense. As we sifted through our work during the fall semester of 2006, we engaged in a bit of foreshadowing, because now, as teachers in the same profession, our Sundays typically consist of much of the same tasks on the same evening, albeit in preparation for the week's lessons at our respective high schools as opposed to completing homework.

The conversation back then was familiar, though. If she was at my apartment, I might offer her a turkey burger and oven-baked fries on my way to slowly gaining fifty pounds over the course of my four years in Urbana-Champaign. At Cassie's apartment, her expertise was spaghetti, or every college student's favorite affordable gourmet meal, Maruchan ramen noodles. Not the fancy ones you find at an Asian restaurant either, these cost about two to three dollars for a pack of twelve.

On these Sundays, we'd be nestled together on our beds, leaning against our room's apartment wall with our laptops on a pillow sitting on our laps.

The topics I engaged in enthralled me. The topics Cassie engaged in confused me. I wrote about the historical periodization of African American culture from slavery to the present day, whereas she took courses with invisible numbers and mathematical theory. Seriously, she had some books that did not have one number in them, yet it was a math course. That confusion solidified the academic path I was taking.

We'd watch either the comical minstrel show-esque exploits of hip-hop icon Flava Flav on VH1's *Flavor of Love* or NBA basketball on ESPN. However, our choice of show didn't really matter, nor did the meal of choice, because there were segments of time when we were so hard at work that not a word was uttered and not a head lifted toward the television. That's what it's like to enjoy the work that you do. That's what it's like to be working on something you are passionate about.

I didn't even view these assignments as work. I viewed them as deposits of information that would equip me with the necessary skills to be an effective educator and leader in the future.

Over the course of the semester, I wrote about fifteen papers of at least two pages. Often, I actually wrote between four and five pages because the topics captivated me immensely. Over the course of the semester, I would have typed what amounted to a sixty-page journal. That taught me the method that I could invoke while writing this book because little by little, a little becomes a lot.

What's more, the papers flowed effortlessly as I wrote. I never recall having writer's block, and the only time I truly paused was to access more information from Dr. Alkalimat's website. Much of the information I encountered was new to me, so I was on a constant journey of exploration and revelation. For example, to learn of the creativity my ancestors sustained while enduring such intense subjugation was exhilarating; from being sold, raped, beaten, castrated, overworked, and underfed, my ancestors had the fortitude and gumption to create songs that would emit messages that relayed that it was the appropriate time to escape.

Songs like "Wade in the Water" were used by enslaved Africans on their path to freedom to communicate that they needed to switch paths and lay low in the water so that they would not get caught by the hounds and slave catchers (the policemen of that time) as they sought freedom in the North or Canada. "Wade in the water, wade in the water children. Wade in the water. God's gonna trouble the water."

Not only did we use music as a form of activism through artistic expression, quilts were also sewn to proliferate maps that would allow enslaved Africans to move stealthily when they ran away in pursuit of freedom.

...when he changed his name from Gerald to Abdul

As I began to critically think about the lessons I was learning, I considered the current state of art in Black culture and its commercialization. Previously, Black art, especially music, was at the nexus of creating a balance that allowed us to persist and survive the subjugation while also motivating and informing us about how to best escape our condition. However, in the mid-2000s, it seemed that our music only served one function commercially, and that was to exploit our creative geniuses, entertain excessively, and keep the populace induced in a mass slumber. This didn't sit right with me.

Why did I have to be exposed to thought-provoking hip-hop by white friends, professors, or illegally through Kazaa or Limewire? Why wasn't it the norm? Or more practically, why wasn't there balance being provided? I loved Three Six Mafia, Lil' Jon, 50 Cent, T.I., Young Jeezy, and Jay-Z, but I needed more substance. Kanye West seemed to be the only one allowed to have such an impact commercially. What impact did this have on our culture and the paradigm of Black folks in the 2000s? Was it a case of art imitating life, or life imitating art?

As I stood in 2006, the collective consciousness of my people seemed to be in a sunken state. Yes, I was growing aware of my true self, but only because of the privilege I had of being at U of I and being led to this course by divine intervention. What about my boys back in Chicago? How would they gain access to this? Would it change their life?

Understand that the internet in 2006 was not the same as it is now in 2020. Not everyone had a smartphone. In fact, I didn't get one until 2010. Also, not everyone had internet access. Although Facebook was growing, as was YouTube, they were still relatively new. Remember, Facebook was still only a college social networking site, so the spread of information was still limited to newspapers, nightly news, and email newsletters. Nowadays, consciousness has risen in our communities because of access to information and the propensity of our celebrities to shed light on our struggles, but back then there was a huge void. Caught between a decade in the '90s that had the Rodney King video and trial, the Million Man March, and artists like NWA and KRS One to chronicle our condition, and the 2010s that had Oscar Grant, Trayvon Martin, Michael Brown, Eric Garner, and Tamir Rice, the 2000s seemed to be a decade devoid of a proverbial match to light the fire.

However, courses like this were the breeding ground for the activism and rise in consciousness in the next decade. We weren't dead, we were just seeds preparing to burst through the surface.

As the semester continued, I grew, not just academically but socially. Professor Alkalimat was a student of Malcolm X, and that was apparent. One specific lecture has impacted me immensely to this day. In October of that semester, the professor discussed the topic of Black nationalism throughout our history.

> You had to convince them that what you wanted them to do was righteous and adequate through terror. You had to convince them that when they look in the mirror, they see ugly, but when they look at *you*, they see beauty and intelligence. For example, during the Renaissance they made Jesus white, but the Bible says he was brown with hair like wool. How you gon' make up down and right left? It happened! (Alkalimat)

I had to meet this man personally. (I was as enamored with his style as I was with Michael Eric Dyson's, who I often saw and studied to increase my vocabulary by listening to his loquacious speeches.) Sure, I had gone to his office hours to clarify certain curricular information, but I needed more. Having delved beneath the surface during this semester, Dr. Alkalimat picked up where Professor Lang left off for me, as he continued to connect our past to the present.

Soon enough, in November, we met at a local coffee shop and had an enlightened conversation.

...when he changed his name from Gerald to Abdul

Thankfully, this highly intelligent man was as kind as he was passionate about Black studies. He opted to pay for green tea. Since I was a broke college student, I appreciated this. It was a warm autumn day, so we were able to chat and sit outside. I was able to learn that Dr. Alkalimat was a native of Chicago who grew up in projects and later went to college in Kansas in the '60s to pursue a career in activism and African studies. He changed his name from Gerald McWorter in part because of Malcolm X's influence with the Nation of Islam. He wanted his own identity to be separate from the slave name that was forced on him. Malcolm X had a significant impact on his life, as he did on mine, so this was refreshing to hear as he allowed me to delve deeper into my appreciation for Malcolm via his website, which included speeches and research on Malcolm's life.

"Here, take a copy of my CD."

When Professor Alkalimat uttered those words, I was shocked, to say the least. As we transitioned to a conversation about the role the internet was having on the transmission of information and knowledge, we also talked about the role hip-hop had in continuing the oral tradition of African culture, going back as far as the griot in West Africa.

The CD he gave me included a project he did with some students of his at the University of Toledo. It detailed their experiences in Ohio and combined them with the content knowledge he had espoused that semester. At the age of nineteen, I had still placed limits around the social construct of age, so I couldn't believe that this sixty-four-year-old man had taken an interest in hip-hop to that degree, outside of just playing an occasional song in his class as students walked in.

From this conversation I learned the importance of also being in touch with the newest forms of technology to relay and obtain information related to the African Diaspora. Alkalimat's websites provided access to important information regarding Black studies to anyone across the globe at any moment. As society slowly adapted to having this overabundance of information available with the world wide web, broadband, and smartphones, most scholarly books still had to be purchased or accessed through a university account. Alkalimat broke the mold then, and now it's the norm. Imagine a sixty-four-year-old, not a thirty-four- or twenty-four-year-old, contributing to changing how we use technology to access information, particularly in the realm of Black studies.

"We all have a role in this struggle, Ernest. This… This information that I teach is still living."

Those words and that meeting were thought-provoking and left me in an intellectual stupor. I started this class in pursuit of knowledge, searching for myself. However, over the course of the semester, Alkalimat took the wool from over my eyes and slowly revealed to me who I was, even more so during our personal meeting at the local coffee shop. Before we departed, I slipped him my mixtape as if he was a record executive searching for new artists, shook his hand with a firm grip, and told him thank you.

As the semester concluded, I continued my familiar trek back home with a new vision and hope for my life. Although I wasn't certain what role I wanted to take yet, I was certain of one thing. I wanted to teach African American history and studies as either a professor or a certified teacher. I was certain that this information would change the trajectory of my people and the way it changed me. The feeling was further cemented for me when I returned home for winter break. As a told my mom about how enthralled I was with Dr. Alkalimat's course, she sheepishly asked me what his name was. I quickly told her that his name was Dr. Abdul Alkalimat, and that he was previously known as Gerald McWorter. What she said next shook me to my core.

"Ern. Shut up!" my mom responded colloquially.

"That was the professor I had at Circle (another name for the University of Illinois Chicago's campus), who inspired my approach as a teacher. He was my favorite professor! This was when the university first started to offer African American history. Gerald was amazing!"

"Ma, stop playing." I was stunned.

To know that the same professor who inspired her pedagogical approach had also unknowingly inspired my career choice and approach thirty years later, at a different university, was stupefying. To me, this was further confirmation that my decision to go into education was fate, and of divine order, and not just a mere coincidence.

CHAPTER 13
. . . WHEN JENA 6 HAPPENED

It had been over a year since the racist party protest had occurred, and the platform I had created on Facebook had grown. The group Students Against Stereotypes had roughly 1,000 members at a time when Facebook was still limited to college students, so in hindsight, that was a big achievement. The group had lost its initial focus, because there had not been much to galvanize behind on campus. Much of the conversation in the group focused on spreading awareness on a variety of issues I wasn't as aware of, such as the war in Iraq, the ongoing illegal occupation of Palestine by Israel, and LGBTQ rights. Although those issues are important and certainly impact the Black community in varying ways, my vantage point was limited at that point in my life to what my immediate experience was as a young Black man.

As I grew in my knowledge, I regularly posted online about what I had learned from Alkalimat and Lang, relating it as much as I could to the present day. Many of the topics I ranted about on Facebook and in my music were limited to interpersonal conflicts relating to our struggle, though. I was hypercritical of our consumerist mindset and propensity to focus more on the new Jordans than on investing in knowledge and academic resources. Although my critiques were valid, they weren't stated constructively. Also, I did not yet know about the nuances of systemic racism and how the global white supremacist structure, which aligned with capitalism, created the multitude of barriers which made our progression difficult. I was slightly misguided, but Jena 6 made me more aware of the various barriers we face, even in the educational system.

With the first semester winding down during my sophomore year, I was perusing online on a chilly December day devoid of snow. As I continued to scroll through Facebook aimlessly, seeding what would later become a social media addiction, I came across a story with a picture of three nooses as the focal point. Knowing the historical ramifications of such an image, I had to stop, especially when I noticed it had been shared several times by my Facebook friends.

I clicked on the story and began to read the details and became alarmed. This couldn't be true. Maybe this article was on *The Onion* and I had not noticed. I scrolled up quickly to check, but I was wrong. It was a reputable site. What I read was the worst case of injustice I had been exposed to in my nineteen years of life.

A group of six Black boys from Jena, Louisiana, had been charged with attempted murder. Initially, that doesn't sound strange until you read the rest of the details. These Blacks were teenagers who got into a physical altercation and beat a white kid unconscious after three consecutive months of racial harassment. The apex of this harassment was an incident where three nooses were hung from a tree on the school campus a day after a Black student had sat under the same tree. This tree, however, was known as the "white" tree—Black students knew not to cross that boundary to congregate there. This was a typical case of de facto segregation within the confines of a high school campus.

The white kids who were responsible for this despicable act in September of 2006 were recommended for expulsion by the principal, but that was immediately overturned by the superintendent, who described it as a childish prank.

Therein lies the problem: hanging a noose, especially in the presence of Blacks, is far from a joke. Rather, it should be viewed as a terroristic threat, and a misdemeanor at the very least.

For more than 100 years following the supposed abolishment of slavery, Blacks were terrorized, lynched, and hanged from nooses by whites throughout the South as a means of violent intimidation to restore and maintain white supremacy and the social order that had been created two hundred years prior. It should be noted that lynchings and other vile forms of abuse, such as being staked to the ground, decapitated, and castrated occurred during slavery as terroristic intimidation as well as a means of punishment. Slaves, however, weren't viewed as people, so their outrage wasn't deemed valid.

From 1877 (the end of Reconstruction) to 1950, nearly 4,000 lynchings of Blacks (and whites to a lesser degree) occurred throughout the South. That amounts to roughly fifty-one lynchings per year, or one every week (NAACP). Although this figure is alarming and amounts to a death toll greater than the 9/11 Twin Tower attacks (3,000), it's misleading for several reasons. For one, it does not track the lynchings that occurred after slavery ended (or rather transitioned to the prison industrial complex) in 1865. The Reconstruction period is conspicuously absent, as if violent white supremacists had taken a twelve-year break before continuing the pathological terrorizing of Black communities. On the contrary, according to Professor Shawn Alexander in the PBS documentary *Tell Them We Are Rising*, "between 1866 and 1872, approximately 20,000 people are killed, Blacks and whites in the South, all because of this perceived threat that education will unlock something." How ironic, then, that the Jena 6 case occurred at a school in the South and revolved around a noose, symbolic of racial terrorism and a reaction to the perceived invasion of segregated white spaces. But why aren't these statistics included with the lynching statistics? Why start in 1877?

It would seem as if these acts of terror were such a fixture in American society that there may have been resistance toward compiling them. Viewing these acts of terror as obscure and something to repudiate and charge criminally was likely not something Americans saw as a necessity, especially those who believed Africans were inferior. Similarly, keep in mind that Blacks have always had a tumultuous relationship with law enforcement, but according to available data, police killings weren't tracked until the 1990s. Even still, police departments aren't mandated to tally or reveal such information to the FBI. So, much like the period following slavery's abolishment (or transition), we have a segment of the American population that is resistant to tracking acts of terror, possibly because they don't view it was an issue. The more things change, the more they stay the same. The very idea of propagating these stories became commonplace due to the work of activists and journalists like Ida B. Wells, who was inspired to expose the tragedies after a friend of hers was lynched for having a successful business next to a white man in Mississippi.

Lynchings were a sight to behold to the racist community. Imagine trying to decide what to do on a hot summer day with your family and opting to grab your picnic basket to attend, not a local fair or park, but the public execution of a Black man near a large magnolia tree located around the corner from your church with friends and colleagues who attend that church. Did I mention that your kids, no matter their age, would also be present during this demonic occasion? It was common for the victim to be castrated, burned, and/or decapitated. These body parts would be sold as souvenirs at local shops in the town. Additionally, pictures from the event would be sold as postcards for the attendees. It was seen as a joyous occasion.

Take, for example, the lynching of Thomas Shipp and Abraham Smith. These two young African American men were lynched on August 7, 1930, not in the South as most would expect, but in the northern Midwest state of Indiana in a small town called Marion. These two men were beaten to death and subsequently hanged from a tree near the courthouse in front of a crowd of 5,000 whites. It was a public spectacle that garnered as much attention as a sporting event (NAACP).

What was the cause of this catastrophe? These men were convicted of murdering a white coworker and raping a white woman without any substantial evidence. It was later revealed that the men were innocent. Like most lynchings, the horrendous and grotesque action that took place was usually justified, in the minds of the terrorists involved, by proclaiming that a white woman's chastity had been taken or that a white man had been murdered—social taboos that, if true, would still warrant a Black suspect more prison time today (NAACP).

Blacks are more likely to receive the death penalty for murdering someone white than the other way around (NAACP). Certain types of murders are typically only considered morally wrong in America when the victim is white, due to the pathological dehumanization and denigration of Black people who, through concerted and perpetual propaganda, have been represented as subhuman and criminal for centuries, to justify their enslavement and subsequent terrorization.

Staring at the picture of the lynching of these two young men, you're able to witness, in full display, an exhibit of the worst of the American spirit. The celebratory nature of extrajudicial executions of Africans, particularly male. Many of the attendees, which include young couples holding hands (maybe he was taking his girlfriend there for a romantic date) and clueless senior citizens, seem to be elated at the atrocity they have witnessed, with sinister smirks in the presence of dangling corpses. The victims' heads were slumped over and tightly entrenched in a rope, while blood soaked through their raggedy clothes.

How ironic is it that the main character in this picture is a tattooed white man pointing at the dangling corpses with a mustache that would be made infamous by none other than Adolf Hitler later that decade? Yes, the same Hitler who credited America as an inspiration for the Holocaust due to their treatment of indigenous people and (enslaved) Africans. This is a part of America's legacy that is often neglected and excluded from textbooks (Moya-Smith).

So, when a white student purposely hangs a noose in a tree, it has a tremendous amount of history tied to it. The culprit is unleashing a lifetime of trauma and terrorism that was never vindicated with justice. It's more than a threat or a warning. It appears as an ominous display of what will happen to the intended Black target (or sympathizer of Blacks). It's a warning to retreat and vacate the premises if you desire to live to see another day.

Can you imagine if a Jewish kid came to school, and a group of kids placed a sign that read "Auschwitz" over their locker? What would the penalty presumably be? From my perspective, they'd undoubtably be expelled without any questions asked and likely face criminal charges (depending on their age). Why was this treated so differently? What was the value of a Black life in America in 2006? Likely the same as 1906. Likely the same as 2020.

Considering this backdrop, the Black community in Jena, Louisiana, took these noose hangings seriously, especially since the repercussions faced by the white students involved were trivial. Over the course of the next few months, there were several incidents that caused racial tensions to swell as several fights erupted involving friends and acquaintances of the parties involved. This would all culminate with a melee that occurred on December 6, 2006. This is what caused the entire country to support the aptly titled Jena 6. The events that happened on this day and the days after propelled the story to insurmountable heights.

On this day, five days after a party to which a group of Black males were denied entry and subsequently jumped, there was another party where six Black male teenagers between sixteen and eighteen got into an altercation with a seventeen-year-old white male classmate named Justin Baker. Details are murky about how the confrontation began. The six Black students claim that Baker hurled a racial slur in their direction, whereas he states that he was minding his business and was blindsided. Baker was beaten unconscious with a swollen eye and fractured jaw (Foster).

This attack, although heinous, is not what grabbed the attention of the country, however. What propelled this story to the spotlight after Baker's beating was the charges against the youth who allegedly responded to a racial slur. Three of the six youth were charged with attempted second-degree murder. The consensus from the Black community across the country seemed to be that this punishment was too harsh, especially when you consider the leniency that was administered toward the white youths who hung the nooses.

My sentiments were the same. Although I did feel that it was unfortunate that Baker was beaten unconscious, I can understand the angst felt by the students considering what preceded the attack. I had a hard time believing that he was completely innocent in this scenario. From my vantage point, persistent contentious provocation and agitation is not always best met with pacification, especially when intimidating and pernicious symbolism and words are used to mock those from a community rife with untreated trauma. Additionally, how hurt could he have been when he attended a school function later that night? My assumption is, if you were beaten to the brink of death, as they asserted, then the victim should have been physically and mentally incapable of carrying on with his regular proceedings for that day. Attending a high school football game, for example, would have been the last thing on my mind if I was beaten unconscious by six people who supposedly almost killed me.

The public outrage seemed to reflect my position. As I retired from Facebook for the night, I knew that I had encountered a story that was controversial; however, I did not realize that it would remain at the center of the public sphere for so long.

Social media coverage of the issue spread like wildfire as it was shared more and more leading into 2007. The case quickly became a social media phenomenon. In fact, I would go out on a limb to say that this was the first polarizing case involving race that was heavily covered and shared on social media platforms like Facebook and Twitter. How would this impact the proceedings? No longer did people have to wait for network news to cover stories deemed important. We the people now had the power to dictate to them what was pertinent. If they neglected a story such as this, our propensity to share it widely, due to its controversial nature, forced the mainstream media to do the same. During this time, televised and print media were undergoing a drastic change and shift as they sought new ways to adapt to the explosion of digital and social media. Essentially, they had to follow our lead or get left behind in journalistic purgatory.

Each day in 2007 the story seemed to grow, especially when celebrity activists Al Sharpton and Jesse Jackson latched onto it. As my sophomore year progressed, the heightened social media attention seemed to have a positive impact on the case. Of the six young men charged with attempted murder after the beating of Justin Baker, five had their charges reduced to battery, but one teen, sixteen-year-old Mychal Bell, remained with an attempted murder charge due to his having a prior record. I'd also add, due to my own exposure to the justice system, that it was because he was Black. What if Justin Baker and five other white friends were the culprits? I doubt he'd still have a charge.

Just look at Ethan Couch, a white teen from Texas who, at sixteen, killed four people in a car accident while under the influence of drugs and alcohol. His attorney used the "affluenza" defense (stating that he was too economically privileged to understand the ramifications of his actions) and was successful in helping his client avoid any time in the penitentiary.

This just doesn't happen with Black children, who are criminalized from birth. The school-to-prison pipeline critique, which asserts that traditional methods of public school culture prepare African Americans, and other children who are minorities in America, more for a life in prison than a life of professional success, is very real. Case in point: Black preschoolers (children as young as three) are four times as likely to be suspended as white preschoolers. Additionally, they make up nearly 50 percent of all suspensions while only accounting for 19 percent of the preschool population (Rock). Sounds a lot like the discrepancy between white and Black imprisonment: 13 percent of the general population and 40 percent of the prison population (NAACP). This is systemic racism at its core. Our children can go a lifetime without experiencing the level of overt racism I was exposed to, but still be victimized by codified elements of racism in this country's structures and institutions which can have an impact that is just as deleterious.

As my junior year began in August 2007, the Jena case continued to grow, especially with Mychal Bell still facing attempted murder charges at sixteen for his role in the group beating. Something had to be done. On September 20, 2007, thousands descended upon Jena to voice their complaints, led by the raucous Al Sharpton and Jesse Jackson, who felt that the inequality in the judicial proceedings was comparable to the noose hangings, and coupled with the public outrage, led to a reemergence of a civil rights movement. I agreed. Little did I know, however, that there would be several more cases, much worse, that recreated the eerie ambiance of the 1960s.

Financially, I couldn't afford to attend the rally in Louisiana, but I had several friends who did. I supported them from afar as I watched in real time on September 20 and 21, glued to my janky laptop in the corner of my apartment on Randolph Street in Champaign.

During my first year at U of I, I was thrust into the reality of racism on a college campus as I witnessed my heritage being mocked for the amusement of white fraternities and sororities, which was reminiscent of vintage minstrel shows. However, that story remained local (although it seemed to happen on a multitude of college campuses across the country). The Jena 6 story, however, was national and experienced in real time.

We didn't have to wait for CBS, ABC, NBC, or Fox to get to the scene to report on what occurred. With camera phones and digital cameras, I was able to experience what happened from a point of view I trusted. To see so many friends and acquaintances joined with activists both young and old from across the country to bring awareness to this issue was encouraging. I didn't realize it at the time, but this would be the first major news story involving racism on a grand scale to gain leverage and popularity based on social media interaction on Facebook. Coincidentally, three months prior to Justin Baker's beating, Facebook expanded to allow everyone to join, regardless of their collegiate status. This also coincided with the noose hangings, which served as the unfortunate foundation of this entire case. Initially, my friends and I were upset with the now omnipresent nature of Facebook. It had felt exclusive, but now anyone could join, including our parents. Facebook wasn't viewed as a potential online resume for potential employers, so there wasn't much motivation to censor party pictures or statuses until this was revealed. Although I didn't agree with it initially, seeing how the Jena 6 case panned out made me grateful that Zuckerberg made that decision.

This story had a long arc to justice, but it eventually came. Although Mychal Bell did serve some jail time and attempted suicide, he eventually had all his charges dropped. He would go on to play college football, as he always wanted, and graduate from Southern University in 2015 (Renegade).

I wish this served as a happy ending for the story of racism and for the story of inequity and injustice in the American judicial system. Sadly, it does not. I've come to learn, while living in a system of racism, that a singular victory is meaningless if you're losing the overall war for equity and justice. The people won, this time. Bell was able to persevere despite having an entire system set on diminishing him to an inferior status devoid of constitutional privileges. Most, however, wouldn't be so lucky.

CHAPTER 14

. . . WHEN TUPAC WAS WRONG

"Ern?! C'mon! We're ready to go," my mom exclaimed as she grabbed her Coach purse and scurried to the garage with my sister Nikki on a sunny Monday in July 2007.

I was almost done getting dressed. In fact, I had plenty of time to be done by 4:30 p.m. as my mom had requested, but I always found a way to procrastinate with even the simplest of tasks.

"Okay ma, here I come!"

I gently placed my laptop on my desk before departing, ensuring that it was plugged in so I could download T.I.'s *T.I. vs T.I.P.* and Pharaohe Monch's *Desire* while I was gone.

I slipped my shoes on and ran to the garage door and noticed my mom and sister were in the driveway preparing to pull off. As soon as I hopped in, my mom backed up her car and departed.

"Where are we going again, ma?"

"To a campaign meeting for Barack Obama," my mom responded immediately as she turned the corner.

"Who?!" My sister and I said in unison.

As we approached a white building in the south suburb of Country Club Hills, I noticed that the parking lot was full, but I was still unsure why. More importantly, I still didn't know who this person my mother spoke of was. Would we meet him? Would he be speaking? I would soon find out.

Because the lot was so full, we had to park on the street and had a lengthy walk to the front door. My sister and I walked in hesitantly, being led by the certainty of our mom. Slowly, we went up the old creaky stairs of the park district building, impatiently wondering what awaited us. As we reached the top, we were met by a boisterous volunteer (a white woman) who directed us into the packed room that was nearly standing room only.

"Welcome! Come right this way, please!"

We all signed our names and added our email addresses and looked for a seat. I was raised to be a gentleman, so I couldn't sit in one of the only available two seats I saw. Those were reserved for my mom and sister. I found a spot on the wall next to them near the window, so I spent my time posted against a blue and red wall and a coffee table with a delicate-looking lamp. It didn't seem to be a safe place to be if I wanted to assimilate myself into the crowd, but it was either that or stand up for what might be an ungodly amount of time. The volunteer we met at the door continued:

"Right now, we need volunteers that are willing to knock on doors and make phone calls."

As we departed, I left not knowing much about Obama except for the fact that he was a Black guy with an odd name for a Black (American) guy who was going to run for president and likely lose. See, I subscribed to the Tupac belief that, "even though it seems heaven-sent, we ain't ready to have a Black president." I thought it was wishful thinking and a crapshoot.

Boy, was I wrong.

I hadn't planned on doing any campaigning for him, but I reluctantly gave his suburban campaign manager my email address. The onslaught of messages asking for money began. I gave $5 at one point, but that was enough for me. The emails were quite annoying, and after a while they were quickly deleted. I had more important stuff to look forward to in my email, I thought. Like emails from professors or an mp3 file from one of my rap friends requesting a verse.

Over the course of the next year, my perspective on Obama changed drastically. I was getting excited about this guy. Could Tupac be wrong after all? From speeches on YouTube to media coverage and fanatical admiration by my mom, I joined the bandwagon as I entered my senior year at U of I in August 2008.

Some Republicans tried to say we only voted for Obama because he was Black. There's some validity to that. Keyword: some. Even if we only voted for him because he was Black, how was that different from the logic they used to elect the previous forty-three presidents? It's partially the reason we root for anyone Black on award shows and game shows. We almost never have genuine representation, so when we have someone who looks like us and speaks up for us, it's exciting! You didn't see Black folks trying to elect Ben Carson or Herman Cain, right? So much for that fallacious theory.

It wasn't just the fact that he was Black. Obama said everything I wanted to hear as a twenty-year-old Black kid who was going to get the opportunity to vote for a president for the first time as a senior in college.

It seemed like fate that this opportunity would simultaneously arise as I discovered my passion for Black studies.

Obama stood on a platform that was progressive and attractive. When I watched clips of his 2004 Democratic National Convention speech, the one that would propel him into the spotlight and a successful run for US Senator in Illinois, I realized why so many were enamored with him. I realized why it was standing room only at the campaign meeting I had attended with my mom and sister a year earlier. He spoke with eloquence, dignity, and passion. His oratorical execution and optimistic tone and delivery united the masses much like Dr. King in the '60s. He perfectly enunciated every word and seemingly made eye contact with everyone in the crowd as he enthusiastically spoke on that which united Americans. I hung on every word because I believed he could lead our country into an era where Black people received true equity and justice in a country that had always viewed and treated us as second-class citizens.

"There is not a liberal America and a conservative America—there is the United States of America. There is not a Black America and a white America and Latino America and Asian America—there's the United States of America."

This rallying cry in 2004 would be his coming out party to the masses. It sought to unite all people under the perilous, uncertain Bush administration, to believe that we could still come together, regardless of race, to achieve the American dream and bring forth true democratic principles. In hindsight, it perfectly encapsulated President Obama's approach as he neglected Black folks' true legislative needs.

Although he spoke eloquently, it proved to be nothing more than a neoliberal rhetorical device. It's almost insulting to look at now because it's akin to a white person saying, "I don't see color." It sounds great because you feel as though you'll finally get judged by your character, which was at the foundation of King's overly quoted 1963 speech. When you have been the target of white supremacist legislation historically, and are currently, simply coming together to hold hands with those who have received advantages and privileges over you won't mend those open wounds. Being solely a "United" American and no longer a "Black" American means you would not receive the reparations you are owed to rectify the targeted legislation that placed you in a disadvantaged position in society.

Calling for colorblindness erases my unique heritage, existence, and plight of inequity. It seeks to call a truce without an apology and return of capital. In 2007 I was fooled by that jargon. In 2019 it infuriated me. I can't say if that was his intention with that statement, but it sure felt that way.

Nevertheless, I was on the Barack Obama bandwagon like everyone else. Not only did his 2004 speech unify many, he spoke on issues that had left the lexicon of past and present politicians.

He promised to close down Guantanamo Bay (a prison that was established in 2002 by the United States, soon after 9/11, on the far coast of Cuba where prisoners of war and suspected terrorists are held and often tortured without receiving a fair trial or an explanation of why they're being held); bring home the troops from the wars in Iraq and Afghanistan; provide healthcare for all with the Affordable Care Act, which has affectionately been known as Obamacare; and end the mandatory sentencing disparity between crack (normally in Black communities) and cocaine (normally in white communities) offenses, where perpetrators would receive a minimum five-year sentence for having five grams of crack whereas those with 100 grams of powder cocaine would receive the same sentence. Additionally, he claimed he would repeal "Don't Ask, Don't Tell" (which forced those in the LGBTQ community who served in the military to remain silent about their sexuality), tax the wealthy more, create financial restrictions that would appease the Occupy Wall Street movement, and pass immigration reform that would allow for a more seamless path to citizenship for immigrants.

These were all positions I supported, especially as a progressive-minded, optimistic college student. However, there was a conspicuous absence in Obama's platform that would ominously lead to a drastic shift in my political paradigm and view of his presidency. In 2008, I was excited, though. I felt that Obama had an inclusive platform and the leadership skills, integrity, and rhetorical skills to lead this country in the right direction for all people for the first time in American history, as far as I was concerned.

When my senior thesis class for my African American Studies minor began in late August, we discussed Obama and watched clips of his most recent speeches nearly every class as my professor found a way to connect his recent commentary to the primary sources we were assigned to read beforehand.

There was such a widespread buzz from the largely liberal campus, especially since Obama, the underdog of the Democratic Party, had secured the nomination in June, beating Hillary Clinton who previously sought to make history herself. Up to that point, everyone assumed his candidacy, and victory, would be a long shot. Personally, I thought his run would be symbolic, like Jesse Jackson's in the '80s, and further pave the way and set the stage for a future candidate. Humorously, I also thought about how Obama was on the path to help me accomplish my destiny to become the first Black president of the US, but I digress.

Being a supporter of Obama at this time while taking my courses was akin to being a seed in fertile soil in June after a rainy day. I was in the perfect environment for my adoration to grow. The defining moment of his candidacy, for me at least, came when past remarks from his pastor, Reverend Jeremiah Wright, were exposed by conservative publications such as Fox News. Wright, who was also the mentor of my childhood pastor, Reverend Dr. Ozzie E. Smith Jr., was a fiery and passionate preacher who was an unabashed critic of American affairs, domestically and internationally.

During one sermon following the 9/11 attacks, Wright made controversial remarks that were similar to Malcolm X's "the chickens have come home to roost" comment that followed JFK's assassination in Dallas.

The words were in rotation on every news outlet in the spring of 2008. The grainy footage from Trinity United Church of Christ, which was presumably never meant for news networks, showed Wright passionately espousing comments viewed as inflammatory to the average white American: "Not God bless America, God damn America!"

That was all anyone had heard. What about the context, though? As a social science teacher, I'm aggravatingly repetitious with the demand that my students analyze the occasion and context before dissecting a primary source. My favorite method is showing them a picture of children saluting the flag while reciting the pledge in the 1930s. The students are all standing with their arms extended forward with a slight slant pointing toward the flag. Everyone assumes that I have shown them a rare German photograph because they assume they're viewing a class of children doing a Nazi salute. To the contrary, these children are American. Before it became the norm to place your hand over your heart, it was common to salute the flag with a straight arm and hand until Hitler's reign caused the world to reimagine its symbolism in the same way they erroneously assume Charlie Chaplin's small mustache was inspired by Hitler. So simply viewing a short clip of Wright's speech wherein he damns America causes a gross misrepresentation of the true nature of his comments.

Wright gave the comments on Sunday, September 16, five days after 9/11, during a time when Americans of all races were uniting behind a common enemy. Our government had quickly purported that Osama bin Laden and al-Qaeda were the culprits, which would lead to an onslaught of racial discrimination against brown-skinned Muslims or anyone who appeared to be of the faith based on their ethnicity. Additionally, this was the breeding ground for our never-ending foray into Afghanistan and Iraq for seventeen years and counting. Everywhere you drove, you saw signs and marquees displaying "God Bless America," "United We Stand," and "Never Forget." These ubiquitous melancholy feelings were warranted, but most people didn't consider the abuse Middle Eastern, African, and Latin American countries were subjected to since the 1950s as a result of American foreign policy.

Between the '50s and the '70s alone, the US government, through the CIA, overthrew the governments of Iran ('53), Guatemala ('54), Congo ('60), Dominican Republic ('61), South Vietnam ('63), Brazil ('64), and Chile ('73) (Stuster). What's more, as the American empire sought to expand, they even indirectly funded Osama bin Laden's rise as they gave millions of dollars in resources to the mujahideen, who sought to remove the Soviet Union (and communism) from Afghanistan in the decade-long Soviet-Afghan War ('79–'89) (Otieno). During the Cold War, American foreign policy led to the death of millions of Black and brown people abroad, mainly from the countries accused of committing terrorist acts against the US currently. This is what we unfortunately must refer to as "blowback."

With that ammo, Wright critiqued American imperialism, faux unity, and the false notion of exceptionalism:

> The United States of America government, when it came to treating her citizens of Indian descent fairly, she failed. She put them on reservations. When it came to treating her citizens of Japanese descent fairly, she failed. She put them in internment prison camps. When it came to treating her citizens of African descent fairly, America failed. The government put them in

chains. She put them in slave quarters, put them on auction blocks, put them in cotton fields, put them in inferior schools, put them in substandard housing, put them in scientific experiments, put them in the lowest paying jobs, put them outside the equal protection of the law, kept them out of their racist bastions of higher education, and locked them into positions of hopelessness and helplessness. The government gives them the drugs, builds bigger prisons, passes a three-strikes law, and then wants us to sing God Bless America...no, no, no. Not God bless America, God damn America. That's in the Bible, for killing innocent people. God damn America for treating her citizens as less than human. God damn America for as long as she acts like she is God and she is supreme. The United States government has failed most of her citizens of African descent. Consider this: for every Oprah, a billionaire, you've got five million Blacks who are out of work. For every Colin Powell, a millionaire, you've got ten million Blacks who cannot read. For every Condoleeza Rice, you've got one million in prison.

I didn't find a lie. However, I can sympathize with how hard this message was to digest for most white Americans who had viewed this as a rare American tragedy. The truth is, we had experienced terrorist acts like 9/11 by way of domestic terrorists since being forced to come to this country many years ago. His introspectively scathing comments on the truth surrounding American hypocrisy were reduced to a soundbite in the same manner that Colin Kaepernick's protest against racism, the justice system, and police brutality were unfairly lambasted as a protest of the anthem and flag.

The media's bombardment of his "God damn America" soundbite was sensationalism and propaganda at its finest. The sad thing is it worked.

The pressure was now on Obama. As a member of Wright's church, Trinity United Church of Christ, and someone who considered him his pastor (Wright officiated at his wedding), he was faced with a difficult predicament. Many white Americans, liberal and conservative, expected him to immediately disavow his association with someone so radical and critical of American affairs.

Obama responded to Wright's comments in a speech entitled "A More Perfect Union" in March of 2008. In my senior thesis class, we watched it in its entirety. During the speech, he expressed his sentiments regarding racism unlike any other presidential candidate before him, because, well, he was the only Black presidential candidate to receive a major party nomination ever. And similar to his 2004 speech's rallying cry of "One America," he resorted to a similar tactic, using the tragedy of 9/11 to springboard his statement:

> As such, Reverend Wright's comments were not only wrong but divisive, divisive at a time when we need unity; racially charged at a time when we need to come together to solve a set of monumental problems—two wars, a terrorist threat, a falling economy, a chronic health care crisis, and potentially devastating climate change—problems that are neither Black or white or Latino or Asian, but rather problems that confront us all.

To Obama, exposing the tendencies and pernicious behavior that possibly led to a despicable terrorist act by some groups who have a hatred of America due to our flawed imperialism and foreign policy, was not worth bringing up at this moment. I disagree, but again, I can see why some would be frazzled. Maybe he should've said "God bless America" before beginning.

What's interesting is, white candidates have never been made to denounce racist friends, associates, or pastors in the past, so why was a Black candidate seemingly forced to denounce a pastor who rebukes the tenets of racism and subjugation? My theory? Racism is the status quo in America, whereas any outspoken repudiation of this malevolent norm is viewed as disruptive, cantankerous, and decidedly un-American. For example, I recently had a video blocked and removed on Instagram with the title "They portray us like dogs and kill us like dogs," explaining the correlation between blackface, negative media coverage of Blacks, and lynchings. My exposure of racism was referred to as "hate speech," although I was simply stating a fact.

Being Black at a PWI or majority-white environment is nerve-wracking, especially once awoken to the injustices of America and regality of Black history. The more knowledge I gained, the more paranoid I became. I'd walk through the quad past white folks, cautious and apprehensive, wondering if they were racist or not. Especially after a lecture in which I was exposed to countless images of white racists mutilating, raping, and lynching my Black brothas and sisters for their melanin content. Coupled with my personal exposure to racism on U of I's campus, and the overt racism Obama endured on the campaign trail, my paranoia was validated.

Mentally, it was debilitating to live that way, though. All white people aren't racist, but how would I not at least protect myself with a cautious approach, considering what had happened and continued to happen to us in America without widespread intervention by so-called progressive or liberal whites who claimed to be allies? For instance, if I'm against domestic violence, and it's so widespread that it happens constantly without conviction, how would I proclaim an alliance with women and walk past public instances where men abuse women without intervention? How would I not advocate for the reparations that women never received? I'd be a hypocrite if I did that. A phony.

Still, at the time, I overlooked this and made excuses. "He'll reunite with Wright during or after his presidency," I foolishly thought.

As Obama's popularity rose precipitously, another public figure was, in a bit of foreshadowing, becoming more vocal about politics publicly. That person, former president Donald Trump, emboldened racists as if he was grooming them for his 2016 presidential run. Obama also emboldened them inadvertently with his very presence as a Black man. His presidency symbolically represented the transformation of America to a new age of acceptance of diversity, which angered many who wanted to, as Trump said, "Make America Great Again" by explicitly subjugating Blacks and other minorities in America.

Trump, who has historically donated to both Democrats and Republicans, led the anti-Obama nonsensical racist brigade by questioning his citizenship status. This absurd and asinine assertion served as a subliminal message and dog whistle for white supremacists who sought other avenues of resistance against the potentiality of Obama's presidency. Trump did not start the rumors, although, as a celebrity billionaire, his stamp of approval in 2011 made the assertions mainstream. Although Trump's push for Obama to reveal his birth certificate gained nationwide exposure in 2011 due to Trump, the claims began primarily in 2008 on conservative websites.

The reason why was obvious. Obama's culture and racial background was a cause for alarm for many racists. Obama didn't have an upbringing that most Black Americans could relate to. He was born in Hawaii to a white mother and Kenyan immigrant father, and given a traditional Muslim name that rhymes with the name of the person the US government claimed was responsible for orchestrating the 9/11 attacks: Osama. Furthermore, his middle name is the last name of a former American ally turned enemy (Hussein) who supposedly had weapons of mass destruction and was later executed on television, much to the pleasure of then President George W. Bush. His unique background led racists to fallaciously assume that he had been born in Africa. So, when they yelled, "Go back to Africa!" they truly meant it.

...when Tupac was wrong

The racists had a field day with Obama. *How do we know he wasn't really born in Kenya? Is he truly American? Is he a Muslim? What do we really know about him? Why won't he show his birth certificate to prove he was born here?* These are absurd critiques because they assert that Islam is synonymous with terrorism. Arguably, more have suffered at the hands of those who have claimed to be Christians while violently proselytizing and spreading their gospel. When's the last time you saw someone get mistreated for having a Christian name?

The questions and demands were absurd. Questioning the legitimacy of Barack Obama's citizenship was the equivalent of demanding freedom papers from a free or escaped enslaved Black man or woman. Show your papers or risk being enslaved again, which in this case would mean social ridicule, political slander, and accusations of malfeasance with the goal of imprisonment.

Once you prove your freedom by showing your papers, the interrogation will take another form and move to another realm, and you'll once again be the victim of a racial audit. The true motive for this interrogation is racism. To racists, you don't belong here, but to not seem explicitly racist, they demanded proof of birth to veil their intentions. The self-hatred and feelings of inadequacy amongst racists who express their loathsomeness through the questioning of Black success is what this is.

Blacks will never be acceptable or permissible in the eyes of a racist, so trying to prove legitimacy by revealing freedom papers (or in this case, birth certificates), dressing appropriately, or conforming to other white-approved social norms are an utter waste of time. You don't belong in America or in their space, from their perspective, because you are a threat to the survival of their race. You are a perpetual outsider.

President Obama felt compelled to prove his Americanness by releasing his birth certificate in 2012 while running for reelection, and of course the criticism from Trump and his ilk didn't end because it was never truly about that.

The racist symbolism that harked back to slavery didn't end there. There were times when I saw footage of Obama effigies being burned during Republican rallies in the South. These effigies were life-size mannequins or dummies, hanging from a wooden post with a noose around their necks and set ablaze. It was 2008, but the images were reminiscent of those I had seen of Black men like Jesse Washington who were lynched and burned in front of a crowd of gleeful whites.

Other instances included rallies with protest signs with the words "Hang in there Obama" with a noose, or signs calling him the Kenyan village idiot, or signs that also attempted to portray him as a primitive Kenyan with limited clothing and a bone through his nose (Delong). Obviously this was not done to celebrate his ancestry, but to attempt to denigrate him and associate him with the propagandized Western view of Africa.

It was also common to see Southern whites holding signs depicting Obama as a monkey. This pernicious and vicious symbol of racism harks back to the pseudoscience theory of phrenology that was first popularized in the 1700s and sought to assert that there was a correlation between brain size and intelligence. The creator of this theory attempted to find a way to legitimize the idiotic perspective that Blacks were inferior to whites by proclaiming they were savages who were justifiably enslaved in accordance with the laws of nature. Phrenology morphed into an even more fallacious theory when scientists in the mid-1800s began to write books and scientific journals asserting that Blacks were essentially the direct relatives of monkeys and apes, whereas they (whites) were mankind's highest point of evolution. Pseudoscience served as the justification for chattel slavery for racist whites. Although these asinine assertions have been proven wrong, the impact these ideas had on the minds of white racists was indelible and longstanding. For many years after, the American mainstream, through ad agencies, movies, cartoons, and other forms of entertainment, still depicted Black people as apes or ape-like.

The protest continued, even more surreptitiously. The attacks on his perceived Muslim faith intensified due to his last name and country of origin despite his proclamation of Christianity. I recall a lady at a campaign rally for his Republican opponent, John McCain, claiming that she did not trust Obama due to his supposed alliance with Islam. McCain quickly corrected her, which is a commendable thing. He should have taken it a step further, though. Instead of just reiterating how much a Christian Obama was, McCain should have also assured her that Islam should not conjure feelings of anxiety and distrust due to perception that the 9/11 hijackers were Muslim. It goes without saying that Islam, as a faith, is commonly associated with brown people and Black people. There's a common theme developing here.

Other detractors accused Obama of intending to enslave whites if elected and implementing socialism through a radical increase in taxes without Congress's approval. Then, of course, there's the Affordable Care Act, a law passed under his presidency, which has been affectionately dubbed Obamacare by detractors and supporters alike. Obamacare is not universal healthcare, but it was advertised as such by the right-wing media. In short, it is a policy that expands healthcare coverage to Americans, regardless of their employment status. It's understandable why some would agree or disagree with this policy. However, some simply veiled their racist critiques of Obama by labeling him a socialist who would morph into a dictator if elected. Some of these critics could not fathom having a Black man lead what they perceived to be their country.

As October approached, the possibility of having a Black president felt more likely, but apprehension still existed. It seemed almost too good to be true, but I was here for the experience. With less than a month until the election, I began wearing two Obama shirts that I ordered more frequently around the largely white campus.

The anxiety I felt while wearing them existed because I felt every white person's eyes staring a hole through me while every Black person's nod let me know that they were raising their fist in solidarity inwardly as they walked past me on the quad or saw me in class. To avoid most of these awkward interactions, I fed my introverted, pessimistic, nonconfrontational side and kept my autumn jacket zipped three fourths of the way to avoid what my mind deemed a worst-case scenario.

The only time I relented was when I was sitting in the back of my token classes, that is, the courses I had where I was one of only a few Black students. I'd be in the back of the class, listening to a lecture I could care less about on Renaissance art, slowly unzipping my jacket. I was more apathetic to opinions in this situation simply because you could hardly make out what was on my shirt when I was sitting down.

My Black studies courses remained my refuge, as they had been since the second semester of my freshman year. Donning my Obama shirt wasn't a big deal there. It was the norm. It was celebrated. My peers would ask where I got it. Without having that space of comfort and acceptance, I wouldn't have survived college.

"I'm so nervous, you all!" Professor McKnight exclaimed in my African American Studies senior thesis course as the class began. The daily lesson had been restructured every week to allow us to discuss any new Obama updates. This Monday was no different, except it was the day before the biggest election of our lives and arguably the biggest election in American history.

As we sat in our normal circle of desks, we all began to situate ourselves by taking out our laptops, notebooks, and weekly articles. A classmate named William chimed in after a few moments had passed.

"I'm nervous too, but I'm ready. Now is the time for change. America betta' not mess this up again. I need Florida to get it together this time!"

The class erupted in laughter as we settled in to prepare for the class discussion. In the back of our minds, we'd probably all agree that we felt the sentiments of both Professor McKnight and William. We were nervous. We forced ourselves to be hopeful, but truthfully, we were really scared. Florida, for example, was notoriously known for conveniently and surreptitiously losing tens of thousands of votes from its Black residents in the 2000 election, which ultimately swayed the election in Bush, Jr.'s favor. Why wouldn't they do it again? Likewise, how did we know that white supremacists wouldn't be bold in their approach, since the stakes were much higher?

We held our collective breath. As class ended for the day and I headed home, the uncertainty weighed me down. I had no idea that this was the last time America would be able to hide its ugliness through covert means and tactics. It would also be the last time that America would solely present the face of a white male to the world and country as the leader of the "free" world. This would also be the last time that I remained in the box of the traditional paradigm expected of Black Americans, especially when it comes to political alignments.

Then came Judgement Day: November 4, 2008.

Election Day was finally here. I arose with vigor and nervousness. Luckily, Tuesday was a slow day for me. I only had two classes and they concluded by twelve o'clock.

"Yooo, you ready?" I called my roommate, Greg, as soon as I got out of class to see if he was ready to go vote as we had planned.

I hopped in my car, picked him and a few other friends up, and headed to the polling place. All we could talk about was our nervous excitement and what we expected to see at our polling place.

"Check it, those white folks are gonna have the doors blocked so we can't vote. We gotta be careful out there, fa' real! Ain't no telling what they're gonna do." Everyone in the car was laughing hysterically while jokingly adding their input.

It was a joke, but we were serious.

As we pulled up, we didn't know what to expect, but one glance at the parking lot and door confirmed what pundits predicted. The parking lot was full and there was a line outside, wrapped around the corner, that seemed to never end. It was as if you went grocery shopping, only to head to the checkout line to notice that there was only one lane open. You despise the scenario, but you realize that you don't have any other option, because if you want your food, you're going to have to wait patiently. That was our situation.

As we got out of my packed Grand Am, we searched for the beginning of the line and began to lightly jog to the location, which was near the park at the south end of the school, to secure our spot before someone else jumped in line.

Although it was November, the weather was respectable. It wasn't overwhelmingly hot or cold. It was hoodie season. The sun was shining and the breeze that caught our faces wasn't overbearing or daunting. In short, it was the perfect weather to wait in line to vote for the first Black president.

The line moved slowly and methodically. Our conversations went from anticipatory and jovial to impatient and antsy. After waiting in line for an hour and finally making it inside, some of us opted to sit down on the carpeted floor while others leaned against the wall. Although it was frustrating having to endure such a wait, I was able to take a step back amid the chaos to realize what I was experiencing. Surely, this type of turnout had to be because of the potentiality of electing the first Black president in Barack Obama. Before I neared the front of the line, I took a deep breath, observed the environment, and became grateful and full of humility.

"I'm really experiencing something historic," I muttered to myself. After nearly three hours, we finally reached the front of the line. I glanced back to see how far we had come and noticed that the line had proceeded to get even longer.

"Next," the voting judge called for me and I stepped forward. My heart was beating rapidly as I grabbed the ballot and inched toward an open booth. Within a few minutes I walked out of the polling place, a local elementary school, with an "I Voted" sticker and the biggest smile on my face.

As we returned to our apartments, the only thing on our minds was the result of the election. My roommates and a few other friends grabbed some chairs and the remote and plopped ourselves in front of the TV in our living room, as we quickly turned to CNN and waited for the ballots to be returned. It was a long night of waiting. CNN anchor Wolf Blitzer assured us that the results would soon be forthcoming.

"Y'all wanna drink?"

Greg grabbed a beer for everyone and a few bottles of champagne before he came back into the living room and reclaimed his seat. We were still nervous because, although Obama had been projected to win, we were still in America, meaning anything was possible, for good or bad. In my mind, the whites who stated that they would overwhelmingly vote for Obama might have had a change of mind when they entered the voting booth. Hindsight is 20/20, but the 2016 election would prove you can't trust the projections.

"Yo, I'mma be *pissed* if he don't win. Swear I'mma snap on every white person I see!" Anthony said jokingly. He revealed a very real uncertainty that existed in all of us. None of us had been particularly fond of our treatment as Black men in America so our doubt was valid. Then the moment of truth came.

As the results came in, it started to seem like the impossible would happen in my lifetime. I sat there with Greg, Anthony, Terrance, Ben, and Jermaine in eager anticipation. As Obama neared 270 Electoral College votes, we glanced at each other with scrunched eyebrows, revealing our collective confusion and disbelief. See, we weren't from our parents' or grandparents' generation, but we understood how historic this moment would be. We were twenty-one and twenty-two. Old enough to have experienced Rodney King and the lynching of James Byrd in 1999, but young enough to not have experienced Jim Crow segregation.

"G, it's gon' happen!" Anthony blurted out with a wide-toothed grin revealing his excitement.

Anthony and Terrance each clenched a bottle of champagne, anticipating the announcement so that they could let the corks fly in celebration. And then it happened. Wolf Blitzer stated what we wanted to hear.

"With 270 Electoral College votes, Barack Obama is your new President-elect."

"Ayyyyyy! *Yeaaaaah!*"

We sounded like members of Lil' Jon's choir the way we collectively yelled, "Yeah!" excitedly. It finally happened! America would have a Black president! We did it! We made it! So, we thought.

Immediately, corks popped and flew over the room. Champagne spilled onto the carpet and drenched our socks as we celebrated. We felt as if President Obama had done this for us. We felt that President Obama was us. We felt as if we had reached the finish line.

Unable to contain our boisterousness, we ran into our apartment building's lobby and began screaming with even more excitement. Terrance ripped off his shirt as if he was Hulk Hogan and waved it around.

"Obama! We did it!"

Not satisfied, we took to the streets. We walked toward Green Street, the main street on campus, and the Alma Mater statue, because we figured there would likely be a celebration on campus after the announcement.

"Honk for Obama!"

We yelled that at every car that went past, hoping that they shared our excitement. Most times they did. You couldn't take the grins off our faces. As we continued to walk, we noticed a crowd of people gathering. Eventually, as we got within two blocks of the Alma Mater statue, we couldn't move anymore. Green Street was filled with people. Not the sidewalks, but the actual street. People had to turn their cars around or park and get out and celebrate.

I had never seen anything like it. As I looked up, I saw white guys on top of the light poles, waving their shirts and screaming for President Obama. People in the streets were chanting and singing excitedly. The Alma Mater statue was filled with people climbing her. Coming from a redlined community in the most segregated city in America, I had never in my life seen so many people of different backgrounds and races come together in such a celebratory fashion outside of sporting events.

President Obama had done the unthinkable. He had seemingly caused America to heal and come together, and he had not even taken office yet. Surely this would be the straw that broke the racist back of America. Hate would no longer fester, because we had the hope and change we had always wanted. Regarding my future, America's future, and race relations, I was at my most optimistic immediately following President Obama's election. Like Kevin Garnett's exclamatory remark following his first championship win, I felt *"Anything is (was) possible!"*

I couldn't wait until he took office in January. If his win created this level of unity immediately afterwards, I couldn't wait to see what would happen when he potentially advocated and passed legislation to help Black people.

Before I knew it, it was nearly midnight, and I had class in the morning. As a freshman, I would've kept the party going, but after nearly flunking out of school I had to change my values. Now, as a senior, I had different priorities. My friends opted to stay, but I needed to make my way back home so I could get up for my ten o'clock class. Ultimately, my goal was to graduate with a 3.0, so I had to remain focused even though I was in my last year.

As I walked home, I couldn't wipe the smile off my face. I knew exactly what I was wearing to my WWII class tomorrow. For the first time, I didn't feel nervous or anxious about wearing one of my President Obama shirts. I didn't care what anyone thought anymore pertaining to my fanaticism. Besides, I was rolling with a winner.

The following day was refreshing. It was a bright yet frigid day in November, and the first day in America when a Black man was the leader. I felt rejuvenated. I dared a racist to say something foolish to me out of bitterness or contempt. I'd laugh in their face!

The soundtrack for the day, much like last night, was undoubtedly Young Jeezy's "My President is Black."

I walked to class with my coat open with an impeccable swagger. As I made my way down Green Street toward the campus, I placed my earbuds in and blasted Jeezy's song at a volume level that should've put my hearing at risk.

"My president is Black, my Lambo's blue, and I be God-damned if my rims ain't too. My momma ain't at home and daddy still in jail. Tryna make a plate, anybody seen the scale?"

I wasn't fazed by the stares or glances that I might've received due to my shirt. I was on cloud nine and in another world. I firmly believed that America would finally start working for Black people. I believed "Justice for all" would finally be true. I thought "All men are created equal" would no longer be a hypocritical statement uttered by a slave-owning Founding Father and president (Thomas Jefferson), but rather a truth that would not be denied to any citizen.

In short, I was naïve. But on that day, you couldn't tell me nothing! In the span of four years, I had nearly flunked out of school, found my passion for Black history and education, and witnessed the ascension of a Black man to president.

President Obama's success affirmed what my mom told me when I asked her why there hadn't been a Black president. Although that dream had long dissipated from my mind, being able to witness the actualization of a feat many thought was impossible was inspiring. I was reminded that I could accomplish whatever I put my mind to with intense focus, determination, and an intelligent, pragmatic work ethic.

I walked into my WWII class, sat down, took my earbuds out, and wrapped my headphones around my iPod. I then positioned my book bag on the ground against the leg of my desk and slowly unzipped my jacket. As I slipped my arms out of my jacket and pushed it down behind me, I was equipped with a smirk so sly, a fox would be jealous.

When class concluded, my white professor who had barely spoken to me the entire semester approached me as I was packing my belongings before departing. He looked at me with the widest grin, pushed his glasses up the tip of his slanted nose toward his face and gleefully said, "That shirt is awesome! After yesterday, I'm proud of our country."

I nodded in agreement and engaged in a jovial conversation with someone from whom I had previously distanced myself due to a preconceived notion that we didn't have anything in common.

For the first time in my life, I felt that the "our" he alluded to included me and my African American brethren. Unfortunately, it wouldn't be long before that privilege and feeling was taken back with a vengeance.

PART III

CHAPTER 15
. . . WHEN I NOTICED WHITE-ON-BLACK CRIME

Blair Holt's murder was tragic to me because it felt personal. As I was finishing my second year of college and preparing for final exams, a young brotha three years younger than me was murdered on a CTA bus. Having grown up in Chicago on the South Side in the '90s, when murders would top out at over 900, compared to the 400–500 that's normally tallied nowadays, I was no stranger to hearing the malicious melody of gunfire on Sangamon, Morgan, or across Halsted. Fortunately, I never lost a friend or loved one to gun violence as a child, but the repetitive sounds of shots, followed by the shrieking sounds of ambulance sirens, while I tried to go to sleep at night was traumatic. As a Black child growing up in Chicago on the south or west side, you don't feel safe in your own neighborhood. If it wasn't gunshots, I witnessed individuals get jumped at the bus stop or "up top" across the street from Morgan Park. The streets are cruel and hungry. If you aren't careful, they'll devour you.

That's exactly why Blair's murder was so significant to me. Blair attended my high school's rival, Julian (the school I student-taught at), which was only a mile away from us. The Julian Jaguars and Morgan Park Mustangs didn't typically get along for the same reason gangs didn't (for no apparent reason other than competition and tradition). In fact, if your bus route stopped near your rival school, it was likely you'd get jumped if you were outnumbered, slick at the mouth, or just because.

...when I noticed white-on-Black crime

Blair attending Julian didn't mean he was my rival, though. He was my brotha, although we never met each other. With his cornrows, he looked just like most of my friends from high school who mimicked Allen Iverson's swag and attire. He likely lived in a neighborhood that I was familiar with and had gone to some of the same establishments and businesses. I'll assume that he was a Bulls fan like me as well. What made his murder even more heartbreaking was how it happened. He was riding a CTA bus. I took the same route every day for three years in high school.

Did I mention that his murder was recorded by the CTA surveillance cameras? This was 2007, two years after Facebook began, so social media was still relatively young. We had not yet conceptualized seeing people get murdered on camera and having it broadcast on our newsfeeds and nightly news channels. Police brutality was still just something we discussed amongst ourselves. It wasn't a global phenomenon yet, with the UN condemning the US's lack of action in protecting Black folks (*Huffington Post*). Up to that point, gang violence, or what has been incorrectly dubbed "Black-on-Black crime," was the most pertinent issue to me growing up because it involved my neighborhood's livelihood daily, and with this murder, it became international news.

The video showed a young man named Michael Pace walk onto a CTA bus and immediately draw his gun and callously open fire into a crowd of commuters without regard or compassion. One of those commuters, Blair Holt, wasn't the intended target. Neither was his friend, but Holt shielded her as the wayward bullet from Pace's gun was discharged in their vicinity. Holt, along with four other people, was shot by Pace that afternoon as he intended to settle a gang dispute. Holt was the only one who died. It's one thing to hear about a shooting, or read an article about it, but it affects you differently when it happens on camera, separate from a movie or music video. "That could've been me," was the thought that continued to run through my mind after I watched it repeatedly.

For a while, I thought we were the problem. I thought that if we simply adjusted our mindsets and stopped killing each other, that we could change our lot in life. I knew racism was bad, but, as mentioned previously, I didn't know the intricacies and nuances of systemic racism as in-depth as I do now. I was overexposed, like we all were, to the myth of "Black-on-Black" crime. What I didn't understand, as my disdain for Black gang violence grew, was that gun violence was at a forty-five-year low when I began working in unfamiliar neighborhoods on the South Side of Chicago. However, you couldn't tell that when you were trying to survive daily.

The media seemed to begin to cover the gun violence in our community as if it were a weekly competition to outdo the previous week's total (I'm not sure if this happened before social media). It was as if someone in Vegas had placed a bet on our lives, or taken out individual life insurance policies, and had a stake in our self-extermination. One week they'd count ten murders. The next, seven. The following week it might be fifteen, then three. No matter the number, it would make headlines as if our world was crumbling due to what they advertised as our propensity for violence. Isn't that the pot calling the kettle black?

Like most issues surrounding violence in our community, Blair's murder was politicized. As I worked on the South Side in 2010, trying to manage my caseload and counsel young brothas like Kenny, the murders were politicized even more. In 2013, the entire nation stood still when another honor student, Hadiya Pendleton, was mistakenly murdered while sitting at a bus stop outside her high school (Kenwood), the high school once attended by the first lady, Michelle Obama. This young lady had just returned from performing at President Obama's inauguration some weeks earlier. This story, like Blair's and every other case of murder in Chicago, is extremely sad. In hindsight, I'm able to see the game and political nature of the national discourse that follows. They'll quickly condemn a young brotha for killing another Black man or woman, but they won't condemn their own for killing us with the same malicious intent. We're portrayed as inherently evil people who need law and order and stiff penalties to correct our behavior, whereas they need counseling or a paid vacation to correct their actions.

Admittedly, I was highly critical of our brothas in the street who were committing murder against each other while refusing to place any of the blame on centuries of systemic racism. I didn't understand that intraracial violence is primarily a matter of proximity. Over 90 percent of Black people are killed by other Black people. Similarly, 80 percent of white people are killed by other white people (Massie). The grand conspiracy of "Black-on-Black" crime that right-wingers talk about as a rebuttal to the Black Lives Matter movement and other grassroots movements for government accountability is a myth. This violence happens primarily because America is so segregated (much like the resources). Those who commit crimes tend to lash out against those who are near them. Imagine someone going halfway across town to specifically target another person they feel anger toward. Imagine someone waking up, loading an assault rifle, hopping in a car, and driving fifteen minutes to murder someone at a school, for instance. Oh, wait. If America was more integrated and not stratified in such a way as to benefit white society socially, politically, and economically, then this false phenomenon of "Black-on-Black" crime would not be a term worth using.

What should be noted is the historical context in which Black murder occurs in the hood, compared to "white-on-white" murder. My conjecture is that whites murder other whites as a result of sentiments related to social or economic ineptitude. Our white brethren are descendants of people who migrated here, primarily for social and economic mobility, which was often made possible by a previous generation's unmitigated violence. So, contextually, their violence might be an unconscious response to reclaiming what they perceive to be theirs through the lens of privilege.

In terms of my brothas, we must understand the traumatizing nature of slavery, trauma that has never been counseled or properly repaired. For every action there is a reaction. For every cause, there is an effect. That is a universal law. We, as humans, with our primitive understanding of the metaphysical, can't properly conceptualize just when the effect or reaction will take place, however. To properly understand the current plight and degradation of Black society now, you must have a firm grasp on what was illegal for Blacks during slavery, in terms of social interaction, and more importantly, what punitive action was legal for whites to inflict upon Blacks.

If history is a vast early warning system, as Norman Cousins asserts, then we shouldn't be surprised when we see the onslaught of so-called "Black-on-Black" crime in government-sponsored redlined Black ghettos across the country. If we were to rewind to 150–200 years ago and insert ourselves as a fly on the wall of an outhouse on a plantation in South Carolina where my paternal ancestors once labored against their will as slaves, then we would witness the phenomenon that set the stage for "Black-on-Black" crime—that is, white-on-Black crime, which essentially reflected the white-on-white crime and torture that occurred in Europe for centuries prior during the Middle Ages.

Disregarding the trauma of being captured from your homeland and being placed on the bottom of a ship in chains for anywhere from one to three months, immersed in feces, urine, repugnant bodily odors and fluids with people you could not effectively communicate with because they were from different villages or tribes. After docking in America, you'd now be subjected to further inhumane treatment. You'd be stripped naked, placed on an auction block in front of curious, heartless onlookers and wealthy white bidders who were looking to add you to their ensemble of destitute enslaved Africans. They'd inspect your muscles, anus, and genitals to ensure you could reproduce at a rate that met the demands of the American empire, which profited from the cotton you picked solely to generate wealth for the whites that owned you and the government.

After being sold, you'd be branded and shipped to your new home, where you'd be forced to take your new slave name. If you did not willingly take that new name, which would be drastically different from your African name, you'd be beaten into submission. For those of you who have seen *Roots*, based on the book by Alex Haley, you know exactly what I am referring to. In the fictional story, which was based on what occurred on plantations, Kunta Kinte was a slave who refused to take his new name, Toby, after being purchased like cargo. The overseer, who was dissatisfied with this, tied Kunta's hands together around a wooden post and proceeded to viciously beat him until he adopted his slave name. The barbaric deed was never punished. In fact, it was expected and accepted. If a Black man got out of line, physical violence at the hands of white men was the norm. They were protected by law, which means that if you fought back physically, you'd be punished severely or even killed.

Floggings for refusing your new slave name was just the beginning. As an enslaved person, the beatings were common and severe enough to enforce the false notion of white supremacy and Black inferiority in the American caste system. For instance, Anglican abolitionist James Ramsay describes the beatings he knew of in the 1700s as follows:

> The ordinary punishments of slaves, for the common crimes of neglect, absence from work, eating sugar cane, and theft, are cart whipping, beating with a stick, sometimes to the point of breaking of bones, the chain, an iron crook about the neck…a ring about the ankle, and confinement in the dungeon. There have been instances of slitting of ears, breaking of limbs, so as to make amputation necessary, beating out of eyes, and castration… In short, in the place of decency, sympathy, morality, and religion, slavery produces cruelty and oppression. It is true that the unfeeling application of the ordinary punishments ruins the constitution and shortens the life of many a poor wretch.

The social stratification that was created was maliciously ingenious because it created division by proxy. For instance, white indentured servants began to receive monetary benefits from dissociating from enslaved Africans in the mid-1600s, which led to the creation of race as a social construct to divide and conquer those at the bottom of the economic ladder, while the elite prospered. Furthermore, Black and white romantic relationships were criminalized and Blacks who owned guns were punished while whites who abused and killed Blacks faced no such sanction.

It would seem, then, that the first instance of perpetual violence in America should correctly be categorized as white-on-Black crime. What's even more insidious is how this charade could continue. Consider that an average of 32 percent of white families owned slaves, not 100 percent (Pruitt). That's about one out of every three. Some states, like Mississippi and South Carolina, had a 50 percent rate, while others like Arkansas had less than 20 percent (Pruitt).

What did the others do, then? They benefited from the system created by the elite white landowners. They'd hire these whites to manage or oversee their plantations to ensure that the enslaved Africans were working efficiently to meet the goals of the plantation. These whites weren't nearly as wealthy as their bosses, the ones who owned the plantation, but they were much better off than the enslaved African. That was the con game they played. This system leeched off the work of both the overseer and the slave, but the poor white was too ignorant and selfish to realize that they had more in common with the enslaved than the owner, whose only commonality was their skin color. These white overseers were supposed to keep "the Blacks" in order by any means necessary. For instance:

> I remember how they kill one nigger whipping him with the bullwhip. Many the poor nigger nearly killed with the bullwhip. But this one die. He was a stubborn Negro and didn't do as much work as his massa thought he ought to. He been lashed a

> lot before. So they take him to the whipping post, and then they strip his clothes off and then the man stand off and cut him with the whip. His back was cut all to pieces. The cuts about half inch apart. Then after they whip him they tie him down and put salt on him. Then after he lie in the sun awhile they whip him again. But when they finish with he, he was dead. (W. L. Bost, Federal Writers Project)

What's more, this was often a public spectacle that was required viewing for all on the plantation. Imagine the feeling of potentially witnessing a brother, sister, wife, husband, or even a child be subjected to this type of brutal treatment without the opportunity for recompense. What is the psychological toll for this exposure? What effect has that had on us? Are we currently acting out our trauma in our neighborhoods, unknowingly? If the animosity and hatred you feel isn't aimed at the overseer or "massa" for what they're engaging in, it's possible that that displaced hatred and anger become visited upon your brethren. This makes sense, theoretically, because you'd subconsciously strive to be like your oppressor, since they were the ones in power with privileges in all facets of society.

In other instances, Black-on-Black crime on the plantation was forced; other times it was preferred, as Blacks were sometimes employed as overseers by the plantation owner. These Blacks, like the whites before them, assumed they'd receive special privileges for flogging their comrades. Others, like Solomun Northup, resented it and couldn't bear to engage in such a horrid practice. For example, Northup states:

> Then turning to me, he ordered four stakes to be driven into the ground, pointing with the toe of his boot to the places where he wanted them. When the stakes were driven down, he ordered her to be stripped of every article of dress. Ropes were then brought, and the naked girl was laid upon her face, her wrists and feet each tied firmly to a stake.

Stepping to the piazza, he took down a heavy whip, and placing it in my hands, commanded me to lash her. Unpleasant as it was, I was compelled to obey him. Nowhere that day, on the face of the whole earth, I venture to say, was there such a demoniac exhibition witnessed as then ensued.

Mistress Epps stood on the piazza among her children, gazing on the scene with an air of heartless satisfaction. The slaves were huddled together at a little distance, their countenances indicating the sorrow of their hearts. Poor Patsey prayed piteously for mercy, but her prayers were vain. Epps ground his teeth, and stamped upon the ground, screaming at me, like a mad fiend, to strike harder.

'Strike harder, or your turn will come next, you scoundrel,' he yelled.

'Oh, mercy, massa!—oh! have mercy, do. Oh, God! pity me,' Patsey exclaimed continually, struggling fruitlessly, and the flesh quivering at every stroke.

When I had struck her as many as thirty times, I stopped, and turned round toward Epps, hoping he was satisfied; but with bitter oaths and threats, he ordered me to continue. I inflicted ten or fifteen blows more. By this time her back was covered with long welts, intersecting each other like network.

Epps was yet furious and savage as ever, demanding if she would like to go to Shaw's again, and swearing he would flog her until she wished she was in h--l.

Throwing down the whip, I declared I could punish her no more. He ordered me to go on, threatening me with a severer flogging than she had received, in case of refusal. My heart

> revolted at the inhuman scene, and risking the consequences, I
> absolutely refused to raise the whip.
>
> He then seized it himself, and applied it with ten-fold greater
> force than I had. The painful cries and shrieks of the tortured
> Patsey, mingling with the loud and angry curses of Epps,
> loaded the air. She was terribly lacerated—I may say, without
> exaggeration, literally flayed. The lash was wet with blood,
> which flowed down her sides and dropped upon the ground.
>
> At length she ceased struggling. Her head sank listlessly on the
> ground. Her screams and supplications gradually decreased and
> died away into a low moan. She no longer writhed and shrank
> beneath the lash when it bit out small pieces of her flesh. I
> thought that she was dying! (Northup)

The bureaucratic and capitalistic dynamic of the slave plantation created an environment ripe for intraracial division by duping the enslaved Africans into believing that they could relinquish the chains of slavery and systemic racism, simply by individual achievement, rather than group merit. By granting a certain contingency privilege, they could keep them divided from those with whom they had more in common.

For example, poor whites had more in common with enslaved Africans than wealthy whites, but they were given systemic privileges that entrapped them in their whiteness, relinquishing their European cultural and ethnic identity, such as the case of John Punch in 1641, who received life as an indentured servant in the English colonies (thus making him a slave) after he was captured running away with two European indentured servants. His European counterparts were only forced to work a few more years as punishment, in comparison. They could have used their privilege to speak up for Punch in this instance, but they didn't, and they were rewarded for that. The hope was that by abiding by these meritocracy-based laws that they'd eventually reach the status of the plantation owner.

Likewise, some enslaved Blacks would be granted access to work in the house to become a house slave based upon their lighter skin color or propensity to align themselves with the malevolent desires of their owner. Others would be chosen to oversee the plantation with the task of keeping their brethren in line. The deception in this is, as an enslaved African caught, captured, and taken to a foreign land, you'd assume that people with the same melanin content, who have been victimized similarly, would sympathize with your struggle. The bewilderment that would exist after experiencing such brutal treatment from your kin could presumably cause a rift amongst the enslaved. You no longer see a potential ally. Your desire to escape your predicament has caused you to maneuver down the path of capitalist individualism.

This was an example of a Black face placed on the hate that white oligarchs created. Now, my frustration toward my predicament and unfortunate circumstances will be placed on those who had no control over their social standing either, as opposed to those who perpetually enslaved me. And with that, the so-called Black-on-Black division began. Combine this unfortunate root with 100 years of apartheid in the form of Jim Crow segregation, redlined policies that created ghettos, a lack of reparations and protection against white supremacist terrorist groups, the War on Drugs, the crack era, and mass incarceration, to name a few. We've been bombarded since this country's inception and placed in less-than-ideal situations in which we have fought each other as opposed to the system that placed us there. Instead of focusing on why one person owns ninety-nine of the 100 seats in the theater, we, all ninety-nine of us, bicker amongst ourselves, fighting over the only available seat.

Whenever the nightly news read off stats of the weekend shootings in Chicago, they never included vital information like this. There was never a *why* question asked. This absence of critical thought would lead the viewer to assume that we were merely savages, even though the most barbaric acts known to man occurred in the United States, with the targets being the descendants of chattel slavery and our indigenous brethren.

These news segments never talk about the other component of American history that has had a profound influence, not just on the shootings that occur in hoods across America, but on gun violence in general.

Imagine you're an eighth-grade child who gets picked up from middle school daily by your father. Occasionally, when your father picks you up, he's frustrated because he has received a call from an administrator detailing how you were involved in several physical altercations that you clearly started without remorse. Your father reprimands you harshly. However, while berating you, your father pulls the car over to the side of the street, parks the car, and turns the ignition off. He then slowly gets out of the car and walks up to an old man in front of a store. After a few words are exchanged, your father proceeds to physically assault the old man, causing him to stumble and fall. After he falls, your father stomps him until he is bloody and unconscious. You don't budge because you're used to it. Your father gets back in the car, continues to berate you while concurrently engaging in the same behavior at least five more times on the way home.

When you return home, your father notifies you that you'll be on punishment for the rest of the week and lose the privilege of using your phone. As you sit in your room staring into space, confounded, you finally realize that you're simply repeating the behavior that you've been exposed to and, as a result, subconsciously learned.

This is our scenario in America. We are constantly demonized for the way we conduct ourselves as historically oppressed and traumatized people. However, this same critique and criticism is rarely ever levied toward the US military, which gets 50–60 percent of our budget and tax money to perpetuate the military-industrial complex globally. Why is it that our troops are still in Iraq and Afghanistan? How is it that a country that has been in a war for 93 percent of its existence is able to avoid such ridicule? In a two-week span of school, which is ten days, that would be like a student fighting nine times. That's absurd and reprehensible.

Consider that America, through the vehicle of white supremacy and capitalism, has been responsible for ruining indigenous cultures across the globe. Ravaging the indigenous people in America was just the start. When the government ran out of space as they expanded westward, they eventually began to island hop. They overthrew Queen Lili'uokalani of Hawaii as well as the leaders and people of Puerto Rico, Guam, Cuba, and the Philippines in the 1800s and early 1900s. In more modern times, they tried to assassinate former Cuban leader Fidel Castro over 600 times unsuccessfully, because he defeated America in the Cuban Revolution and Bay of Pigs and maintained an economic system that this country was vehemently opposed to in communism (Oppman). The CIA was devoted to murdering Castro, having tried to poison his cigars, swimsuits, pens, and even potential lovers.

Although they failed in Cuba, the American government was highly successful with their other targets. For instance, they assisted in the assassination of Che Guevera, who fought in the Cuban Revolution; Dag Hammarskjold, who was a Swedish secretary general with the United Nations; Dominican Republic dictator and former US ally Rafael Trujillo; Ngo Dihn Diem, who was a South Vietnamese dictator and former US ally; Patrice Lumumba, the first democratically-elected leader of Congo; and Chilean leader Salvador Allende (All Time 10s).

What these individuals had in common was the potential to disrupt America's imperialism globally by aligning themselves with socialism as opposed to capitalism and American hegemony. These actions should not come as a surprise, though. Megalomaniac and former US Secretary of State Henry Kissinger stated it plainly: "The illegal we do immediately. The unconstitutional takes a little longer."

Since 2004, to "prevent terrorism," America amped up the use of drones overseas for their military operations. These drones were supposed to decrease the likelihood of American casualties while also leading to more accurate killings of "terrorists." This sounds good, I assume. However, a slew of questions should arise after hearing the previous statement, the first of which should center around the idea of "terrorists." How do we know these people are actual "terrorists" outside of conjecture? What's the proof? Will there be civilian casualties as well? What if a civilian is walking down the street with "suspected terrorists?" What would be the course of action?

As you can imagine, the results were and have been disastrous. According to the Bureau of Investigative Journalism (as of November 2018), since June 2004 there have been nearly 5,000 strikes in military operations outside the US. From those strikes, between 8,000 and 11,500 people have been killed. It is estimated that 800–1,600 of those have been civilians and 250–400 of those have been children. Let that marinate. 11,500 over the course of fourteen years is an average of about 820 murders a year. That's also 114 civilians and nearly thirty kids annually (the Bureau of Investigative Journalism).

American citizens have not been exempted from this treatment. For example, we have Anwar al-Awlaki, his sixteen-year-old son Abdulrahman al-Awlaki, Jude Mohammad, Ahmed Farouq, and Adam Gadahn. To be fair, most of these men worked as recruiters for al-Qaeda. However, it seems as if homegrown terrorists rarely get any attention. What about Dylann Roof? He murdered nine Black Christians at their church in South Carolina in 2015 after they welcomed him in to attend their Bible study.

Domestic terrorism is the biggest threat to Americans, according to the FBI, but the media would have you believing that a brown guy with a long beard, who professes to be a Muslim, is going to fly halfway across the world and kill Americans (Wray).

It took until the end of 2021 for American troops to withdraw from Iraq and Afghanistan (with about 2,500 troops remaining in Iraq in an advisory role). This military occupation, which was an extension of Manifest Destiny and American imperialism, lasted roughly twenty years. Considering that, how can the media, government, and American citizens then scrutinize my Black brothas for engaging in the very same tactics that they have unfortunately learned from their abusive father? Maybe America can begin to fix the hoods of America when they discontinue their violence abroad. While that's highly unlikely, remember that a child learns by what they see rather than what they are told to do. America will praise Dr. Martin Luther King annually (when they wanted him dead when he was alive), while concurrently continuing its oppressive hegemonic abuse abroad.

The similarities are staggering and ominous. America engages in war abroad for territory. Likewise, gangs in the hood claim blocks (neighborhoods) as their territory. America is the world leader in weaponry usage and sales. Similarly, gangs in the hood can maintain their power and dominance by the excessive use of weapons that were initially used by the military. The gangs in the hood typically use drugs to generate wealth. These drugs typically come from countries that America is at war with. The big difference, however, is that the gang members in the hood get punished when caught. America does not.

It must be understood that the sins of the hood won't likely diminish until America comes to peace with its warmongering ways. The nerve of them, calling us criminals and thugs when we have been the targets of sociopathic violence and criminality for centuries.

When I began to come to grips with America's role in our plight, I began to bury myself in YouTube videos when I wasn't conducting home visits in my role as a caseworker. I'd sit in my cubicle with my headphones on, inputting data from home visits with a playlist of videos ranging from Tim Wise to John Henrik Clarke, Dr. Amos Wilson, Yosef Ben-

Jochannan, Michael Eric Dyson and Cornel West, to Noam Chomsky and Malcolm X. Malcolm, Cornel, and Dyson were familiar to me, but discovering Chomsky and Wise was an interesting development because for the first time in my life I had seen privileged white men speak out against racism unabashedly as if they were affected like people with melanin. Concurrently, delving into Clarke was intriguing because he provided a paradigmatic shift in my approach to African (American) Studies. The moment I heard him utter, "If you start your history with slavery, you can only become a better slave!" I knew I had to commit to digging deeper into our history and discover a broader spectrum of who I was as an African man in America, prior to 1619 or 1526.

Chiefly, that profound statement caused me to ponder, "What was the crime rate like in ancient Africa?" That question, of course, was rhetorical in statement and thought, because although our ancient African cousins did have conflicts and wars like all other civilizations across the world, they existed in ethnic and tribal societies that didn't have a concept of race, or systemic dehumanization, so within their societies intracommunal violence or crime did not happen to the degree that it needed to be propagandized or politicized.

West African societies were based on communal living first, not individualism, and all actions within these unique societies were created for the purpose of the collective. Because of this, intracommunal or intraracial violence in West African societies did not occur in the same manner as the violence that emerges from Black communities that have been deprived of resources intentionally and systemically within a white supremacist framework in America.

This is most evident with the pre-colonial Kingdom of Benin in West Africa, where many Black Americans descend from. The Edo people built the Walls of Benin over the course of about 600 years with over 150 million hours of labor, to protect the king with moats totaling nearly 10,000 miles long and 2,500 square feet. This is important to understand, not just because it is a remarkable architectural feat with precision of symmetry, proportionality, and "fractal design," but also because of the extravagant homes that were built within these walls, which were built without doors because theft was so uncommon. Ironically, many of us can attest to similar living conditions as Black Americans. Despite the circumstances I was raised in on the South Side of Chicago, where the murder rate sometimes surpassed 900 in one year in the '90s, we often kept our doors unlocked all day as my sister and I played outside. Yes, there was violence in my neighborhood occasionally, but there was also an inherent sense of community that served as proof that our cultural antenna had not had its signal completely disrupted.

Dr. Amos Wilson's videos challenged me as well, mainly because he wrote and published a book on this exact phenomenon in 1990 entitled *Black on Black Violence: The Psychodynamics of Black Self-Annihilation in Service of White Domination.* In this book he masterfully purported how the effect of the pathology of Black intracommunal violence is intentionally orchestrated, for the purposes of maintaining and supporting a system of white superiority and domination, through a perpetual causation of structural violence. Dr. Wilson says, without acknowledging the social context that this violence emerges from, you'll find yourself blaming the victim with a belief that those engaging in violence within this context are inherently violent, rather than critiquing those whose unmitigated violence begets this violence. In other words, if we are to agree that the pathology of this racist system has yet to cease, then why would we think that the violence that laid the foundation has ceased? You might think of violence in terms of the officer's gunshot to the face that killed our sista Sonya Massey as she begged for her life in Springfield, Illinois, but withholding vital resources from fellow citizens in a dire situation and creating a system that operates in a similar manner is also violent.

To Dr. Wilson's point, this system produces violence by design. It is the result of structural coding, which primarily operates off a cause-and-effect schema. In other words, because "I" (politicians who are in power) craft legislation that makes it difficult to purchase housing, the impact will be a lack of businesses and capital circulation, fresh food, recreation, and a properly-funded educational system. And because "I" also craft legislation on a macro level that allow weapons and drugs to enter these communities in place of educational, recreational, and economic opportunity, the effect will ultimately be self-destruction and mass chaos as people fight for the remnants of the few available resources.

Consider what was done to us during the aftermath of Hurricane Katrina. We were trying to stay afloat, and in an attempt to survive, we decided to take what we need in an environment of scarcity, only to be labeled looters and thugs. When we screamed for help on rafts, we were merely waved at and flown over by President George W. Bush, who had the means to solve this problem. Are we looters or doing what we need to survive? Are we responding to our environment we were intentionally bred in?

As American society "progresses," it would appear as though we have not elevated our collective conscious away from these primitive ways. Rather, we seem to have transitioned to a more modern, technologically advanced, politically correct form of brutality that extracts violence from us as a form of entertainment and economic necessity.

This analysis made even more sense to me when I read portions of Dr. Frances Cress Welsing's *The Isis Papers* and realized that white supremacy was quite simply the practice of Europeans and non-white co-conspirators, attempting to prevent what they believe to be their own genetic annihilation. As such, those who believe in this and practice it aren't incentivized to disrupt these structures of racism that lead to higher instances of violence within our community, because in essence, it empowers them and feeds the fallacy of their superiority and focus on the survival of their "race."

It was apparent to me from the hundreds of hours I spent listening to lecturers, professors, and intellectuals like Dr. Amos Wilson, Dr. Frances Cress Welsing, and Dr. John Henrik Clarke, that I had so much more to learn. I was a college graduate and graduate student who had realized what commencement really meant. I had only just begun to procure the knowledge that was necessary to effectively lead myself and my people out of perpetual mental enslavement.

CHAPTER 16
...WHEN IT KEPT HAPPENING AGAIN, AND AGAIN, AND AGAIN

Public exposure to police brutality (or neighborhood watch brutality) as of 2010 was still relatively primitive. Throughout our history in this country, especially since the abolishment (transition) of slavery in 1865, our abusive relationship with the police had been well-documented within our community. As Black folks, we'd often share stories amongst ourselves about the tumultuous encounters we had, often trivializing them and expressing gratitude that we were still alive to tell the story. Stories like the ones I mentioned earlier in the book often remain urban legends. We knew it was a problem, indeed. However, we accepted the treatment as a part of being Black in America because we felt helpless. If previous generations had been so helpless in fighting this epidemic, how successful could we be? This type of defeatist attitude is what leads individuals and movements to the graveyard with the same shackles that were forced on their ancestors. That mindset is a fast track to mediocrity and subservience. Shifting from "Why me?" to "Why not me?" communally and individually would become a pivotal paradigm shift for us all to embrace to demolish these systems of abuse.

The Rodney King beating occurred in 1992 and, although cases like Amadou Diallo in 1999 (shot forty-one times by the NYPD) and Sean Bell in 2006 (shot fifty times by the NYPD on the night of his bachelor party) were also tragic, they were discussed to little fanfare, even though those cops were also acquitted despite hurling a barrage of bullets at two unarmed nonviolent men with the intent of callously murdering them. Their tragic stories remained exclusive to our community without much exposure on mainstream corporate news. In fact, the protests that erupted after the acquittal of the cops in both cases remained local. When Oscar Grant was executed by an officer in Oakland in 2009, and it was captured on a blurry phone camera, though, the collective consciousness of the people began to arise.

When Trayvon Martin's murder happened in 2012 at the hands of George Zimmerman, the people fully arose from their slumber. Trayvon's story was unlike Oscar's, due to the lack of video footage, but it would garner more attention, partly due to it happening during a time when nearly the entire country had a social media account. Trayvon's story felt so much more personal as well because of how it happened and who it happened to. I was in my second year of teaching at the time, and I had regularly taught Black boys between the ages of fifteen and eighteen years old. I was twenty-four years old then, which was not too far removed from Trayvon's age at the time of his murder. What's more, his murder took place during the halftime of the all-star game of my favorite sport and league, the NBA.

During that all-star game halftime, seventeen-year-old Trayvon had decided to buy more snacks to last him for the remainder of the game, so he set out to walk to the store. After a few minutes, Martin purchased the now-infamous pack of Skittles and bottle of Arizona iced tea that would later be found next to his corpse.

It was a rainy night in Sanford, Florida, as Martin walked home with a hoodie on while talking to his close friend Rachel Jeantel over the phone. Martin's objective was to make it home in time for the second half, while George Zimmerman's was to eliminate a fictionalized threat he had imagined in his oblong psychotic cranium.

Zimmerman, a twenty-eight-year-old white Hispanic who had created a neighborhood watch after failing the police exam, observed Trayvon from his car as he walked home. Trayvon was a child, attempting to swiftly return home with a hoodie on to block the rapid rain drops that began to fall that night. Zimmerman didn't see a child, though. He let his racist paranoia run wild. He immediately called the cops and described young Trayvon as a suspicious man who appeared to be looking for a home to break into. The dispatcher said they would send an officer to check things out, but Zimmerman couldn't wait and opted to take matters into his own hands. He proceeded to get out of his car and follow Trayvon as he continued to his father's house, muttering, "These assholes always get away," to the dispatcher. What happened next will forever remain a mystery. Dead men can't give testimony, so all that we had to rely on was Zimmerman's testimony and our common sense. Based on the words of Trayvon's friend, Rachel Jeantel, it would appear that Zimmerman chased Trayvon down in the rain. Trayvon, who initially ran as well, eventually stopped and got into a physical altercation with Zimmerman and attempted to defend himself, as anyone would in a similar situation. While understandably defending himself, he inflicted facial bruises on Zimmerman, who resorted to deadly measures to account for his cowardice. He proceeded to grab his gun and fire it, killing Trayvon immediately.

Initially, Zimmerman wasn't charged, and wasn't even expected to go to court due to a Florida statute called "Stand Your Ground" which asserts that a civilian can use deadly force with a weapon if they feel that their life is in danger. Oh, and I don't think you would be wrong to ascertain that he wasn't charged because he was a white man hunting and killing a Black child. Trayvon's family was outraged, rightfully so, and they started an online petition that garnered the support of millions of people.

It was at this point that I was made aware of Trayvon's murder. Like most of my activist-based discoveries, I learned of this case online.

Look, if you're like me, you'll ignore a chain letter email or petition in a second. Chain letters get deleted on sight, but petitions might get a second glance depending on the mood I'm in. Luckily, I was in a good mood on this particular spring day in March as I concluded another day of teaching at the alternative school in Chicago's Roseland neighborhood. I opened this email out of sheer curiosity. That, and it was sent by my Aunt Monica. Monica didn't always send emails, so I figured it was worth checking out. My assumption was correct. After opening the email, I realized that I had been reading about a case to which I was completely oblivious.

"Trayvon, who?"

I sat behind my desk as my students grabbed their belongings and headed toward the front door exit of the musty former clinic turned school.

"See ya later, Crim!" they said jovially, excited to be done with school for the day.

I couldn't give them more than a quick wave. My eyes were glued to the screen as I read about Trayvon's story from his mom and dad on Change. org. I was enthralled and disgusted. My plan to grade papers and plan lessons for the next day was temporarily on hold. This was a travesty that required my immediate attention.

I copied the link, pulled my chair closer, clicked on the browser and went to Facebook. My goal was to ensure that everyone on my page knew about this. Little did I know that the word had already spread. When I began to scroll, not only did I see a plethora of Trayvon Martin stories, but there was also a ubiquitous display of the attire that Trayvon Martin had on the night he was killed. Person after person on my timeline had hoodies on as I scrolled to raise awareness about the case. The night that Trayvon was callously murdered, he had three things on him that would become infamous. First was the hoodie, second was the Arizona iced tea, and third was the bag of Skittles. These items became political statements as everyone from college friends to colleagues to celebrities, both Black and white, wore hoodies as they posed with an Arizona iced tea and Skittles.

As the world became conscious of this travesty, two topics of discussion began to unfold. One, if this murder happened in February of 2012 and it was now late March, why wasn't George Zimmerman arrested and charged yet? Two, was Trayvon murdered because he had on a hoodie or was he murdered because he was Black?

The hoodie symbolism was powerful. People of all races came together to honor the life and legacy of Trayvon to show that someone's attire shouldn't be grounds for stereotyping or murdering them. Surely, I agree with that statement; however, with Trayvon's situation, it was misguided. And this is coming from someone who posted a hoodie picture as his Facebook profile picture for over a year. Many people began to miss the point. Trayvon wasn't murdered because he had on a hoodie; he was murdered because he was Black. This has been the case since the 1500s in North America and 1619 in the United States. Black men have always been public enemy number one. As such, resistance or noncompliance with a white man, whether they have a position of power or not, can lead to the murder of a Black man, depending on their mentality. They are a protected class.

In fact, America was created to help white men prosper financially and politically. Literally, one of the reasons why the English colonists (Patriots) declared independence was because they feared that Britain would abolish enslavement due to the verdict of the Somerset case in 1772, in which James Somerset gained freedom. So, yes, the American Revolution and American independence was about tea, taxes, and mistreatment by King George III, but it was also about maintaining slavery.However, these truths are constantly denied, or hardly discussed, and we as Black folks deal with the repercussions of those living lies. Take world-renowned Black American comedian Chris Rock, for example. On July 4, 2012, he caught flack and was embroiled in controversy for simply stating the fact that Black people were enslaved on July 4, 1776, and the Fourth was white People's Independence Day. The responses to his comments were egregious and overtly and subtly racist. This plainly stated truth gained so much attention that it was featured on every public forum from *The Today Show* to CBS and ABC, for pointing out the obvious fact that this country was not created with our best interest in mind. It was created for white folks; specifically, men who had wealth. And to ensure that this was done, affirmative action was taken to make it a reality. Blacks, on the other hand, have had their humanity debated and legislated since the establishment of this country's government in 1787. From being counted as three fifths of a person to having amendments passed to affirm citizenship, freedom, and voting rights, our status in this country is only as good as the psyche of those in political power. More times than not, those are white men. That tide, however, is slowly changing.

Meanwhile, I couldn't return to work the following day with this on my conscience, without addressing it. I had lesson plans, but they didn't matter anymore. I was a Black teacher teaching Black children on the South Side of Chicago in one of the most impoverished neighborhoods in the city. How could I not discuss this topic? It could've been one of my students, or even me.

"Bae, hurry up!" My wife shouted from the bedroom as I continued working on my laptop on that gloomy Wednesday evening.

"Okay! I just gotta finish up a few more things!"

That "few more" ended up lasting two more hours as I scoured the internet for the facts of the case in order to be fully prepared for discussion tomorrow. The planning took some time as well, but I eventually settled on an activity that would cause the students to relinquish the stereotypes that had been forced on them by the media in order to embrace their true nature as young kings and queens with ancestry from Africa. In part, I was inspired to take such an approach because I was emboldened with a tremendous sense of pride after watching the *Hidden Colors* documentary (which was produced by Tariq Nasheed), per a staff member's referral. This film helped me realize and learn that Africa had influenced (most of) the world's civilizations. It also caused me to become adept at researching claims made in films. It changed my critical thinking lens moving forward. I now approach non-Black historical topics and achievements from the perspective that we had likely in some way directly (or indirectly) impacted an accomplishment until proven wrong. That's not to say that we have created everything, but it is to say that so much of who we are has been purposely hidden. Because of that, we should approach history from a top-down approach, rather than the down-top approach we are often conditioned to have. In other words, instead of using history to "prove" that we did something meaningful, we should already assume so, and know that we have accomplished great things, and assume that we've had a hand in the things we admire, until proven otherwise.

I had also become even more stern in my rejection of white supremacy and its lunacy. I was only in my second year of teaching at this point, but I had already determined that tomorrow's lesson would be the most important one of my career. I shut down the laptop after saving the document and carefully placed it in my laptop bag.

The next day was important. I approached the school visibly stoic, but internally agitated. As the class period began (our alternative school didn't have a bell, so one of our security guards would yell "*Rotate!*" at the end of every period), I immediately began the class with a remark about Trayvon.

"Who in here has heard about Trayvon Martin?"

Nearly half of the students raised their hands lazily, as they were still wiping the sleep out of their eyes. One student, who was known for being outspoken, reacted.

"Why y'all care so much about that man? My niggas get gunned down all the time!"

I took a deep breath to ensure that I didn't respond too harshly. I was prepared, though, because Malik was a bright student who often played the devil's advocate in class. I'm not sure what happened to this kid, but I always felt that if he was continually molded and guided in the right direction that he'd have the potential to be a great leader and activist with his intelligence and charisma. To me, he was Malcolm X before prison. He showed great potential, but needed to constantly be reminded of the appropriate way to handle things.

"Well, Malik, this doesn't invalidate what has happened to your friends or people that you know. It's just, this is a story that has gained a lot of attention because of the racial dynamic and the fact that the perpetrator hasn't been arrested. This case is symbolic historically."

Malik retorted immediately.

"None of them mu'fuckas that murdered my guys got arrested, so what's the difference, Crim?"

I didn't even care about his choice of language because I knew how passionate and heartfelt he was. Also, his point was so valid I didn't find it necessary to criticize on such a trivial matter as he was attempting to gain an understanding of the American (in)justice system. Internally, I applauded him and his critical thinking skills, but as an instructor I had to provide a response.

"I'm sorry to hear that, brotha. I hope that the potential success of this case can lead to more accountability on all fronts. This represents the racism Black people have faced and continue to face with the judicial system, so it resonates with the public. Not to devalue your friends' situation at all, but I also think that because of the recent popularity, this case needs to be addressed. I'm sorry about what happened to your friend. We can also talk about that if you like."

After hearing my response, Malik nodded his head seemingly in agreement, looked away for a second as if he was considering a response, or contemplating something I said, grabbed his pen, and begin to doodle on the paper I passed out.

The rest of the students seemed split. I saw some who appeared to understand Malik's point, while the other half wished he'd stop talking so that I could continue with my remarks.

I explained who Trayvon was and followed it up by showing the class a video that provided any intricacies that I failed to mention. Having already passed out the papers, I went on to divulge the details. The students who weren't aware were shocked and disgusted. The hands shot up and a lively discussion ensued. Immediately after, I explained the instructions. At the top of the sheet was a picture of Trayvon Martin in a hoodie, which was now the most infamous attire in the country. Under the picture was a phrase that required the students to fill in the blanks. It read:

"The media portrays me as a thug, but I am _____, and _____. I am Trayvon Martin."

It was simple, but powerful. It challenged the students to accept the reality of how white America views them in society, much like Zimmerman viewed Trayvon. Concurrently, it also challenged them to define and create their own positive image separate from the propaganda and sensationalism of the corporate media. This was imperative, because we as African Americans have often accepted the deleterious image that has been forced upon us from the oppressor. Additionally, the fact remains that we cannot conquer the demonic nature of this illegitimate system unless we first believe in ourselves and know that a victory is possible.

As I paced the room, I noticed empty spaces. Every row I'd glance down only to notice that students had refused to fill in the entire sheet. Was it a refusal as I perceived, or an inability to conjure a positive self-image? Without a doubt, it was the latter.

"So, what's going on?" I blurted out as I walked back to the desk. "I don't get this, to be real witcha," bluntly responded a student named Damon. I walked back to the board and began to brainstorm positive adjectives with the students. You would think finding three positive statements about yourself would be easy, but it's not for some students. Even today, when I ask a class of thirty-one students to tell me something positive about their day, the class is mostly mute; however, when I ask them to tell me something bad that's been happening, every hand shoots up.

Much of society has been inundated with a pessimistic mindset. For groups who are targeted by racism, this is even worse when you consider racial battle fatigue. However, I refuse to allow that to persist with my students on my watch.

After the students filled out their sheets, I had them place them in a makeshift box. I had planned on using a small box that would be able to collect all of the papers, but I had to settle on an old tissue box. When the last student placed their folded paper in the box, I pulled them out one by one and read them aloud, while a student wrote the positive adjectives on the board. As we wrote them, I randomly called on different students to repeat the positive affirmations with an "I am" preceding their statement.

"I am...brilliant!" Jasmine said boisterously when I called on her.

Although he probably wouldn't admit it, I could tell I was reaching Malik. He understood the importance of this whether he'd admit it or not. A class that was usually raucous became uncharacteristically quiet as each person spoke. I normally had to yell over them to get them to simmer down as a classmate was speaking. Not this time. This discussion hit them hard.

I left school that day feeling good about myself, but that wasn't enough. That's shallow. What about Trayvon's parents? It would take a while, but their diligence paid off up until this point. It took two months, an online petition, and national outrage, but George Zimmerman was finally arrested for murdering Trayvon. But then something strange happened. He bailed out expeditiously. That wasn't the issue, though. It was how it was done that was so perplexing. Zimmerman was able to bail out of jail because there was a crowdfunding campaign on GoFundMe that amassed millions of dollars in support of his heinous act. Zimmerman was a hero to a segment of whites who viewed his act as justified. They felt Zimmerman eliminated another "thug" from the street, but they couldn't be further from the truth. The problem was that certain media companies corroborated this false narrative.

Instead of highlighting the thuggery that Zimmerman engaged in, the media found it appropriate to disseminate less than flattering information and images of Trayvon. No, they didn't discuss Zimmerman's propensity to frequently call the police on Black minors. The nightly news focused on Trayvon's suspension for marijuana possession and a few pictures online where he sported a scowl, as opposed to his academic or athletic success. Where was the mention of his admiration of flight and desire to enroll in aviation school? Likewise, the media failed to lambast Zimmerman's call to the police almost a year prior because he felt threatened when he witnessed a seven-year-old Black male child walking to school. Yes, that really happened.

As the de facto fourth branch of the US government, the media continued its complicit and explicit criminalization and denigration of Black folks for the state and white supremacist establishment. This racialized propaganda is more effective than you think. I would find out firsthand the following summer when George Zimmerman went on trial for Trayvon's murder in the summer of 2013. On the cusp of the George Zimmerman murder trial, I had just successfully finished my first school year in a large district (which meant job security and potentially a pension) and witnessed the birth of my firstborn on May 27. Needless to say, I was extremely optimistic at this stage in my life. I had married my queen a few years prior and witnessed the manifestation of a few of our goals. For instance, when we initially moved to our southwest suburban home, I was hesitant due to the sixty-minute commute to work in Chicago daily. My wife assured me that things would work out, and considering the price we got the house for, I obliged because it was a deal we couldn't pass up, despite the difference.

A year later, a social science position opened at the school where I am currently employed, and I aced the interview after having applied to nearly fifty schools without a response, successfully securing a salary that was 67 percent more than what I had previously made, just in time for our first child. Additionally, the school was only twenty minutes away from our new home! I felt invincible as I witnessed the results of my work ethic and mindset. I felt that *The Secret* and the law of attraction was real, and I was a living testament. However, I quickly learned that individual prowess or success cannot successfully counter the sufferings of an entire group of people living in an oppressive state.

In late June of 2013, with a daughter nearly one month old, I began my first full viewing of an actual trial. This wasn't Judge Judy or Judge Mathis. This was not for entertainment, and it would not be decided in fifteen minutes. I felt this case would prove the inevitable, which is, Zimmerman callously murdered a seventeen-year-old child due to his own preconceived notions and false assumptions of Black criminality. However, I was sorely wrong.

My schedule fit perfectly around the court proceedings. I was off work for the summer and the only thing on my mind was fatherhood, my queen, enjoying time with friends, and the results of this case. Meaning, I arose daily with the intent of eating breakfast and positioning myself to watch the trial daily until it ended. *TGIF* had long been off the air on ABC, and with the NBA Finals over at this point, I didn't have anything else to look forward to on television. My wife, Cassie, was extremely understanding. After eating, I would grab my work laptop and headphones and get in position at our dinner table. I was affixed to the television as if I was waiting for the calling of my name in a professional sports draft.

My daughter's cries couldn't subvert me from the laptop screen. From nine in the morning to five at night, for about two weeks straight, my time was booked. I took breaks for the restroom, food, and an occasional kiss from my wife and daughter, but then it was back to work. Obsessive? Sure. This was personal though, and I convinced myself that my district was paying me to watch it for educational purposes because regardless of the result, I would find a way to incorporate this trial into a future lesson. Showering? That was an afterthought. Phone calls and text messages? I'd return them later.

As the trial wound down, I felt confident about how the case would turn out. Of course, not having the experience of being an actual lawyer or someone who had viewed several trials, I couldn't accurately assess how well the prosecution did. I was relieved that it was over, because now I could resume my life. My wife was relieved because I began to shower again regularly and the odor I emitted, that likely caused my newborn to cry a few times, would cease to exist.

The next day, I wouldn't have the privilege to sit around waiting for the verdict. Thank God. It had consumed my life, so what better way to continue with my life than celebrating the life of my queen.

July 13, 2013, was my wife's twenty-seventh birthday, as well as verdict day. We met two of our friends, Frank and Keyanna, at Cooper's Hawk for dinner before meeting a larger group later that night at Bar Louie's to begin the celebration the right way. The drinks we had during the wine tasting, while we waited for our table to be ready, definitely helped take my mind off the impending verdict. After a while I forgot that the jury might make a decision on this day.

"Crim, party of four? This way, please," the waitress politely said as she proceeded to guide us to our seats.

As we sat down and looked over the menus, we conversed over everything from marriage to our careers to traveling to life as parents. We were all so inebriated that the conversation was inherently hilarious without trying to be. The bread couldn't get to our table soon enough. We needed it to counter to liquor we had consumed.

"Are you all ready to order?" the waitress asked, after placing the bread on our table on one of the few vacant spots.

We all stared at each other and snickered childishly because we hadn't even glanced at the menu yet. The conversation was too good.

"Not yet!" I blurted out with a wide-toothed grin. "Okay! I'll give you a second."

We still didn't open our menus.

"I love my job. But cleaning up shit from my patients is something I'll never get used to, man."

We all erupted in laughter as Frank continued about the mishaps of nursing. He and his wife shared the same career, similarly to me and Cassie, so they shared this unfortunate experience. Following that comical story, we all got quiet for a moment, realizing that none of us had decided on a meal yet. The waitress would be back at any moment now, so the pressure was on!

And then it happened. My phone buzzed. I had phone etiquette, so I rarely if ever placed my phone on the table face-up during dinner, or texted during dinner for that matter, unless it was urgent. Since we now had a daughter who was nearly two months old, any text could potentially be an urgent matter. I quickly took my phone out of my pocket, since the table was momentarily quiet, and checked to see if it was a text or notification. The text alert was CNN, so I immediately knew that it was pertaining to something groundbreaking.

"George Zimmerman has been found not guilty of the second-degree murder of Trayvon Martin."

My mouth dropped. I was stuck. Shocked. Perturbed. Irate. Melancholy. I immediately sobered up and put my phone in my pocket because I couldn't stand to read any more about it.

"Zimmerman's going free, y'all," I said somberly to Cassie, Frank, and Keyanna.

They looked at me and shook their heads in disgust.

"Are you serious?!" Cassie exclaimed after dropping her napkin. Frank and Keyanna looked away with a stern scowl and said, "What?!" in unison.

Although we hadn't discussed the case with them previously, we all had an understanding and grasp of what the case entailed and what it meant to the Black community. It was a Black thing. This was the biggest story to all of us, because it would validate or invalidate the so-called justice system in America. Many in my age group, who had been born in the '80s, had known of injustices that had become pop culture phenomena, like Rodney King, for instance, but we were unknowingly raised under the guise of respectability politics. Meaning, we believed that, since we got our college degrees and followed the arbitrary rules for what it took to be successful as a Black man or woman in society, we could escape the grasp of white supremacy and the inadequacies of the justice system. Trayvon was murdered doing what we all had done, regardless of educational attainment. He was walking with a hoodie, as a Black man, and was profiled as such.

I was aware of the Oscar Grant case, which had occurred a few years prior, but still, I felt this case would go differently. What did this mean for me as a Black man? It solidified the notion that a white man, not even a cop, could get away with murdering us simply because his imagination and implicit (and explicit bias) instructed him to further investigate what business we had roaming the United States as freemen. The Stand Your Ground law that was used to defend Zimmerman was simply a statute that white supremacists could use to murder us when they imagined fear and wanted to dispose of us in the manner America had always done.

What perturbed me even more was my setting. I was with my wife and two close friends in a classy suburban restaurant surrounded mostly by whites, who didn't seem to have the same feeling of disgust. I wanted to go up to the nearest person I saw and confront them. Did they know what happened? Did they know about this case? Were they aware of the verdict? Did they support Zimmerman or Trayvon? I felt isolated and alone in a room full of people. I was supposed to be jovial and enjoying my wife's birthday, but I couldn't concentrate or focus anymore.

What did all of this mean if I had to live with the paranoia of possibly being murdered without justice being served by a racist with a vendetta against Black men? My last day could be on my wife's birthday for all I knew.

We sat still for a moment, not sure how to proceed and continue after hearing such tragic news. The conversation began again awkwardly, in the same manner as an elevator conversation about the weather, but eventually reverted to its original element.

By the time we arrived at Bar Louie's, it was still fresh in my mind. We met with a large group of friends and had a great time, but with every sip of alcohol, I felt myself repressing the feeling of depression regarding the case. Something in me must've still had faith in the American judicial system at this point in my life. Otherwise, I wouldn't have been so disappointed. I was hoping that this case would lead to a broader systemic change due to the outrage and protest that followed. When Joliet had a rally to honor the life of Trayvon and express displeasure with the verdict, I was there marching angrily, hoping this release of frustration would assist with the depression I was experiencing.

The onslaught continued. I'm sure the injustices have at least remained constant over the course of American history, but these cases seemed more pernicious. Of course, not being alive in the Jim Crow era, I don't have a personal experience to compare it to, but it's telling when my seventy-something-year-old great-aunt tells me that she believes things have gotten worse, solely due to the illusion of progress that exists during our era, especially during Obama's administration.

Trayvon Martin garnered attention from around the world, but for me it became business as usual as an adult. There was Oscar Grant, who was executed in 2009. The following year, in 2010, his murderer would only serve eleven months. In 2011, Troy Davis would be executed in Georgia for the murder of a white cop without evidence. In 2012, Trayvon's murder became a headline story with a 2013 acquittal of the murderer. In the midst of this, there were two lesser-known, presumably race-based murders that caught my attention. One, Rekia Boyd, occurred close to home in Chicago and was supposedly over a loud conversation. The twenty-two-year-old left a party with a friend in Chicago in March of 2012, nearly a month after Trayvon's murder, to go to the liquor store. While talking, they were confronted by a white off-duty officer at around 1:00 a.m. that night for being too loud. One thing led to another and the officer, Dante Servin, pulled out his gun and shot her in the back of the head and killed her. He claimed he saw her friend taking out a gun, but what he actually had was a cell phone.

Later that year, another seventeen-year-old, Jordan Davis, was murdered in Florida in November of 2012 by a belligerent white man because, according to the culprit (Michael Dunn), Jordan's music was too loud. Davis's mom would use this unfortunate experience as the impetus toward a successful congressional election in November of 2018, in which she ran on a platform of gun control in Florida. If you ever wanted an example of someone constructively using hurt, pain, and inconceivable trauma proactively to inspire and change, look no further than Lucy McBath. How inspiring!

In 2013, Kendrick Johnson, a seventeen-year-old Black teenager from Valdosta, Georgia, was found dead in the gym of his high school at the bottom of a gym mat. I learned of this story because the pictures of his disfigured face went viral online, the same way Emmett Till's picture did in *Jet* magazine in the 1950s. Authorities claim that Kendrick got stuck while attempting to retrieve a shoe. Allegedly, because of the placement of the mat, Kendrick was not able to maintain his balance or climb out, so he suffocated and died. The cause of death was determined to be positional asphyxiation. After the initial autopsy was done, it was revealed that Kendrick's organs weren't returned for the examination that was to be done by the family's private pathologist. Instead, Kendrick's body was completely stuffed with newspapers. It was alleged that his organs were destroyed due to the position of his body in the gym mat. If this story is

...when it kept happening again, and again, and again

true, it still doesn't explain why he was stuffed with newspapers, which is against protocol.

If that doesn't make sense to you, you're not alone. Trust me, though, it gets worse. For one, the private pathologist found evidence of non-accidental blunt-force trauma to the right side of Kendrick's neck that could not have been self-inflicted. This contradicts the claim that his death was accidental. What's more, there was blood on one of the doors in several spots at a relatively high position near the door's window. The spots also had a stream of blood under them, which seems to indicate someone was slammed in those spots and bleeding to the point where it trickled slowly. However, authorities claimed that those spots were not related to the case or Kendrick at all. Whose blood was it, then? Why didn't they conduct further investigations since it was spotted at a crime scene? That wasn't it, though. What about the shoes that were next to Kendrick's body with a red substance on them that was determined to not be blood? What about the hoodie that wasn't Kendrick's, according to his parents, that was found on the scene, right next to the mat but not taken in as evidence?

Over the years, this case has taken more turns than a NASCAR race. Each state autopsy reveals positional asphyxiation, whereas the family's autopsy reveals a murder, even as recently as January of 2020. Additionally, some assert that the prime suspect in this case is the son of a former FBI agent, a man named Brian Bell, who apparently had a gripe with Kendrick dating back at least a year before his death. As of 2024, Kendrick's family is still fighting for justice, and refuting the claim that the death was self-inflicted.

His body laid there rotting in the hot summer sun of Ferguson, Missouri.

That was how I was introduced to this lynching. Much like Trayvon, we didn't have a video recording of the incident, but based on the result, it seemed as if they were trying to send a message to the surrounding Black community. Why else would a dead Black child's body be left in the sun for hours without being removed or at least covered up?

I was shocked and disgusted like everyone who saw this picture, but I had no idea that this picture would be the beginning (resurgence) of a movement for Black liberation. A picture is worth a thousand words, they say. Well, this one had lynching written all over it, one thousand times. The only thing that was missing was the gathering of smiling white families. Well, they could now celebrate behind their computer screens and phones, so who's to say that this wasn't still happening, as the picture surely made its rounds on white supremacist forums online. It became more apparent at this point that this was a common practice that we were just being exposed to with the advent and ubiquity of social media. Entrepreneur Gary Vaynerchuck said it best when he stated that social media hasn't changed us, it has just revealed who we always were.

Mike Brown and his friend were confronted by Darren Wilson while walking home in the middle of the street in Ferguson, Missouri. Wilson claims he politely asked them to get on the sidewalk, whereas Brown's friend Dorian Johnson has a different recollection. Johnson claims that Wilson irately yelled and ordered them to "Get the fuck out the street!" Johnson then states that he responded by telling the officer that they were almost home.

Wilson claims that Brown responded with, "Fuck what you have to say!" He then claims that when he drove up on them and tried to open his door, it was immediately slammed shut by Brown, who yelled more obscenities at him, which frightened Wilson. Brown then punched Wilson for some reason, so he grabbed his gun in an effort to protect himself. Wilson goes on with his egregious claims and asserts that Brown attempted to wrestle the gun from him while simultaneously saying, "You're too much of a p***y to shoot me." After grabbing hold of his gun, Brown began to run away. He then paused, looked at Wilson with a menacing, deranged look and ran toward Wilson before being shot at least six times and dying.

Dorian Johnson, on the other hand, asserts that Wilson, who admitted to having a history of using racial slurs toward African Americans on the police force as well as having complaints filed against him alleging racial discrimination, flung his door open, after blocking them with his car, causing it to ricochet off Brown's body. Wilson, presumably upset at this moment, reached through the window to grab Brown to gain control and assert himself as the dominant authority figure. This caused a tussle, according to Johnson, wherein Wilson reached for his gun and fired a couple of shots at Brown, one hitting Brown in the hand. Wilson claims Brown reached for his gun, but Johnson claims that never happened. After the initial shots were fired, Brown and Johnson attempted to flee the scene, naturally. Rather than taking this as compliance, Wilson decided to remove himself from the car to continue to fire at Brown as if he was a rabid animal on the loose in need of being tamed. He fired more than ten shots during this ordeal, six of which hit Brown in the head, shoulder, and arm. At one point, Johnson stated that Brown stopped and turned toward Darren Wilson and placed his hands up to show that he was submitting to the maniacal nature of Wilson's orders. Wilson, however, did not care that Brown submitted and continued to shoot to kill as if he were an imminent threat.

Soon after, the media began to criminalize Brown, as if to say he deserved to be shot down like an animal in that instance. As I used to tell my Black Student Union students, they portray us as animals, so that when they shoot us down like one, people are less sympathetic.

Ferguson immediately became the site of a new civil rights movement, and our cry became "Black lives matter!" in an effort to bring awareness to the unjustified and unfairly adjudicated police brutality cases. The Black Lives Matter movement sought to proclaim that we, too, are human and deserve to be treated as such. For far too long in America,

Black bodies have been brutalized without repentance or punishment. For too long, Black death has been viewed through the lens of justifiable homicide, whether the culprit be a white cop or a gang member. Black Lives Matter was a cry for equity in the justice system, similar to the way sanitation workers in the '60s chanted "I am a man" to demand proper treatment in accordance with the law. Furthermore, it served as a duality by demanding that whites view us equally, because the Lord knows that if their sons or daughters were killed at the rate that ours were, they'd receive better treatment. Black Lives Matter also served as a form of empowerment to Black communities that have often been taught to view themselves negatively and as less deserving of the same rights, privileges, and opportunities as whites due to the conditioning of a society that regularly promotes the propaganda that asserts Black criminality and inferiority and white angelism and superiority.

We live in a time when the racism that used to be explicitly stated is now implied. As I watched the nation continue down its usual path of divisiveness in the summer and fall of 2014, as Mike Brown's murder reached an international audience behind the chants of "Hands up— don't shoot" to commemorate Brown's sign of surrendering, and "Black lives matter" to assert Black equity, some whites began to outwardly rebuke the notion of the latter. The counter became "All lives matter," and the argument was that Blacks and supporters of Black rights attempted to promote the notion of Black supremacy. To the contrary, Black lives have never mattered in this country. They still don't. In terms of this topic, Blacks represent 13 percent of the population but account for 31 percent of people killed by the police, as opposed to whites who are 61 percent of the population but account for 52 percent of those killed. What's more, 39 percent of those killed by cops while not posing a threat are Black, whereas 46 percent are white. This means that if you are white, you are less likely to be murdered by a cop, in accordance with your percentage of the population (61 percent), but if you are Black you are 2.5 times more likely to be killed and three times more likely to be killed while not posing a threat, relative to population (Vox). As of 2015,

99 percent of cops involved in these cases are not charged with a crime (Mapping Police Violence).

But wait—Mike Brown wasn't the only Black man that was killed under questionable circumstances in 2014. Another situation happened in New York City that caused just as much outrage because, unlike Mike Brown, it was filmed. Eric Garner, a forty-three-year-old Black man, was strangled to death by an NYPD officer named Daniel Pantaleo in July of 2014, using an illegal chokehold. Garner was frustrated with the fact that he was stopped by these officers (as part of New York's Stop and Frisk program, which has led to Blacks and Latinos being disproportionately stopped, under the suspicion that they're breaking the law, in direct violation of the Fourth Amendment) for simply standing in front of a beauty supply store. These officers suspected that he was selling loose cigarettes and told him to leave.

Garner refused, and they attempted to arrest him because of this. Garner was not selling anything and attempted to pull his hands from the officers' grips. After this, Pantaleo began to choke him, while the other officers piled on him. Garner repeatedly screamed, "I can't breathe," but none of the officers cared. Moments later, Garner was dead. This was the climate in New York in 2014. It can be argued that this remains the climate today.

> "Get away [garbled] for what? Every time you see me, you want to mess with me. I'm tired of it. It stops today. Why would you…? Everyone standing here will tell you I didn't do nothing. I did not sell nothing. Because every time you see me, you want to harass me. You want to stop me [garbled] selling cigarettes. I'm minding my business, officer, I'm minding my business. Please just leave me alone. I told you the last time, please just leave me alone."

> —Eric Garner

Murdered while shopping? John Crawford was callously murdered by officers in Beavercreek, Ohio, while shopping at a Walmart on a Tuesday evening in August of 2014. Crawford was shopping while talking on the phone to his fiancée. As he continued shopping, he eventually picked up a BB gun that he intended to buy, and a white man named Ronald Ritchie, who was surreptitiously watching him, called the cops on him. This man claimed he was brandishing this gun at customers, and the police entered the store, and shot and killed him, without any questions asked. No one was charged, but Crawford's fiancée was threatened by the local police for speaking up.

As the summer transitioned to autumn and the school year was in full swing, the consciousness of the people began to grow with each publicized incident of police brutality. As someone who had already declared himself a "woke" teacher, I felt I had to increase my intensity and incorporation of current events into my class. For me and many of my African American and Hispanic students, the omission of this information and failure to relay it in a constructive and applicable manner could be life or death. That was the challenge I had the pleasure of shouldering, but I willingly accepted that responsibility. Imagine taking the hurt, anguish, and emotional trauma I had embraced to a job where I was expected to quietly acquiesce to corporate America and sit isolated in a cubicle for eight hours a day, remaining silent about the pain I had inherited. I looked at teaching as a privilege and responsibility, and an opportunity to change the world one student at a time by relaying to them the truth about themselves, their heritage, and the country, so that these things are no longer taught through the skewed imperial angle of American exceptionalism. Knowing that I was charged with the task of teaching American government and US history this year made my responsibility that much more important.

It was my mission to bridge the gap between general American history and the abuse of innocent Black folk that likely came across their social media feeds all summer as well. The Stono Rebellion, the Declaration of

Independence and American Revolution, the Boston Massacre, the Bill of Rights (particularly the First and Fourth Amendments), the Fugitive Slave Act of 1850, the abolitionist movement, and several other topics in the course were directly connected to the roots of white supremacy and the conspicuous prevalence of police brutality that serves as an obscure branch from the roots of this racist doctrine. How was the Boston Massacre different from what had happened to Mike Brown, John Crawford, and Eric Garner? How were the uprisings and protests in Ferguson different from the American Revolution? Why does America praise certain instances of subversion but ridicule all others involving people with melanin?

As I explained this to my classes, which contained Black, white, and Hispanic students, while also showing the videos, they were appalled, outraged, and disgusted. Above all, they realized that this was a problem as much as I did, and they were furious, too. Hope springs eternal in the youth, the blossoming flowers in a corrupt world. The trick is reaching and teaching them the appropriate way before society corrupts and inundates them with the perpetual, perilous mindset of yesteryear that has continually kept us divided and unwilling to tackle the elephant in the room, which is racism.

As the week of Thanksgiving approached, I had another reason to be furious. On Sunday before Thanksgiving, November 23, 2014, to be exact, as I was doing lesson planning, I had received a text from a friend with a headline relative to a Black child being murdered by an officer. I was in shock, so I stopped and clicked on it. What I saw was absolutely appalling, and it was caught on video. Tamir Rice was only twelve years old, y'all.

As Tamir played with a replica gun in a park in Cleveland, someone called the police. As soon as the police car arrived and got near Tamir, who was stationed in the middle of the park, you see an officer jump from the car as if he were approaching a dangerous armed suspect, immediately shooting him to death within seconds. Contrary to the claims in the police report, the officer did not attempt to warn twelve-year-old Tamir by instructing him to drop his "weapon." Young Tamir wasn't given the benefit of the doubt. He was viewed as a thug, and a criminal, even as a young child. Once again, the cops lied on their police report. Oh, and in case you were wondering, the officer who murdered Tamir, Timothy Loehmann, wasn't charged, either. In fact, after being let go from his position with the Cleveland Police Department several months later because he lied about why he was terminated from his last position (he was deemed unfit to serve), he was later hired by another Ohio police department. He quit a few days after due to protests.

With all of this on my mind, I still had to return to work the next day, the last day of school before Thanksgiving Break.

The school year was emotionally daunting for me because, as one of three Black male teachers in the school and one of four in the entire district, I felt isolated. The classroom became my sanctuary, my place of solace. I was a preacher; the front of the class was my pulpit, and my students were the parishioners. I didn't realize it at the moment, but the tangents I would go on in class during this time and during my Brother-to-Brother mentoring club meetings about these topics became the fertile ground for which my career as a speaker began.

If my class was heaven, then the hallways, half-day staff meetings, and teacher's lounge visits were hell. Imagine, if you can, losing a family member or friend, having it broadcast all over the news and social media, only to return to work and not have a soul reach out and offer condolences. That was the feeling I had after the Mike Brown grand jury decision revealed that Darren Wilson wouldn't be charged. This feeling felt worse than when I found out that Zimmerman wouldn't be charged with killing Trayvon, because in this situation, I had to return to work the next day. Making copies in the lounge was a daunting task that day because I didn't want to look anyone in the face besides my students.

I was tired of the façade, the mask I wore, and the role I was expected to play as one of the token Blacks in my school district. I didn't want to see any of my white coworkers unless they had the wherewithal to acknowledge my existence, the pain my people felt (the pain they also should have felt), or simply reach out to express the same frustration. The story was on nearly every station the night before. Surely, they knew. Right?

I was fed up with abiding by the notion that to be successful, I had to master DuBois's theory of double consciousness. I was furious. The frustration and isolation I felt in this moment reminded me of the times I was the only Black person in my college classes. It wasn't a good feeling at all. Maybe I expected too much of them. How would they even go about approaching me or other Black coworkers in the district? Wouldn't that be a tad bit awkward? Don't they have their own issues to tend to? Should I have been the one to initiate the conversation? I don't know, but I can say that my direct supervisor, who I affectionately called Pat Summit (because she was such a great leader and coach like Summit was), always provided support because she knew how passionate I was about social justice. Unfortunately, though, she was the exception.

I can't speak for the vast majority of the white coworkers I had during this time period, because I didn't and still don't know them personally, but I honestly think that their privilege afforded them the opportunity to ignore or disregard such travesties. That's one of the problems, though. In such a divided country, we have too often viewed issues not as American, but rather as specific to a demographic. I don't feel that we'll ever make progress toward King's utopian dream until Black issues, for instance, are viewed as American problems, and not just Black problems. Factually speaking, we didn't create our tribulations, so why are we viewed as the ones that are solely responsible for solving them? Regardless, I'm proud to say that they have constantly worked to ensure that that doesn't remain a reality moving forward, as a school district.

"Hey, Crim… How's it going?" a white coworker muttered as I stood over the copy machine with my head down, attempting to avoid all human contact. With heavy eyes and a flared nose, I said, "It's going!" with a fake smirk. I had been trained well. I couldn't even break script for a second and be honest about the pain I felt.

I proceeded to grab my copies and walk across the hall back to my class. I sat down in my seat, leaned back, begrudgingly threw the papers down, and let out a sigh of relief as I pondered if I'd even use the copies for class. My mind was racing too much. I knew what I had to do, but I hadn't yet decided. Before I could get too comfortable, the bell rang. I slowly got myself together and approached the door, unlocked it so that my students could enter, and positioned myself outside to greet them. I wasn't in the mood at all, but forced myself to smile for them.

After a few more minutes, the tardy bell rang. I took a deep breath, turned around and entered the class, and wiped the smile off of my face. I walked toward the front of the class to address the students. As I did, my tear ducts filled, and my eyes felt heavy. I tried with all my might to push my tears back. If I had been able to, I would have positioned my index and thumb near my tear ducts to prevent myself from crying. I did what most men who have a false sense of masculinity and manhood do. What makes it worse is that I was aware of the danger involved in the widely perpetuated notion that "real men don't cry."

"I'll be real with you all, I'm really not feeling it today. I just need a break… It's too much." My words were scattered and genuine. The class, which was talking vociferously prior to my arrival at the front, was completely silent at this point. I then quickly grabbed a vacant chair, dragged it across the floor, sat down, rested my forearms on my thighs, and listened to the silence. They were all ears and anxiously awaiting my next comment, so I continued.

"Y'all, it's just hard. Being Black in this country is like walking around with a shooting range target. I just don't…"

...when it kept happening again, and again, and again

As I continued, I felt my eyes swell again. And then a tear fell. To this day I'm not aware of how obvious it was, but I'm certain a few students noticed it.

"Remember the Mike Brown case we've been talking about periodically this year? Yeah, it was revealed yesterday they won't even charge the officer. The grand jury doesn't think it's necessary to even take him to court. This is why I told you all on the first day... This is why I told you all that I don't stand for the pledge or national anthem. It wasn't written for me...for us. I don't even know what to tell y'all right now."

I spoke to a room that represented the best of America. I spoke to a room that represented the future of America, a group of open-minded young adults from various racial backgrounds (Hispanic, Black, and white) who realized that I was telling them the truth. They realized that the case I highlighted was wrong, no matter the race. They got it. However, the people with "power" didn't, and at that point it seemed as if they never would. I continued, and we spoke for the entire class period. "I wish I could tell you that reaching a certain level of education or economic status meant that you'd escape the terror of living in a racist country, but I can't. I'll say this though... Y'all give me hope for the future. This is the only place I'd want to be now...besides Ferguson."

When the bell rang at the conclusion of class, I realized that I had given the students something that's sorely needed in America, and that's honest dialogue. I like to think that I helped them, but the truth is, they helped me more. Had I not gotten that off my chest, I would have sunk into a proverbial abyss of stress and depression, especially considering the environment I worked in. I felt better, but feeling better isn't enough. It must actually get better. I began to plot my next moves as soon as the day concluded. I would not allow this to continue or persist. I was determined. I'd get results for these kids and my kids or die trying. Soon after that, it was revealed that Eric Garner's killer would go free, too, so I didn't have time to waste, in my mind, anyway, especially when I found out that the only person who was imprisoned regarding this situation was the person who filmed the murder. He, Ramsey Orta, became a target due to his vigilance and fortitude when filming and posting the catastrophe. Suddenly, the NYPD became concerned with an old gun and drugs charge that he had.

The first thing I thought of was empowering my students so that they would know their rights, just in case they ever encountered a situation such as this. I wanted to empower them in the same way the Black Panthers empowered their members through political education. The Panthers knew the law more than the police, it would seem. Huey P. Newton (the co-founder) often talked about how they would trail police and pull over with their guns drawn to monitor them whenever they pulled over an unsuspecting brotha or sista, to hold them accountable, so that they would know they were being watched.

After asking around at school, I was able to make a connection with several Black officers in the area from the Black Police Officers Association who agreed to come and speak to my kids to give their perspective on the current state of affairs regarding issues pertaining to police brutality. This was important because I had never spoken to an officer personally about issues as serious as this, and neither had my students. So, when Detective Randy Williamson came to speak to my American government class during second period later that school year, I was just as attentive as they were. I made myself comfortable on the left side of my class in the back, to give myself the chance to hear the message while also monitoring the students. There was no need, though, because they were alert. What I learned was alarming. I went into this thinking I was doing the proper thing by simply educating my students on their rights when encountering cops. They were educated on this facet by two amazing people who happened to be officers. The lessons they taught were vital for every citizen to learn, especially when dealing with an unreasonable officer. The problem that I later came across is, cops are legally allowed to be the judge, jury, and executioner if they simply perceive the person they have encountered to be a threat.

Now, when you're dealing with a reasonable person who takes pride in their job and duty in protecting citizens, this wouldn't be a problem. However, what happens when the people who are trusted with the responsibility to "protect and serve" are born and bred in a system that fosters and produces racism, whether implicitly or explicitly? Detective Williamson explained that two court cases in the '80s made this possible: *Tennessee v. Garner* and *Graham v. Connor*, which unsurprisingly were ruled during Reagan's era as president, set this precedent. The Garner case involved police shooting and killing a fifteen-year-old Black child named Edward Garner (how's that last name for irony) who fled the scene after stealing $10 and a purse from someone's house. The police defended their actions by saying that they had to shoot and kill Garner because he was a fleeing suspect and thus they had to protect the public, because based on their perception of the situation, he might be a danger to anyone else he encounters.

In *Graham vs. Connor*, the victim survived an incident of police brutality. Simply put, the Supreme Court ruled that officers can justify using excessive force if they perceive it to be "objectively reasonable." But what does that mean in a country when our perception is primarily formed from the chairs we sit in at home in segregated cities and towns, learning about each other through a mass commercial media that regularly proliferates racist propaganda on minoritized groups like African Americans for the purpose of profit?

Allowing cops, who are flawed human beings, to respond lethally, based solely on their perception, is ludicrous. Who has gauged their biases? Who has defined or quantified their perceptions? I've seen firsthand where students are disciplined or treated differently due to the color of their skin because the teacher perceives them to be a threat based entirely on their own flawed perception and understanding. How might this play out when someone has a gun and works a stressful job that is often a situation of life or death? Obviously, I respect officers who try their best to incorporate compassion into a profession that does not demand it. It's a difficult job that often exposes rational people to the worst behavior known to man. It expects them to solve problems created by racism, classism, and capitalism by providing handcuffs and prison cells. I can't provide a ratio for how many "good" cops exist versus the ones perpetuating the harms I just discussed, but I can tell you that there's an FBI report that states that they are concerned about the increasing number of white supremacists infiltrating law enforcement. Likewise, I can say with certainty that we have more "nice" people performing the role of cop than "good" people. "Nice" people who are cops see the problem, but refuse to report it because they need to maintain the peace and keep their jobs, whereas "good" people who are cops are driven to expose these injustices as whistleblowers.

Maybe we should require officers to take an implicit bias test. Maybe teachers should, too. Maybe we need to revisit those controversial Supreme Court decisions. Maybe there shouldn't be a "maybe" in front of those statements. Let's just do it for the sake of our progeny. In American government courses, we constantly enshrine the sacred concept of checks and balances. Why not here, where it really counts, where human lives hang in the balance? I walked away from Detective Williamson's presentation feeling inspired but conflicted. I didn't want to simply teach my students how to be respectable to avoid an irrational officer. I wanted to teach them how to change and uproot a system that was set on denigrating and even ignoring their very humanity, and the fundamental rights that pertain thereto. Laws that aren't aligned with virtue enable the avaricious nature of men whose power was established on a faulty foundation of immorality for the purpose of economic gain. The only true laws that exist are God's universal laws. Societal laws are merely our way of attempting to create an illusion of justice that is based on our perception and limited scope of reality and the concept of "fairness." With that said, to some, the murder of Crawford, Brown, Rice, Bland, Grant, and countless others *is* justice.

And that's precisely why this problem still exists.

CHAPTER 17
...WHEN THE HATE WAS INHERITED

The school I worked at for most of my teaching career in the southwest suburbs of Chicago was unlike anything I had ever experienced. Consider that I grew up in a redlined community that was 99.99 percent Black and attended an elementary school that was over 95 percent white, only to then graduate from a high school that was also 99.99 percent Black. As activist John Carlos once said about his high school, my high school was so Black that the only white people were the ones in the book. I then experienced varying levels of diversity in college, but as a professional, I had grown accustomed to Black management and Black staff members. Imagine my surprise when I began working at a school where the student demographics were akin to the future of America and the staff was virtually all white. I was one of five Black male teachers in a district of well over 6,000 students. That's the norm, though, when you consider that only 1.7 percent of all teachers are Black males. The student body consisted of over 50 percent Hispanic (Mexican) students, with Black and white students somewhere near 20 percent each. Additionally, more than 80 percent of the students were low-income. Since this was my first time teaching such a diverse student population, I would learn a vast amount about America that I had not previously known.

I didn't know what to expect with this new endeavor. I was a good teacher at the Black school I taught at, but would my approach translate to a different demographic? I was shocked because, for the first time in my life, I had encountered, on a broader scale, the effects of classism in American as it pertained to whites. I knew how racism affected Blacks and Hispanics, but through this experience, I became well-versed in what white folks struggled with in America, as well as the misinformation they were fed that allowed the racial divide to continue and widen.

This school had Blacks from the hood as well as from upper-middle-class backgrounds. There were Hispanics who were undocumented, and some whose families had lived in America for over sixty years and could not relate to the experience and fear some students had of Immigration and Customs Enforcement (ICE) and Trump's presidency. My school also had conservative whites who lived in a rural town close to the school and who loved to hunt and fish. Conversely, there were whites who were impoverished and identified with Black culture, while others lived an upper-middle-class experience and labeled themselves as progressive liberals. With that said, most of the school was liberal, but there was enough parity involved in class discussions to teach me more about conservatism than any of my college classes or imprudent social media debates.

Kenneth, a slender 5'11" white kid with square glasses, a buzz cut, and a sinister smirk, helped me realize, more than any other student during my career, the power of the propagandized teachings of Fox News and the deleterious effects parents can have on their children's racial socialization by either including them in racist conversations or fostering an environment for hate at home. How else would a sixteen-year-old child learn to hate those of another race with the same vitriol as a white kid from the '50s or '60s?

When I had Kenneth, he was one of three white kids in my US history class, and the only student who expressed his conservative viewpoints unabashedly. Make no mistake, conservatism isn't inherently evil. In fact, I think most humans are a combination of liberal and conservative, depending on the topic. Kenneth's conservativism, however, was

...when the hate was inherited 251

entrenched in hatred, racism, and skewed teachings. It was the direct result of Fox News's propaganda machine. The signs were there, but I didn't catch them. Maybe it was because Kenneth was an A student who had the highest average in my class, or maybe it was because he was always polite and well-mannered when we spoke. Whatever the case, I was naïve.

Sure, I had kids who erroneously assumed that the Black Panthers and KKK were equivalent in some way, but they were receptive when I fashioned a lesson that allowed them to research the purpose and actions of both groups. In fact, they left with a renewed perspective. Kenneth was drastically different.

"Obama's horrible."

He'd find a way to randomly insert his disdain for President Obama with a devilish smirk and grin no matter the discussion while looking around, daring someone to challenge him. Most students would just roll their eyes as if to indicate that they were sick of his nonsense. Occasionally, a short, slender, highly intelligent black-belt-holding Black kid by the name of William would tell him to calm down, but that was the extent of it. As the school year progressed, another outspoken student, a tall, muscular, curly-haired white kid named Paul with whom I had several conflicts throughout the year, would tell him to his face that he thought he was racist and that he needed to shut up. Kenneth never provided a plausible response when his peers challenged him; he'd only continue to smirk and fold his arms as if he'd won the debate by simply initiating the conversation.

"Why?" I'd reply calmly.

"Because…he's forcing business owners to pay for healthcare with Obamacare. He's awful. He's a socialist, and Obamacare is the worst thing to happen in the history of this country!"

"Seriously, Kenneth? The Affordable Care Act *just* passed. It's impossible to gauge whether it's been good or bad already."

My responses were consistent. I required the same thing from Kenneth that I did of all students who had political views I agreed with: proof. It was fine to me that he didn't like President Obama. In fact, as of 2014, I hadn't been the most ardent supporter of his anymore, although our reasons were vastly different. I felt that he had sacrificed his progressivism for a brand of neoliberalism that capitulated to the demands of the Republican party. Furthermore, he was steadfast on continuing the commander-in-chief's longstanding tradition of extending the American imperial empire by force as a means of sustaining the military-industrial complex. I just couldn't understand how a man who ran on such a progressive platform could concede so many of (what I assumed to be) his morals. The drone strikes were endless, for instance. That, and I didn't think he was a strong enough advocate for reparations, provided a plausible solution for police brutality, and a myriad of other Black issues.

The key difference in our mutual criticism of President Obama was that mine was rooted in disappointment and an expectation of liberalism, while Kenneth's was rooted in bigotry, racism, an outsized sense of entitlement, and an infatuation with conservatism.

Kenneth was relentless. He even did his History Fair research project on the failure of Obamacare without adequate research and proof. I warned him that his grade would suffer due to the absence of sufficient evidence, but he did not heed my warning. He instead took a reduced grade and reveled in being able to present his hatred for President Obama to a class that mainly consisted of Hispanics and Blacks, without having actually called him a "nigger" publicly.

He was very strategic in his criticism of President Obama during his time in my class. There was a reason that he had the highest average

...when the hate was inherited

in my class. His intelligence was in his ability to express his hatred surreptitiously. But unjustified hatred is a form of ignorance from my vantage point, so receiving an A in a class does not equate to intellectual prowess in all aspects, particularly the arena of common sense. Although he would soon reveal himself to be explicitly racist, he knew that it was best to conceal his true intentions while in class. Whereas most of my students were more consumed with sports, video games, fashion trends, and music, Kenneth religiously subscribed to the religion of white supremacy, in conjunction with pickup trucks and bass fishing.

The irony in this whole situation is that I recall him losing his niece to an ailment that school year because she didn't have access to healthcare. The year came and went, and I chalked it up to Kenneth being some uninformed kid. I felt he would eventually grow out of this phase due to the environment he was immersed in at this school. I also felt I'd have the same luck I had with a white student named Billy. Billy wasn't like Kenneth in his critique of Obama and obvious racist sentiments, but he came from the same nearby rural community, was in a similar social circle, and displayed a Confederate flag on his pickup truck. By the time Billy was done with my class and graduated, however, I was able to, through my teachings, convince him of the truth of what the flag represented. As such, it came down. He even sent me an email of appreciation after graduating when he passed his military entrance exam, praising me for being the only teacher who believed in him. I assumed I'd have a similar impact on Kenneth, who was two years younger.

I was wrong. Dead wrong.

His views were so irrational in class that I didn't take them seriously enough. Maybe it was the smirk. Maybe it was his grade. Maybe it was simply because his critiques were illogical. Whatever the case, I should have paid attention.

During the Ferguson uprisings, as I like to call them, it was revealed that Eric Garner's murderer wouldn't go to trial, either, because the grand jury didn't think there was enough evidence to charge him, although the whole debacle was on camera. Apparently, Garner resisted arrest and deserved to die from an illegal chokehold. By the time winter break came (2014–2015), the uprisings continued across the country, especially in Ferguson. I had participated in a few myself in Chicago to release some frustration.

I reviewed videos of citizens being beaten, tear gassed, and shot with rubber bullets. Was I surprised? No, because this is America. Blacks who stand up against injustices are met with more hostility than whites who provoke violence. But I was frustrated because I saw a 2014 version of what I taught and assumed only happened in 1964. The brutal treatment wasn't livestreamed for the world to see, though. Yet the police wouldn't stop. They didn't care because they knew they wouldn't be held liable.

As I scrolled through social media, I saw a screen clipping that kept reappearing on my timeline. The posting was made by a conscious white sister named Ariana, who graduated from Central in May like Kenneth. She posted it on her Tumblr initially, and it went viral locally. When I clicked on it and read what was included, I was appalled.

It was a clip of a Facebook post by my former student, Kenneth, who had a picture of a Blue Lives Matter police badge as his profile picture and a Confederate flag as his banner.

"I'm sick of all this Ferguson shit and now this Eric Garner shit. I'm sick of Holder, Sharpton and Obama. There would be no crime in America if Blacks didn't come here. #WhiteLivesMatter #WhitePride #BlackLivesDontMatter."

That's not all, though. Additionally, Kenneth stated:

"Exactly. All the looters, rioters, thugs, gangbangers, naacp [sic], Blackpanthers [sic], Al Sharpton and Eric Holder all need to be beat, shot, raped, tortured and killed for all the shit they have caused America, Ferguson, the white race, and Darren Wilson and his family."

I was enraged. How had I taught this kid? How had I shared the same classroom with such a vile and despicable racist for nine months without overhearing something so repulsive? Kenneth had always had these sentiments, but he was able to manage them surreptitiously. Instead of ridiculing Trayvon Martin, Eric Garner, or Mike Brown in class when those discussions came up, he'd steer the conversation to a critique of President Obama and his policies. Although his view toward Black people was evidence of a primitive mindset, he was clever enough to manage his racist, white supremacist views in order to form a cordial relationship with his only Black teacher. This type of relationship afforded him the opportunity to get an A in my course, join the National Honors Society, and be regarded as one of the most astute students in the school. If the measure of a student's success is solely based on academic merit, Kenneth was proof that our criteria needed to evolve.

I had to do some soul-searching as this story continued to spread online. I knew that Kenneth had been racist all along, but I was in denial. As a young teacher, I felt I could transform the life of every Black, brown, and poor white youth I encountered with my teaching prowess. I had no idea, until I met Kenneth, that my encouraging and inspirational nature would gravitate toward an obviously racist student to transform his degenerate mindset. Subconsciously, I had taken on that task. I knew that Kenneth had never said anything explicitly racist, so it wasn't like I could write a referral. What would I say? "Student dislikes Obama and states it daily?" I knew Kenneth had to have come from a household that fostered and nurtured his racist views. So, I felt that I could give him a glimpse of his ignorance and hopefully inspire him to change in the nine months that I had him. I was entrapped by the naivete and gullible nature of a young teacher.

The response online was swift. Students who graduated with him were ready to pummel him the next time they saw him. I couldn't blame them. I wanted to lay hands on him as well. A few teachers reached out because they knew that I had taught him. Some even thought he had directed his statements toward me. I assured them that he didn't, but he really did. I am my brother's keeper. I am the Black students he hated and the Black protesters he wished death upon in Ferguson. A degree and title of educator does not separate me from the common struggle that we all share.

Ariana had positioned herself as a modern-day teenage muckraker. She had done something that some white people had gotten lynched for not too long ago. She sided with Black people and even exposed someone who was racist, directly opposing what he stood for. Now, it goes without saying that Black people could get lynched for simply breathing in the direction of a white person on any given day, but it should be mentioned that white allies have served a purpose in the struggle. Imagine how quickly institutional racism would dissipate if more stepped up, as Ariana did, and relinquished their privilege for the benefit of Black folks. I never saw nor talked to Kenneth again. I didn't want to and didn't care to. For some reason, though, he assumed that I wanted to hear from him again, as he sent me an email fifteen months later with the jovial subject "Your Old Student." The email asked how I was doing and included his college major and career aspirations. He concluded the email wishing me and my family well. No mention of his comments. No apology (although it would not have been accepted). No repentance. I, of course, ignored him, but was amused at his attempt. How can you wish me well, while simultaneously wishing people in my community, with similar political views, were raped, beaten, tortured, and killed?

The same summer as Kenneth's comments, a Black church in South Carolina was the target of a white supremacist terrorist named Dylann Roof, who had a look and profile eerily similar to Kenneth's. The way he callously murdered those nine Black parishioners while seamlessly blending in during their Bible study in June 2015 reminded me of Kenneth's ability to momentarily acquiesce to the cultural norms needed to survive four years at a school that was mainly Hispanic and Black. Kenneth will likely live a coddled life in which his rants will rarely if ever be mentioned or discussed. In fact, it's probably a secret to most in his circle. Roof was coddled on his path to death row. Immediately after his massacre, even though he had fled the scene of his horrendous crime, the officers took him to Burger King before jail because he said he was hungry. You could construct a very long list of Black suspects who were never afforded such an opportunity.

The scariest thing about people like Kenneth and Dylann Roof is the polarity involved. Relatively speaking, it is rare in this century for a racist to go on a murderous rampage. The majority of racists, though, are perhaps even more dangerous, as they carry out their hateful acts in a surreptitious manner. Kenneth possibly learned his lesson early on, so he might have the ability, like most racists, to obtain a job that allows him to hold sway over and impact the lives of Black and brown folks, like a teacher, lawyer, doctor, judge, entrepreneur, or scientist. Imagine Kenneth as a doctor, refusing treatment or to relay information to a Black patient about an important procedure that is needed to save their life. Imagine him as a public defender, refusing to give his Black client the best representation and potentially creating the framework for a vicious cycle of poverty and imprisonment. These things do happen in America, but because "nigger" doesn't precede them, society doesn't view it as the most pertinent matter. It's all about what you prefer, then: a slow death or random explosion.

I often wonder if racism could persist if our education system, instead of extoling imperialism, capitalism, and the ways of the American empire through the admiration of people like George Washington, Christopher Columbus, or Thomas Jefferson, sought to teach white children their history through an anti-racist lens. For example, during the same period that these aforementioned figures existed, there were also white

Americans committed to ending slavery. However, most Americans likely can't name five white people who fought against racism, or slavery, in American history. Can you? For example, do know about Warner Mifflin (a nearly seven-foot-tall white man who advocated for reparations for enslavement during the period of the American Revolution), John Quincy Adams (the sixth president and son of the second president who devoted much of his time as a congressman to radical anti-slavery efforts, which led to the "Gag Rule"), John Brown (who sought to lead an armed revolt with enslaved Black folks to end slavery in the mid-1800s), or Anne Braden (who, during the Civil Rights Movement, recruited white people to protest racial injustice and once helped a Black family buy a home in a white suburb to counter redlining).

Kenneth and Dylann Roof were the products of an American system that would like to forget people like that, however, and their behavior revealed itself as part of a growing trend in America in 2015. The summer of 2015 was in some ways the rebirth of hate. Wait, let me correct myself. 2015 was the rebirth of the popularity of overt racism. It became trendy again, as it had been in the 1960s and every year prior. It would also serve as an ominous warning sign of what was to come in America.

That summer, Donald Trump emerged from the shadows of Trump Tower and *The Apprentice* with an announcement that grabbed every headline in the country. Trump announced he would be running for president. He promised he would be committed to securing the southern border to prevent "illegal" Mexican migration to the territory of the United States—a southern border that used to be Mexican territory prior to the massive theft that occurred during the Mexican-American War. This war, which began in 1846, concluded in 1848 with Mexico ceding territory that would later become the states of California, Nevada, Arizona, and New Mexico.

Trump stated:

> When Mexico sends its people, they're not sending their best.
> They're not sending you. They're not sending you. They're
> sending people that have lots of problems, and they're bringing
> those problems with them. They're bringing drugs. They're
> bringing crime. They're rapists. And some, I assume, are good
> people. (*The Washington Post*)

While some thought the abrasive nature of his comments would be an immediate turnoff to the American public, the silent majority agreed with Trump. It was as if they had been waiting for someone to speak their language again. In an era where white celebrities and actors are ridiculed for even thinking of the utterance of "nigger," it seemed to be refreshing for them to hear a bold white man giving voice to their innermost and hateful thoughts. He moved candid conversations that were previously held in the privacy of a racist's home, from the '70s onward, amongst like-minded family members and friends, to the forefront of political discourse, and he was applauded.

Trump's comments reeked of nativist talk which emerged from the 1800s as white Protestant Americans held to the belief that immigrants (ironically, most were European immigrants) should not be allowed because they weren't born in America.

Trump played to the fear of his constituents who felt that they had lost their country while Obama was president, regardless of their political party. Trump's elementary rhetoric was one that could appeal to a wide range of individuals, from the whites who dropped out of school prematurely, to the college-educated white man who wanted immigration done the "right" way. All in all, he made them all believe that they would lose their country even further if they didn't tighten up security at the border by building a wall that would be high enough to keep Mexican immigrants out.

That this rhetoric caught on so quickly proves the effectiveness of this age-old scare tactic. In the 1600s, race was used as a device to pit poor whites who were indentured servants against poor Blacks who were initially indentured servants in the English colonies. This was so that whites would view the eventual subjugation of Africans through chattel slavery as rightful while they sought rewards and benefits from their wealthier white superiors. This divisive tactic worked then, and it continues to work now. Trump created an enemy that whites could believe in, shifting the blame away from economically prosperous individuals who choose to cheat the system and profit off our divisiveness. Three and a half years earlier, Occupy Wall Street had exposed the increasing wealth gap that exists in our country. Centuries later, the age-old game of divide-and-conquer remains, unfortunately, an effective one.

With one speech, Trump galvanized a conservative base that believed Mexican migrants, who often start companies that create jobs, were their enemies and barrier to success. Furthermore, he convinced white Democrats, who had previously voted for President Obama, to change their course and trust in a man who had inherited his empire. There was also a small fringe group of Blacks and Hispanics who believed his rhetoric because they believed that American politicians failed to focus their efforts on those who were here "legally."

Some felt that his ridiculous racist portrayal of Mexicans was his only sign of bias, but Trump had a long history of racism that convinced me that he was not a friend of anyone with a tinge of melanin in their skin. From contributing to the redlining of America during the Jim Crow era by refusing to rent to Black tenants, to calling for the death penalty for a group of Black teens (the "Central Park 5" who are now known as the "Exonerated 5") who were erroneously charged with raping a white woman—and more recently leading the absurd charge that President Obama wasn't born in America and thus should not have been allowed to be president—it was apparent that Kanye should have continued his

...when the hate was inherited

261

ridicule of Republican presidents by asserting that Trump didn't care about Black people the same way he boldly reprimanded George W. Bush on that score many years ago.

White women, surely you can see that he doesn't respect you as his equal, either. He bragged of grabbing your "pussy" and forcing his tongue down your throat, and had been accused of sexual assault by countless women. Yet, most of you continue to support him. Why?

The world was shocked by Trump's comments. I too was shocked initially—not just by the comments, but because he had previously been a supporter of Hillary Clinton and a donor to both Democratic and Republican campaigns. His speech seemed to be a deliberate ploy to galvanize a demographic who felt overlooked during Obama's presidency. It worked. The exposure he received was enough to catapult any average Joe to the White House. It was free of charge, but amassed millions of viewers for cable channels like CNN, MSNBC, and Fox News.

None of us believed in 2015 that this imbecilic man would win the presidency, but here we are, still trying to figure things out as he enters his second term as the country moves further to the right. Isn't that an accurate portrayal of the state of affairs in America, though? We change the rhetoric, language, tone, and display, and assume that the visceral nature of the threat changes as well. Unbeknownst to us all, it just causes it to grow like a peace lily at your parents' home, requiring little water and care, but capable of engulfing your entire house.

I returned to work for the 2015–2016 school year completely dismissive of Trump's ascension. I was in my first year of teaching AP United States History, so the demographics of my classes had changed drastically. Whereas before I had mainly male students in STEM who were apathetic toward politics and had an affinity for working with their hands, entrepreneurship, and trade schools, most of my new students were aware of the political cycle; thus, I often went off on tangents with them as we discussed Trump's latest gaffe.

They were nervous, understandably so. During their early years, they had been exposed to what has been described as King's dream actualized, with the election of President Obama. Now, they were seemingly seeing their country implode right before their eyes.

"All right, let's go to OneNote and check out last night's homework…"

I attempted to transition and connect our ten-minute discussion on Trump to our lesson on the Mexican-American War, but I was interrupted by the always spunky and charismatic April. April was a great student. Besides excelling academically, she was also one of the school's top actors in the drama program and a stellar orator on the speech team. Her body language, from her wide glasses and giddy smile to her spirally body motions and optimistic attitude, made her a tremendous asset to my class for discussion and classroom activities requiring participation and engagement.

"Mr. Crim… Do you think he'll actually get elected?"

I responded with the utmost confidence.

"Trump? No. Don't get me wrong, he has a lot of support, but this is just a ploy for him to get more exposure. He's a businessman who lacks any political experience outside of his preposterous Obama criticism. He won't even make it past the top five. I don't agree with Republicans on hardly anything, but I think they're intelligent enough to pick a more qualified candidate than this guy."

I had no idea that I'd be wrong about this twice.

We continued with our lesson, which required the students to draft an essay addressed to Trump, and anyone in general who was unaware of how the United States stole Mexico, educating them on the evolution of America's border and treatment of migrants throughout history.

Hate crimes rose and hate was popular again. Hate was no longer something to be ashamed of. Hate didn't have to be hidden systemically anymore. Metaphorically speaking, white supremacists were able to take their hoods out of their closets. They didn't have to wear them, though. That's both good and bad, depending on your angle.

I couldn't keep up with the outlandishly racist videos I had seen on WorldStar, Facebook, and Twitter as some whites were frequently caught yelling "nigger" at unsuspecting Blacks or lambasting Hispanics for speaking Spanish as opposed to "American." Through the power of the internet, most of these people were rightfully shamed, but it didn't deter them.

With the rise of hate came anxiety, not just for myself, but for my Hispanic students, who justifiably were fearful of Trump's ascension as some of them were undocumented.

"Crim, is he really gonna build a wall?"

"Crim, you think dude is really gonna round us up?"

"Crim, why does he have so much support?"

As the days passed, the questions increased.

Again, I tried to reassure my students that they didn't have anything to worry about. I repeatedly stated that, although the racist rhetoric was disturbing, it was likely Hillary Clinton would be the next president. As 2016 progressed, however, I began to seriously doubt my prediction.

The primary elections intensified, with the other Republican candidates dropping out precipitously.

I can only imagine how Black folks who survived the Jim Crow era felt living through what seemed like a reenactment of the worst of the '50s and '60s. Besides vociferously boasting about his plans to ban Muslim visitors and build the wall, he held rallies in small-town America that appeared like Klan rallies. They'd chant Trump's slogans, "Make America Great Again" and "Build the Wall," in unison for minutes as he approached the stage. His most popular statements were blatant dog whistles meant to galvanize white supremacists. Make America Great... again? When exactly was it great for all people?

Meanwhile, Trump promoted violence at his rallies regularly. When it was revealed that protesters were throwing tomatoes at one of his rallies in 2016, Trump responded as you'd expect him to.

"If you see somebody getting ready to throw a tomato, knock the crap out of them, would you? Seriously, okay? Just knock the hell...I promise you I will pay for the legal fees. I promise, I promise." (DuVernay)

When a protester was being escorted out, he made a statement that was directed toward the security guards encouraging violence:

"He's walking out with big high-fives, smiling, laughing. I'd like to punch him in the face, I'll tell you." (DuVernay)

Furthermore, in a climate that had already been contentious between Blacks and police officers, he alluded to cops being too gentle with suspects, encouraging them to use excessive force when detaining someone.

"When you guys put somebody in the car and you're protecting their head, you know, the way you put their hand over [their head]," Trump

...when the hate was inherited

continued, mimicking the motion. "Like, 'Don't hit their head and they've just killed somebody, don't hit their head.' I said, 'You can take the hand away, okay?' " (DuVernay)

When the person running to be the leader of the "free" world encourages violence, it should be no surprise when his supporters use violence at his rallies, or when violence is used to stop one.

When Rakeem Jones was at a Trump rally in March 2016, it wasn't because he was fond of him. Jones came to protest. Placing himself in a hostile situation where he was vastly outnumbered, it came as no surprise that he and other protesters, some of whom were white, were instructed to leave the stadium in North Carolina immediately. As Jones and his comrades were leaving the building, he was viciously attacked with a malicious elbow to the face by a seventy-five-year-old white man named John Franklin McGraw. As Jones turned around in bewilderment, McGraw retreated, and Jones was handcuffed and removed with force as if he were the violent one (Norwood).

After the incident, McGraw was arrested and released on bail. Admittedly, the most surprising occurrence with this entire incident came, not with the punching and handcuffing of Jones, but with the court proceedings. On the day of the sentencing, McGraw was extremely apologetic, which isn't a surprise, but Jones's reaction to his supposed remorse bewildered many.

"Bruh. Really? C'mon, nah."

I saw the clip on Twitter and replayed it several times in disbelief. After the sentencing, McGraw apologized, and Jones accepted it. Immediately after, Jones embraced McGraw, who was placed on unsupervised probation, with a warm hug. I was shocked and I couldn't believe it (Norwood).

I can't help but wonder why we are always expected to forgive white racists who attack us. I surmise that there's an element of fear of mass retaliation, if resentment becomes habitual amongst Blacks. That's coupled with the expectation of Black subservience, compliance, and contentment with second-class status.

When are the abused going to decide that an apology isn't enough unless reparation takes place? When will the abused decide to say "no more" and allow and require the necessary punishment to take its course, as would be the case with them? When will the abused demand more? When will the abused require the justice system to not just look at these cases as isolated, but as branches from the same root of white supremacy? How ludicrous would it have been if the white teenager with special needs, who was kidnapped and beaten by four Black teens presumably because he was a Trump supporter, was expected to forgive the perpetrators for their callous actions? So, why expect the same from us? Until our situational forgiveness leads to a widespread transformation in the justice system, the dispersal of resources as reparations and systemic change, it is meaningless.

Although Kareem Jones forgave his attacker, Chicago didn't. When Trump planned to come to Chicago for a rally no more than a few days after Jones was attacked, Chicago resisted. The display of protest was so strong, persistent, and voracious outside and inside the stadium that the rally was cancelled due to safety concerns. Chicago reminded the world that you cannot be compliant and forgiving when a fascist regime comes down your block. If this had not been done, who's to say that more cases of violence, like the one Jones was the victim of, would not have happened. From the outside looking in, the energy and vitriol present at a Trump rally is the breeding ground for violence toward Blacks and other groups targeted by racism.

The energy that was present in Chicago wasn't pervasive enough, however. Whereas people in major cities like Chicago, New York, and

Los Angeles might reject Trump's rhetoric, the vast majority of America is rural and white, which meant that he had countless other markets to tap into that would not be met with the same vitriol. Trump carried his momentum into November, and despite initial predictions, won the presidential election.

I was in complete shock, as was the rest of the country, but no one felt the ramifications more than my Hispanic students (especially those who were undocumented), who had been the target of Trump since he announced his candidacy. I woke up the following morning in disbelief, but motivated because I was reminded of the importance of my job during such a trying time. I also understood that all politics are local, so I didn't believe Trump's policies would have any effect on my daily life or mindset. I was as determined as I had ever been. Not being Mexican, I didn't consider what my students may have felt that morning, however.

As class began that Wednesday morning, my AP class entered the room in an unusually somber mood. I wasn't surprised. I knew I would have to curtail much of what I had planned to discuss what had just occurred, because it was historic, for all the wrong reasons.

"We might as well address the elephant in the room," I stated to the class after the Pledge of Allegiance was said over the intercom in 1984 fashion.

As the hands shot up, I noticed a soft whimpering toward the back of the class, but I couldn't tell if it was from a stuffy nose or crying. I continued our conversation as I had planned. After a few more minutes, I noticed the shuffling of a few seats and chairs. I had my back turned at the time because I was writing something on the board. However, when I quickly turned to face the class, I saw one of the Hispanic students, Ariel, run toward the classroom door. I followed her to the door, only to be told by one of her close friends that she had not been feeling well because of the election. I asked Ariel's friend to check on her in the bathroom. After a few minutes Ariel returned, sat down, and put her head down for the remainder of the class. I understood why she felt the way she did, so reprimanding her was unnecessary. Rather, she needed comfort and support. Not even twenty-four hours after Trump had been elected had I heard tales of racist remarks in the hall and online. The racist bullying that Trump had infamously initiated and participated in on his campaign trail had now seeped into high schools more pervasively.

During pre-dismissal, I made my way to Ariel and we talked well into the passing period. She expressed her frustration, echoing similar sentiments about the rampant bullying that had already occurred. What stood out the most to me was the fear and uncertainty. She was undocumented and didn't know what her and her family's fate would be. She was, however, certain that the country she and her family came to for a better life was now explicitly hateful and rejecting toward them.

I didn't know what to say, so I just listened and notified her that I was an ally. Her fear was confirmed when ICE was spotted in Joliet, pulling over Mexican residents and arresting those who were undocumented. The fear became so pervasive that many families refused to leave their homes, even during their child's graduation ceremony. I felt helpless until I realized that I could relate. It had been happening to us for centuries. In fact, the vitriol my Mexican brothas and sistas felt now was all too familiar to my ancestors who were sold, separated, and discarded like animals.

There are beautiful and courageous people in this country who get it, without a doubt, but until they scream louder and have the echoes of justice ricochet from every corner, we will continue to endure more of the same behavior and ire. So, reject those who respond with "We're better than this!" whenever an incident of overt racism occurs. America has never been "better than this." In terms of racial conflict, America is what we see now.

...when the hate was inherited 269

If Trump and his explicitly racist supporters are the worst things you've seen from America, you should read a book on Black or indigenous history. The vitriol that Trump has popularized on a mass scale has been occurring for years, under every president, to Black people. What we now see is what happens when you reject the cries, screams, and voices of the downtrodden that have told you for centuries that this problem is real. Legislation can't solve it. A Black president can't solve it. You solve it in your home.

If you're Black, teach your kids that they are regal and come from a prestigious history that goes beyond the label of "Black" in America. Show them the birthplace of all mankind, Africa. Make sure they are proud of it so that they don't associate it with poverty, starving children, and AIDS. Teach them that they are equal, not inferior, to all human beings, regardless of color. Teach them to love their bronze-colored skin and gloriously nappy hair because it is a gift from God, a result of our ability to adapt biologically. Teach them to love one another and let them know that they are entitled to greatness, the type of greatness that does not begin or end with high-end fashion or other material items, but instead emanates from within.

If you're white, teach your children that they aren't better than anybody and that they aren't entitled to something just because of their skin color. Teach them about a heritage and ancestry that extends beyond the label of "whiteness." Teach them their European history and how its roots extend to African civilizations. They'll learn about the supposed "greatness" of America by proxy, as soon as they walk into a school, turn on the TV, or attend a sporting event, so teach them about the repulsive history of this country that lives in the shadows, the history that made Hitler proud to cite America as an inspiration for his treatment of the Jews. I want to see America evolve to being "better than this" but we must be honest and admit that the country has not made it to that point yet. This is evidenced even more when you consider Trump, having been exposed for who he is as a serial rapist, proud racist, and sexist who doesn't have a plan that benefits all of America, outside catering to the white fear of being replaced by minoritized groups and ushering in more capital for his wealthy friends, was still able to win the 2024 election in convincing fashion, thwarting the hopes of Vice President Kamala Harris of becoming the first Black, Asian, and woman president in American history.

If Trump's 2016 election served as a wake-up call for those who believed America had changed at its core, then his 2024 election win served as a reminder that you don't need to close your eyes to experience a nightmare. I sat stupefied the night of November 5, 2024, as the results came in on CNN. A part of me truly did believe that Vice President Harris would win, because having experienced the travesty of his first election, I optimistically assumed that we would collectively want to move forward progressively. However, I was wrong. This was Trump's third election season, and the first time that he won the popular vote. How ironic that this accomplishment came while running against a Black woman.

As I made the decision to finally lay down at a quarter to midnight, confounded and drunken with hysteria, I reflected on the times my mom came home, as a principal, with complaints of how white teachers treated her. I also thought about the experiences my wife had, and what she experienced. I thought about my aunts' stories as well. It was then that I realized that Vice President Harris's forthcoming loss would be more of a reflection of the lack of social progress made by white Americans, because if many of them, as so-called "liberals," couldn't manage their emotions while working under the leadership of a Black woman at work, then what made me believe that the same people who couldn't fathom having Hillary Clinton as their leader eight years earlier would now willingly accept Vice President Harris?

I went to bed for the night, wondering how I'd reveal this upsetting news to my daughters in the morning, hoping that these results would somehow change by the time I arose five hours later. They did not.

As I write this in November of 2024, the question remains: will America ever get it right, and choose a path that enables all of us to prosper collectively in a multiracial democracy? Will America ever work toward creating a country that implements policies and practices that reflect Thomas Jefferson's eloquently stated (and hypocritical, as he enslaved over 600 Black people in his lifetime), "All men are created equal"? For the foreseeable future, that will have to be a decision predominantly made by the white community in America, due to their population and economic influence in our governmental affairs. Is that what they truly want? That remains to be seen, but it surely doesn't seem like it.

CHAPTER 18
. . . WHEN WE HAD ANOTHER RED SUMMER

It was 2016 and the school year was finally over. Summertime is paradoxical for Black people in America. It always has been. It's a time we look forward to now, as many of us live in climates where the winters are harsh, and because the climate reminds us of our homeland. Exposure to sunlight brings out a jovial spirit that can't be matched by the seasonal depression and sadness that comes from Midwest or East Coast winters. But then there was also the torture of slavery and the Jim Crow era and even now, during the Black Lives Matter era. Summers have never been an easy time for us as a people.

Most of us were shipped to warm climates in America, which would allow the "owner" to use us for slave labor year-round. During this period, when the Earth's North Pole is tilted toward the sun, the days grow longer by almost four hours. This of course means that "owners" could maximize their profit margins and consequently torture us more. For instance, during these cruel summers, enslaved Africans could be beaten until their bones were broken. Additionally, they could be flogged severely, confined to dungeons, have limbs chopped off, and even be castrated, according to abolitionist James Ramsay (East of England Broadband Network).

Public beatings during these summer months were common. If an enslaved African refused to work hastily, the "owner" or overseer would force them to strip down and begin flogging them for all of the plantation to see, as an example of what could happen if they were defiant as well. W. L. Bost, a formerly enslaved African who told his story to a journalist of the Federal Writers Project, proclaimed that these floggings would sometimes end in death. According to Bost, there was an instance where one of his comrades was beaten until he lay in a pool of blood in the sun. As he rotted away and later died, the "owner" ensured salt was poured into his wounds to worsen the pain (Library of Congress).

If you were deemed a delinquent slave during these cruel summers, you would be placed in a smokehouse, the place where many Americans slow-cook their meat over the summer for cookouts. If not that, they'd have muzzles placed on them, or spiked collars, or have their fingers placed in thumbscrews. They would sometimes also be hung by an incision made in their ribs (Riley). During these summers, rapes were frequent, long before the #MeToo movement began advocating on behalf of women who had been raped, assaulted, and abused.

Three hundred years after the first African arrived in the British colonies for the purpose of slavery, so-called "free" Blacks endured similar treatment with the Red Summer of 1919. During this summer, the methods of torture had changed slightly (public hangings and burnings at the stake persisted), but the purpose had remained the same. There were twenty-five riots that had broken out in cities and states such as Houston, East St. Louis, Chicago, Washington, DC, Omaha, Arkansas, Tulsa, and Charleston.

In Chicago, the riot started because Black people swam on a beach that was deemed only for white people. There are pictures that even document whites in Chicago walking around, literally hunting Black residents like animals, for thirteen days, destroying Black homes and businesses in the process. The Black community in Chicago fought back too, as WWI veterans raided an armory on the South Side to combat the violence they faced, at a location that is now Chicago Military Academy high school. This brave display of armed defense eventually contributed to the end of the riot.

In Arkansas, whites started a riot because Black sharecroppers protested for fair treatment. More than 200 Black men, women, and children were killed as a result of the three-day massacre (Britannica). In Tulsa, Oklahoma, a thriving section of town known as Black Wall Street was home to over 600 Black-owned businesses. There were restaurants, grocery stores, movie theaters, churches, private planes, a hospital, a bank, a post office, schools, libraries, and a bus system as well. This riot, which happened two years after 1919's Red Summer, occurred due to the jealousy of a neighboring white community that spread a lie about a Black man assaulting a white woman on an elevator. This was the most frequent lie spread during this time as justification for lynching Blacks. Afterward, another onslaught of violence ensued in which the Black residents of Tulsa's Greenwood area were attacked and bombed by the National Guard, which was in cahoots with the local whites.

By the end of the anti-Black riot, more than 300 people were dead. By the end of the summer, tallies show that nearly 1,000 Blacks had lost their lives. Unlike the nonviolent rhetoric that would emerge thirty to forty years after this summer, many Blacks, especially those WWI veterans, armed themselves and defended themselves against their white attackers. It's hard, though, to come away victorious when you are the minority, and everyone is against you, even your own government (Official Black Wall Street Team).

Why did this behavior seem to persist, though? Many scholars attribute the ubiquitous nature and persistence of racial terrorism throughout American history to the fact that white aggressors are rarely arrested, prosecuted, or imprisoned, especially during this time. On the contrary,

...when we had another Red Summer

because of Jim Crow laws, Blacks could be arrested for sitting in the white section of a bus or attempting to dine at a whites-only establishment.

As far as I was concerned, there isn't much that had changed in terms of prosecuting racist acts.

"C'mon, now! Really!?"

I already had an indifferent view of the celebration of the July Fourth holiday because my ancestors were still enslaved while white American males celebrated their freedom from Britain. My views were akin to Frederick Douglass's in his "What to the Slave is the Fourth of July?" speech, and Chris Rock when he tweeted, "Happy white people's Independence Day. The slaves weren't free but I'm sure they enjoyed fireworks."

As far as I was concerned, it wasn't worth celebrating past having a day off and enjoying more time with my family. Juneteenth (June 19), which, coincidentally, is my wedding anniversary, was more worthy of my admiration because it signified when Blacks in Texas found out they were free in 1865.

With that said, July 4, 2016 was great. The quality time with my family was appreciated, but the rest of the week was full of stress, anxiety, and anger.

"Bae, did you see these videos?" I called my wife over to my phone from the kitchen as I sat on our couch, sunk into the comforts of the soft pillows. "I can't take it no mo'!"

Cassie responded irately, having not seen the video yet. She had decided to stop exposing herself, as much as she could, anyway, to the onslaught of traumatic videos that had bombarded social media. I had not yet graduated to that level. I welcomed the trauma, subconsciously, because

I felt I needed to prove to myself what I already knew about our plight living within a white supremacist country.

She walked away, throwing her hands in the air, but I continued watching in repetition.

In the first video, Alton Sterling, a resident of Baton Rouge, Louisiana, is shown being violently subdued after the police were called on him for selling bootleg DVDs outside of a gas station, something I had done for a couple of years in high school, something that would still be prevalent in every hood across America if not for Netflix.

Sterling was placed on the hood of the car and eventually on the ground as officers attempted to arrest him. Once the officers were on top of him, you hear one scream, "He's got a gun!" before shooting him to death. Sterling did have a gun, which is lawfully allowed by the Second Amendment, but he was not using it or brandishing it prior to being confronted by officers on this day. In fact, while subdued, videos show that he was not attempting to reach for it (Hanna). How would he when he was pinned down to the ground in submission?

Neither officer involved in this murder was charged. In fact, it took them two years to fire the man who pulled the trigger after body cam footage highlighted his aggression and threat of murder toward Sterling. A day later, another video emerged. This time it came from an unlikely source on Facebook Live. Diamond Reynolds, the girlfriend of the man who was murdered in Minnesota, Philando Castile, began to livestream after her boyfriend was shot by an officer while in the driver's seat of his car.

Diamond and Philando had been used to being marginalized and harassed for driving while Black. In fact, he had been pulled over nearly fifty times in the span of a year for minor infractions (Corley). While pulled over, the officer, who approached the car nervously, asked Castile for his ID. Philando had seen this play out numerous times. So, instead of reacting hastily, he practiced caution. He told the officer that he was reaching for his ID. He also told him that he was a licensed gun owner who had his weapon on him. However, as soon as he reached for his ID, the cop, who had conjured up a fallacious mental image of Castile as a criminal and thug with a weapon, shot him to death, firing seven shots (Corley).

Reynolds didn't know what else to do, so, in an effort to make the public aware, she started to livestream the commotion.

Immediately after going live, Castile can be heard screaming, "I can't breathe" which revived memories of Eric Garner's last words. As Reynolds calmly described what had just happened, the officer can be seen screaming and panicking while still holding his gun out, pointed toward Castile. Even in his death, he remained a threat in the officer's imagination.

The officer would eventually be arrested, but by 2017 we were singing a familiar song as we were made aware that he had been acquitted of all charges. Facebook Live didn't matter, because apparently Castile deserved to die because he was Black and armed.

By July 18, I was singing a familiar tune again.

"Bae, you remember that Sam DuBose video? The one where the Black dude in Cincinnati was shot in the head by an officer for pulling his door closed after the police tried to force him out the car? Yeah, I'm pretty sure they won't charge dude. The family got paid earlier this year and now I see an article about them moving on..."

Cassie could only nod in disgust. Unfortunately, I was right. The officer who is shown shooting DuBose in the head on camera would not be punished after a mistrial in November of 2016 (Berman). The only thing the family got as solace was money. Often, they murder us and offer money in exchange for justice. We don't just need economic resources, though. We need justice too. Without the precedence of justice, these attacks will continue.

That same summer, I found out that Michael Slager would be charged with the murder of Walter Scott. Scott was shot several times in the back as he ran away from Michael Slager. He was at least twenty feet away at the time, but for some reason Slager thought it was still necessary to murder him.

I wasn't content with him being charged, even though he was later sentenced to twenty years. This is because it still does not solve the broader issues that exist. Why should we be shocked and satisfied when an officer is charged and convicted of a murderous crime they obviously committed? Sometimes they throw you a bone from the table while they continue to dine on the finest cuisine.

Any celebration regarding Slager's conviction would be short-lived anyway. On July 27, 2016, as I watched TV on the couch next to my wife, our program was interrupted by the news that the officers involved with Freddie Gray's murder would be acquitted, despite Marilyn Mosby's efforts to convict. Freddie Gray was a young man in Baltimore who fled from an officer on a bike after making eye contact. He ended up with a severed spine while in police custody. He eventually died from these injuries.

I could only sigh under my breath and retort, "I'm sick of this shit. Fa' real…"

Cassie put her phone down, inched closer to me, and massaged my shoulders as we both grappled with the reality of another Black man being killed without justice being served.

Immediately afterward, an uprising broke out in Baltimore as the citizens expressed their frustration with a so-called justice system that continued to fail them. During this time, people kept screaming that the system was broken. On the contrary, the system was intended to work in this manner.

Another critique came from those, particularly on the right, who frowned upon the violent nature of the uprisings. They ridiculed the Black folks in this community for destroying property and refusing to peacefully protest. Never did they critique the behavior and actions that led to this situation, though. I find it ironic that these same people celebrate the violent nature of American imperialism.

They see no problem in celebrating the Fourth of July, which celebrates America's violent protest against the British. The actions that led to the Boston Massacre are okay, but not a violent reaction from those in Baltimore. The Boston Tea Party was acceptable, but not an uprising from a community that is the sad object lesson for the effects of systemic racism? An uprising against authority was okay then, because it led to the establishment of white American supremacy, apparently, but it's not okay now because Blacks are expected to accept their second-class status with silent obeisance. The hypocrisy was all I could see.

This hypocrisy was further demonstrated in the way white officers normally handled white residents. It goes without saying that whites are killed by cops too. Justine Damond, an Australian citizen, was killed in Minnesota while visiting America, for example. The difference is, the cops are often prosecuted in these cases (Damond's killer was sentenced to twelve and a half years). Additionally, we account for 25 percent of all police shootings and deaths while only comprising 13 percent of the population (Helsel).

In many instances, whites will be shown leniency and restraint while we're shown a gun. For instance, in the case involving fifty-one-year-old Jerry York from Arkansas, in a video shown on YouTube from December 2018, York is shown violently resisting arrest, grabbing the cops' weapons, beating them with their batons, and stealing their vehicle momentarily (Mershon). He did all of this and lived. The police never fired a single shot. Compare this to Walter Scott, who was running away from the cops when he was shot in the back, or Sam DuBose, who was shot in the face while seated in his car, attempting to remain in the car to retrieve his identification. Lest I forget, Rekia Boyd was shot and killed by a cop for refusing to lower her voice when a cop asked her to.

And, although it didn't involve gunfire, I was not still over Sandra Bland's death, or Kalief Browder's, both of which occurred in 2015. Sandra Bland, who was the same age as me and reminded me of the Black women in my life, was stopped by a white officer as she was driving back to the Chicago area from Prairie View A&M University in Texas because she didn't put on her turn signal. Because she wasn't docile or submissive in her responses to this irrational officer, she was forced out of the car and abused before being arrested. She was then placed in a jail cell over the weekend, only to be found hanged in that same jail cell in Texas before the weekend was over. It was declared a suicide, but I don't believe that, and neither do millions of other people, specifically Black Americans. It just doesn't add up.

Kalief Browder's story, on the other hand, reflects how the system slowly kills us mentally. Kalief, who reminded me of the young men I taught, was arrested at sixteen years old in 2010 in New York City for stealing a backpack. However, Kalief didn't actually steal a backpack. There was no evidence that this occurred. However, because he couldn't afford bail, and didn't plead guilty, he was forced to spend three years at Rikers Island jail awaiting trial. While there, Kalief was subjected to the worst types of abuse prior to being released in 2013, after it was determined that he was in fact innocent. In 2015, two years after his release, Kalief hanged himself at his parents' home, having never recovered mentally from his tumultuous experience at Rikers Island.

This is why we're mad. This is why I'm mad.

Through it all, I learned not to expect much from the nation's first Black president, even though I wished and hoped the problems we faced could be solved with the stroke of a pen. I had long ago lost hope in him being a potential savior for our community, because I should've never assumed him to be one in the first place. Rather, I should've put more energy and effort into grassroots activism and leaders who were doing work in their immediate communities during this time. Politicians aren't activists, but they can and should be pressured by activists to pass legislation. Those previously held beliefs in saviorism emerged from a place of political immaturity and naivety. My opinion evolved to one of nuance regarding his presidency. I felt that he did some good things, whereas in other areas I felt more could've been done.

In terms of helping us specifically with legislation, he ensured funds were allocated to HBCUs and created a program called My Brother's Keeper to address the achievement gap experienced by young boys who are targets of racism. Additionally, 19 percent of the federal judges he appointed were African American (The White House).

President Obama's stance on police brutality was clear. He ensured that investigations were done. He showed remorse and wept behind the microphone during some of these cases, but there was never a curtailing or decrease in these incidents. This left me wondering, however, just how much a role a singular person or president could even play in diminishing something that is entrenched in the fabric and culture of America. He also allocated millions of dollars for body cameras, but that ultimately served as another way for us to view our deaths virally. Additionally, he created a police task force that recommended independent investigations into police-involved deaths. On the flipside, he passed the Blue Alert Law, which would set up a nationwide notification system to alert officers when a threat was imminent. I can't disagree with that law. Yes, it's necessary, but the protection of Black lives is necessary as well.

Symbolically, I still admired what he represented as a Black man achieving the highest office in the most powerful country in the world, but honestly, I expected more. Maybe that was the problem, though. Maybe I expected more from him than I expected from us as a collective. I resolved to never again expect that much from an individual. I resolved to only expect that much from myself. Because honestly, that's the only way I won't be let down again.

CHAPTER 19
...WHEN I WAS FACED WITH A HATE CRIME

As July 30 approached, I anticipated an outing I had planned with my wife, but truth be told, I wanted to leave the country again.

We had just returned from Jamaica a month earlier, but I was anxious to go back. It was our second trip there, but this one was better because we left the resort for the first time. Although I haven't been to Africa (yet), I imagined Jamaica was very similar. I felt like I was at home.

I recall cruising along the outskirts of Montego Bay, passing lush and verdant mountains on the countryside, humming Bob Marley classics to myself while engaged in a thought-provoking conversation with our tour guide, Andrew. It all started when I asked him if they celebrated their native son Marcus Garvey, the pan-African leader who empowered Blacks in the 1920s and sought to help us relocate to Africa because he thought equity would never be achieved in America. His influence was so great that the FBI, through the leadership of J. Edgar Hoover (the man who helped sabotage Dr. King, Malcolm X, and the Black Panthers many years later), was able to get him deported and exiled from America.

We also talked about the legendary Queen Nannie of the Maroons, who was Jamaica's version of Harriet Tubman. After escaping from slavery in Jamaica in the 1700s, she established a maroon community in the countryside and devoted her life to freeing enslaved Africans from British control, burning plantations and waging war against the enslavers. "Mon, twenty yurs ago we don' have da KFC like we do nah," Andrew stated, pointing out another KFC as we drove through the town.

He alluded to a corporate takeover that had put out small business owners in Jamaica. Capitalism in America was the same as capitalism in Jamaica, apparently. I was reminded of the food deserts in our community, which were full of liquor stores and fast-food restaurants with a glaring omission of grocery stores containing fresh produce.

From that conversation, I began to understand the depth of the African Diaspora. It was something I had studied many times while sitting in a lecture hall at U of I, but I hadn't experienced it personally until that moment. Their experience with racism was slightly different in the sense that they were the majority in their country. Even so, they were still dealing with the effects of imperial control and systemic racism after only gaining independence in the '60s.

The effects of colonial rule are sometimes just as harmful because of the toxicity of the system's entanglement in every aspect of the oppressed people's culture. In a land of Black people, many of them strived to replicate the Western standards of professional success and beauty, according to Andrew.

Throughout our hour-long conversation, the comment that resulted in the eruption of the most laughter came when we discussed colorism after I asked him how big skin-bleaching cream was in his country.

"Jamaicans love their white Jesus!"

We laughed hysterically for what seemed like several minutes, over the overrepresentation of a man—was said to be born in a region adjacent to Africa over 2,000 years ago—as white with blond hair and blue eyes, but the comment revealed a harsh reality of internalized hatred that was birthed through the seeds of racism. I maintain that racism teaches whites to believe in their false inherent superiority and Blacks are taught to believe in their false inherent inferiority.

Although we have had a long history of valuing Eurocentric standards of beauty, like Jamaicans, I can say that I am most proud of our generation's aesthetic shift. Nowadays, you'll see brothas, partly due to rap artists like J. Cole, sporting high-top fades, afros, mini fros, with twists, dreadlocks, faded locks, and cornrow braids. You'll see sistas, who were the originators of the natural movement, sporting short fros, large bodacious afros, dreadlocks, and a variety of other creative designs with their natural hair, like puff balls. It goes without saying that people can wear their hair however they want, whether weaves or extensions are included or not, but it is impressive that a generation of Blacks who many have cast off as immature, impatient, and out of touch are the ones embracing their natural beauty.

I enjoyed Jamaica, not just because of the excursions, but because of the culturally enriching experience we had with Andrew. I carried that with me the rest of the summer, especially as I encountered the countless injustices that the summer of 2016 had in store for me.

The date approached for the Margarita Festival, our last festive event of the summer before returning to work a few weeks later. We were conscious and woke, but also young and ready to have a great time. This is best personified by the attire we wore. I had on a black, red, and white shirt that read "Knowledge is Power" with six must-read books for Black empowerment included. These books were Marcus Garvey's *Selected Writings and Speeches*, *The Autobiography of Malcolm X*, Chancellor William's *Destruction of Black Civilization*, *Out of America* by Keith Richburg, *Black Power Inc.*, and Assata Shakur's autobiography. Cassie had cornrows and a halter top that displayed a beautiful jet-Black woman with dreadlocks. Each dreadlock had the name of a Black woman who had a profound impact on Black society, from Harriet Tubman to Ida B. Wells to Assata Shakur to Fannie Lou Hamer and Ella Baker. We were walking billboards for Black consciousness and empowerment. In hindsight, our attire made the forthcoming situation even more ironic.

We had looked forward to this trip, not just because we wanted one last outing before school started, but because the previous year we had bought tickets too, but had been so busy that we forgot to attend.

"Maybe turn down that street," Cassie said in annoyance.

We had been looking for a parking spot for nearly twenty minutes. This wasn't shocking since we were in Chicago, but it was still frustrating. Eventually, after about thirty minutes, we found a parking spot. Another wait was in store for us, however. We got to the Margarita Fest, which was at the prestigious South Shore Country Club, only to see a line that seemed a mile along stretching from the back of the Country Club building toward the front entrance.

Before getting in line and waiting an hour, we asked around just to make sure that this was, in fact, the line we were supposed to be in. It seemed too bad to be true, but alas, it was the only option. It was an overall pleasant day, about eighty degrees and partly cloudy. As such, our wait in line became a hassle, not because of the weather, but because we were understandably impatient.

After finally arriving inside between one and two in the afternoon, we immediately sought out a food truck. We were starving! We had not eaten at all that day, and the wait in line only increased our appetite. Plus, we were parched. We came for drinks, but we were prepared to guzzle a gallon of water first.

We nervously searched for food that could accommodate our newly adapted vegan(ish) diet. We had switched over at the New Year and

...when I was faced with a hate crime

had abstained from meat for nearly seven months at this point, and did not want to be taken off track simply because we were at a festival. We eventually came across a food truck that served black bean burger sliders. Not too long after, we'd eat again at a Mexican food truck that served veggie tacos with peppers, rice, beans, and guacamole. Yeah, we were hungry!

After our palate was satisfied, we jumped in line to grab a margarita. The event was named after the infamous drink, so we had to see what the hype was all about. After grabbing our beverage, we walked around for a bit and enjoyed the ambiance. The festival was organized like a backyard party. There was a deejay, a dance floor, areas to sit, a VIP section, food trucks, and games. It felt like a large family reunion, with a mature audience of adults who were gathered to have a great time. Nothing more, nothing less.

After perusing the setup, we went to the beach area. Toward the back of the Country Club where the festival was, there was a small opening in a fence about twenty feet behind a rather large tree that was guarded by the Chicago Police Department. They were there to check wristbands and to ensure that people who sought reentry were paying customers since the beach, although partially secluded, was still open to the public.

We went to the beach and relaxed for a few hours. We reminisced over the summer, parenthood, pop culture, spirituality, the beauty of nature we experienced while sitting on the sand, and the impending school year that was quickly approaching. It was soothing and relaxing. We continued to sip our margaritas and toast to the good life as we soaked up the sun rays and pleasant sounds of the waves from Lake Michigan cascading against the sandy shores of the beach. Our only wish was that we had brought a towel so that we could evade the presence of sand in our shoes. That was the least of our worries, though.

As we got up to head back inside the festival, our movement apparently shocked a large group of seagulls, who immediately dispersed and flew away toward the lake.

"Cash Money taking ova for the 9–9 and 2000…"

We showed the officers our wristbands, reentered, and immediately went toward the dance floor, which was quickly filling up thanks to the sounds of Juvenile's epic anthem, "Back that Ass Up." For any '80s baby, the first few seconds of that song conjures thoughts of timeless party songs from an era when Cash Money, No Limit, Roc-A-Fella, and the Ruff Ryders were notable record labels that ran hip-hop.

We danced as though we were back at one of those house parties at U of I. It was a great time, but we were nearly thirty with two kids, so we were admittedly getting tired. We finished up on the dance floor and walked around a bit more before our planned departure when I noticed something I had never seen at a large gathering like this, much less at a cookout with a small fraction of the attendees. I noticed an open bean bag game. I was later informed that this was called cornhole, but that's beside the point.

"Wait, hol' up!" I put my hand on Cassie's shoulder to alert her about what I had seen. Having the luxury of being able to see over most people at a height of 6'2", I felt obliged to notify her because I knew she couldn't see it if she tried.

"One of those bean bag things is open. Let's check it out real quick." Cassie was down for it, so we began to trek across the field, shuffling through empty tables and chairs in anticipation of engaging in one last activity before we left. When we got there, we realized why it had probably been vacant. There was only one bean bag to play with at this station. I thought this was odd, so we both began to search in the

...when I was faced with a hate crime

immediate vicinity, thinking that maybe we had overlooked them in the high grass.

We searched but didn't find anything. That's when I looked to my left and realized that the group next to us had what seemed to be about ten to fifteen bean bags in their midst. The group, two Black and two white people, had so many bags that they were using the extras as some sort of backboard for the holes.

I tried to give them the benefit of the doubt. Maybe they took the bags because there had not been another group of people who had come by to play. I wanted to make it obvious that we were looking, so I began to pick up the cornhole boxes to possibly locate one, to no avail. It seemed as if they saw us looking, but no one offered. That's when an opportunity was presented to us.

While we were looking, someone from the group threw one of the beanbags far off course, so far, in fact, that it wasn't directly retrievable by anyone that was playing their game. It was near the seats and tables, which were stationed away from the cornhole section to presumably avoid a possible collision.

We waited nearby for several minutes to see if they were going to retrieve the bag, but no one budged.

"I'mma gon' head and grab it!" Cassie yelled over the sounds of the loud music in the distance, elated that we had an opportunity to play the game. I waited by the boards, so that no one else would approach and take our place.

That's when it happened. As Cassie returned with the bean bag, our countenances were immediately struck by the image of a short, petite, scraggly-looking, dark-haired white woman with a demented scowl approaching us from the left. Upon reaching us, she began to yell and scold us over the supposed theft of the bean bag. Mind you, we were at a public venue that we paid to enter just like she did. It would be like claiming a member of a health club stole your basketball as you shot around because they retrieved the item after you ignored it.

"What are you doing!? We were playing with that! You could've just asked to play with us! Give it back!"

We were taken aback by the audacious way this woman, whom we now know to be Jessica Lynn Sanders, approached us. Was she seriously approaching us with this level of animosity over a game?

"You weren't playing with it!" Cassie snapped back. "Whatever…"

I could tell Cassie was frustrated, but content with not dealing with the nonsense Sanders had brought our way. I had already surmised that this woman was not getting the bean bag back, though. You don't talk to someone like that, especially not my wife.

"You look like a fucking whore!" Sanders retorted.

I thought this insult was odd, because for one, my queen is far from a whore. She is, in fact, the personification of beauty, brains, and moral aptitude. She is royalty. Secondly, Sanders and my wife both had halter tops, which weren't revealing. The main difference, of course, was that Cassie had images of proud, intrepid Black women on her shirt. Sanders must've hated that!

"Who the fuc—"

As we were preparing to respond to her egregious assertion about my wife, Sanders interjected and raised the stakes. No one could have predicted that the desire to play cornhole would have led to this, but it did.

"You're both a bunch of fucking niggers!" Sanders said with aggressive certainty and frustration that her previous plea hadn't led to the retrieval of the bag.

"You're acting like niggers. Niggers!"

She kept going. This couldn't have been her first rodeo hurling such a racist insult at a Black person. I was shocked, but I wasn't surprised. I had seen this situation occur countless times, especially on social media. With Trump's rise, it seemed to be a regular occurrence, unfortunately.

Her onslaught continued. She had said it more times than I can remember, but it was well past ten.

"Give it back, you niggers!"

One of her Black friends, a dark-skinned guy a few inches shorter than me with a solid athletic build, stood nearly in between Sanders and me, refusing to make eye contact. He only moved as we did, seemingly protecting her from an imminent attack. Her other Black friend was a light-skinned girl who seemed to be mixed. She stood by with her hands on her hips. Unlike the other friend, she faced us and seemed distraught. Her other white friend remained in the back, toward the cornhole game where Jessica had come from.

We knew this could happen at any time because we were Black in America, but we were still hurt and shocked. I responded with an insult that didn't bother her in the least bit.

"Well, if we're niggers, then you're a cracker!"

The response was weak, in comparison, but it was accurate. "Cracker" is a term rooted in slavery, referring to whites who had a propensity to use the whip to severely beat and punish enslaved Blacks. It echoes the loud cracking sound that came from the whip when used. The whip would ricochet so loudly off the back of the enslaved Black that was the target of the abuse that you could hear the whip and skin crackle simultaneously as blood splattered everywhere. Unbeknownst to many, cracker refers not to skin color, but to a racist act that emitted a grotesquely repulsive sound.

My attempt at an insult had no effect, so she continued. A millennial, I contemplated grabbing my phone and recording the onslaught. I had seen this play out so many times in the past. When the target of the hate recorded it and posted it online, they were usually able to attain social justice with the help of outraged allies who worked vigorously to expose the bigot's racist ways to the public. I intended to do the same. It was my only line of defense, since saying "nigger" isn't against the law. As the verbal barrage continued, I had made up my mind to use my phone. I reached inside the depths of my cargo shorts, pulled out my phone, unlocked it, and went directly to the camera and pressed record.

"Whachu call me?! Say it again!" I yelled emphatically as soon as I pressed record.

Sanders, completely dismayed and irate, immediately slapped the phone out my hand. It went twirling like Simone Biles on a balance beam and thankfully landed in the grass. As I sought out my phone, you could hear the faint sounds of house music in the distance, a cruel irony that represented the experience of Black folks in America. As we struggled with a racist episode and attack, the rest of the festival's attendees, unaware of the situation due to the loud music and distance of our debacle, continued to enjoy themselves since it didn't directly affect them.

I picked up the phone and pressed record again, anticipating that it had stopped because of the hit. However, it was still recording.

...when I was faced with a hate crime

293

Her Black female friend, who stood to Sanders's right and my left, offered support for her friend and assured us that she had not been doing anything wrong.

"It doesn't bother us!"

What's more, her other Black friend, the buff brotha who stood to her left, continued to inch closer toward the gap between myself and Sanders as she continued. Their inaction represented another cruel irony about racism in America. That is, there are Black folks out there who would rather make excuses for white supremacy than address it. I was furious, irate and at a loss for words. At the very least, I expected those who looked like me, who also knew her, to intervene, restrain her, and let her know she was being ridiculous. That help didn't come, though.

Although we have a proud history of Black freedom fighters, we also have an unfortunate history of Blacks who have chosen to relinquish the communal and familial attitude of Black culture in an effort to acquiesce to white society. This is sometimes done out of fear and a haphazard attempt to assert individuality in order to distance oneself from the perceived negative aspects of Black culture. It symbolically screams, "Look massa, I'm not like the others! I'm different!" The so-called justice system begs to differ, though.

With that said, her white friend in the distance, who also witnessed this melee, deserves the same level of blame as her Black friends. She should have also intervened.

"Nigger, nigger, nigger, nigger, nigger, nigger, nigger...nigger...nigger," Sanders continued with her hands above her head, with a cigarette in hand in a celebratory manner, daring me to react.

"So, if I hit her, what happens to me!? She knocked my phone out my hands! She called me a nigger!"

I wanted to grab her and throw her to the ground. I wanted to punch her into oblivion with the strength of Ogun. I felt defenseless, though. I had sought to pose a question in the heat of the moment that had merit. She had been permitted to verbally abuse me, but had I responded in conjunction with her racist provocation, then I would be deemed the bad guy. Such is the experience of being a Black man in America.

My reaction thus far had been the inverse of how I was raised and how I had usually responded to threats or name-calling growing up. By the age of ten, I had fought more times than a heavyweight fighter climbing the ranks before a title match. If anyone on my block looked at me the wrong way or disrespected me or my sister, I wouldn't hesitate to swing on them to defend our honor. As I matured, I calmed down and learned the value of a more cerebral approach. I hadn't felt the need to lay hands on someone since a white friend of mine disrespected me for attempting to play matchmaker with a girl he liked when I was in eighth grade.

"You don't know me, man, I will fu—" I stopped myself. I had quickly remembered why I had begun recording in the first place. This wasn't about me and what I wanted to do to her. This was now about finding out as much as I could about this evil woman. I did not yet know her name, so I was now set on having her relay as much information as possible.

"If you hit me you're a nigger. Go home, you're acting like a nigger!" Sanders was making even less sense than she had been before, but she continued and began to turn and walk away.

Not before I could interject and demand more information, though. "You ac… Keep saying it. And what did you call my wife? Gimme yo' name too! Gimme yo' name too!"

As she began to walk away, she took one step in the opposite direction, pivoted while conjuring up a hefty glob of spit, which sounded like a dental suction device, and catapulted it in our direction. Some of the phlegm got on my arm, but it barely touched me. However, when I looked at my wife to the left, I noticed the slimy, mucous-laden glob of spit had gotten on her right arm.

I immediately turned my phone off, balled my fist, and stared a hole through Sanders. As we approached her, all I could think about was my two beautiful daughters, who were three and one at that point. I then thought about my parents and sister, my students, my mentees, and the pain and trauma I carried daily while enduring the Black experience in America. I thought of my ancestors, who experienced similar treatment on a regular basis and much worse pain I couldn't even imagine experiencing. I thought of 1619, 1492, and the regality I descended from in Africa prior to being enslaved. I thought of the ancestors in my past that sacrificed so much for me to be here that I'll never be able to identify by name. I thought of the power of "nigger" and the powerlessness it had over my life, once I chose to identify myself with my true heritage which was outside of the "nigger" white America attempted to create. I thought of my experience growing up in Chicago in a redlined community and manufactured ghetto. I thought of how I almost flunked out of college until I began taking Black history courses. I thought of the Chicago police officers on duty and the armed security guards in the vicinity who would surely view me as the guilty culprit had we attacked her physically like we wanted to. Would they have felt the need to kill me if we had attacked her? I thought of George Stinney, Jr., Emmet Till, Laquon McDonald, Mike Brown, Trayvon Martin, Rekia Boyd, Sandra Bland, Kendrick Johnson, and the countless others who lost their lives due to their melanin. Conversely, I also thought of revolutionaries like Nat Turner, Harriet Tubman, William Still, David Walker, and Ida B. Wells, amongst many others.

We had a lot to lose, and so much more to gain if we responded in accordance to what this moment in history called for.

It was at that very moment that we made a decision, not for ourselves, but for our progeny. Considering what was at stake, we knew what could potentially happen, despite being innocent. There was an armed cop to my left in the distance who was walking in our direction at that very moment. What if I struck her? What if my wife did? What if I looked at him the wrong way? I could have been another hashtag. I reacted, not out of fear, but out of wisdom. We walked away and decided to fight for justice with the evidence we had. Any other decision could have been life-ending.

Like so many other moments in my past, Black history had saved my life again.

EPILOGUE

My life hasn't been the same since July 30, 2016.

After the attack, I immediately turned the phone off and checked on my wife, since the spit had mostly landed on her. After a few minutes, a brown-skinned Black lady with long dreads and glasses came to our rescue. We didn't think anyone had noticed what happened. Thankfully, we were wrong. As we sat, contemplating our next course of action, an armed Puerto Rican security guard came, seemingly out of nowhere, to restrain our attacker. Because she was so combative, this led to a tussle on the ground in which I'm told she called him racist names well. What happened next is the reason why I had to fight so hard for justice. Instead of arresting her, the security guard forced Sanders and her friends to exit the event. He came back and attempted to pacify us by giving us a free drink and access to the VIP area after we asked for her information several times.

We decided to leave immediately. We then sat in the car for about thirty minutes, talking about what had just happened and, eventually, we contacted our parents. After talking to them, I checked my videos and was relieved. I realized that I had caught the crime on camera. Saying "nigger" isn't technically illegal, but spitting on someone is. I had proof of the whole thing. I went to a video editing app afterwards, merged the videos, uploaded it, and began to pull off.

"What are you doing? Post it now!"

Cassie was adamant that we needed help identifying the woman immediately. And so I did. Our post was short, and our request was, too. Realizing that Facebook made the world smaller, we asked that our friends share the video to help us identify the culprit.

By the time I got home, the video had 30,000 views and hundreds of shares. That night, I emailed the video and story to every local news station and newspaper in the Chicago area to spread the word.

By Sunday morning, we had several messages that identified the suspect as Sanders, and a long list of media inquiries.

By Monday, the video had 300,000 views and Facebook had suspended my personal account, allegedly because someone reported me for using a false name (I used "Ernest C-Three" as my alias to avoid contact with students). As a result, the video ceased being shared until I agreed to submit a copy of my ID and use my real last name.

That was all the motivation I needed, though. I had no time to remain in my shell. I had Cassie create a public figure page on Facebook and I swiftly went to another room to record a video for my new page, called "Are You Ready?" I posted it on my Facebook and YouTube pages, which now also contained the original hate crime video that Facebook had removed by suspending my account.

The last two weeks of our summer break was spent researching lawyers, going to the police station, and trying to maintain a sense of sanity while also lesson planning for the upcoming school year.

I had seen the video posted everywhere. The *New York Post*, *Desus and Mero* (HBO), and various other prominent Facebook and YouTube pages. Newsy, CBS Chicago, WGN, the *Chicago Sun-Times*, WVON, WLS radio, NPR, the *Herald News*, *Daily Southtown*, WorldStarHipHop, and countless other online and print publications covered the story, helping us spread the word in our pursuit of justice. Overall, it had amassed over twenty-five million views.

During the school year, I felt like quitting because the case only moved when I provided my detective with intel, unfortunately. The urgency I felt wasn't mutual, from my vantage point.

Fortunately, people like you kept reaching out and helping. Every piece of information I got regarding this case and Sanders's subsequent arrest came from friends and strangers on Facebook of every color, creed, race, and ethnicity. When I felt distraught in the middle of October, I received an anonymous message, notifying me of Sanders's current place of employment (since several individuals who saw the original video had contacted her previous employer and got her fired). I relayed this new intel to the detective I was working with, expeditiously. Within a week, I had received a call that notified me that she was arrested while deep-frying French fries at the fast-food establishment she now worked at.

I shouted in my car with excitement. Now the real work began. Sanders posted $50,000 bail after being charged with a felony hate crime and misdemeanor assault.

In the meantime, I would now amplify my voice to levels previously unheard because this unfortunate incident had refocused my life's mission and purpose to serving my community outside of the class. I refused to sit idly by while our kids could become the potential target of a hate crime or other injustice without having a firm grasp of who they are and were racially, ethnically, and culturally to prepare them for life in the battlefield that is America. I refused to let my kids grow up in a world that hadn't progressed with providing equity for people that look like us. I was determined, not just to win this case for me and my family, but to also truly win and provide justice for all, as it is eloquently stated in the Pledge of Allegiance.

As such, I started speaking publicly about my experience, empowering children to see their inherent worth. Later that school year, I also started a Black Student Union at my high school with a friend and coworker named Mr. Coatney and an inquisitive student named Janese, whose love for Black history was just as strong as mine.

What's more, I realized that, while racism and evil will always exist, we can all do a better job of creating a judicial system that punishes it equitably. There also needs to be a concerted effort to equip our Black children (and other minorities in America) with the knowledge needed to fight racism progressively with pride and solidarity. If my book and life story doesn't serve as an example of the positivity that can emerge from knowing one's history, a study by two professors from Harvard University and the University of Pittsburgh should surely do it. According to Ming-Te Wang and James P. Huguley, Black children who are socialized and taught to have racial pride perform better academically. As such, the proliferation of this pedagogical revelation is tied with my life's purpose and the mission of our Black Student Union (Wang and Huguley).

This hate crime experience, combined with my experience at a racially-integrated high school, had revealed to me the importance of white allies as well. They have access to a portion of society, because of their skin color and institutional privileges, that Blacks and other minorities in America do not. With that comes a great responsibility. From an educator's perspective, it is imperative that our educational systems teach history in a way that would prevent our white children from being used as tools of white supremacy by those who have been erroneously taught ethnocentrism and by those who profit off of the pestilential divisiveness that is the legacy of racism in America.

White children need to be taught that they do not have to carry the baton of this country's racist forefathers. Rather, they should use their privilege to tear down the walls of oppression that exist in edifices that

Blacks, and other minorities in America, do not have access to. This makes our country better by proxy. The same country that produced anti-racist activists like Reverend Bruce Klunder, who was killed when he put his body in the way of a bulldozer during the construction of a segregated school in Cleveland, Ohio, in 1964 also produced the racists that were hell-bent on the construction of a segregated school for the purposes of educating our children. We need more Reverend Bruce Klunders. Whether that happens or not is up to us. That is a matter that must be taken up with the white American community, as it is within their households that that likelihood has the highest percentage of manifesting.

Who in their right mind would make a case for fighting someone with their index finger as opposed to a fully balled fist? Such is the logic of racists who presuppose that their success can only come at the cost of the subjugation of an entire group of people.

From the time Sanders was arrested in October 2016 until the trial in October 2017, I had several setbacks and accomplishments related to the case and my life's journey. I must truly thank my family, and of course the Assistant State's Attorney's office, for the support they provided us during this time. Nothing was more gratifying in my pursuit of justice, however, than seeing Sanders in court on that fateful day. The sentencing was bittersweet. I was elated, but unsettled. Sanders was sentenced to ninety days for the misdemeanor. The judge decided to drop the hate crime charge because he thought a year in prison was excessive for what she did. I disagree. Additionally, the Illinois hate crime statute is vague. He felt that the prosecutor needed to prove that she went to the festival with the intention of committing a racist act. I disagreed with him wholeheartedly, but was content at that moment.

I was content because I realized that our government had done a horrible job of remedying the problems it created with slavery and racism. It was disappointing but not surprising, and provided more motivation to keep working toward my mission of uplifting our kids and assisting with the creation of a system that provides equitable justice in America. It was gratifying because of the sweat and tears that went into the case. It was a message sent to the world that we weren't going to sit by and accept racism without fighting back. Can you imagine how many people have gotten away with these crimes throughout the course of history? We have photographs from the '60s that captured the moment activists were spat on while integrating lunch counters, but that type of abuse surely didn't start then. This was for them and the countless others who lived in a time when the justice system would openly call them niggers, treat them as such, and get away with it.

You don't often see a news story with a Black man and white woman pictured, involving a crime, where the white woman is the one with a mugshot. Imagine that. We sent a ripple through the course of history together and we will continue to do so.

We did that. We did that together. However, true justice for the crime of racist acts or a racist system can never truly be resolved through the very system that created it. Although, egotistically, I wanted her to serve more time, I can never truly put a timeframe on what justice looks like, especially when so much of what was damaged on that day is still being healed. Especially because the very people who have contributed to harming me cannot help with healing me. Additionally, is prison time truly justice for me and my wife, or anyone impacted by crime? Did she spend time reeducating herself, and was there a massive investment in education that would prevent this harm from taking place again on a foundational level? I doubt it.

Like Mariame Kaba said in *We Do This 'Til We Free Us: Abolitionist Organizing and Transforming Justice,* "A system that never addresses the why behind a harm never actually contains the harm itself. Cages confine people, not the conditions that facilitated their harms or the mentalities that perpetuate violence."

Hate crimes are still on the rise, and will likely increase exponentially under another Trump presidency. The pathologically harmful American education system and society that produces that hatred is still here as well.

So, what's next? I keep fighting. We keep fighting. There's so much more work to do, and we must commit to doing it, one day at a time. Our progeny depend on it.

ACKNOWLEDGMENTS

Thank you, Cassie. I love you with all my heart! This book is the physical manifestation of my dedication to defending you and our love. Thank you, Chloe, Caylee, Caiya, and Caria. You four are the reasons I move with a sense of urgency daily. Let this book be your guide through the rough terrain of America. Thank you, Melody, Ernest Jr., and Veronique, a.k.a. "Da Fam." Your constant support and love are the only reason this came to fruition. Thank you, Ollie Mae Knight, it took a while, but now I understand your approach. Thank you, Millicent, Monica, and Lisa, for always treating me like your son even though I am only your nephew. Thank you, Mark and Regina. This wouldn't have been possible without those Disney trips and weekend sleepovers. Thank you, Ernest Crim Sr., Evelyn Crim, and James Knight; I hope that I made you proud in heaven. Rest in peace. To my editor, Hugo Villabona, and the entire team at Mango Publishing, thank you for taking the time and care to help me tell these stories.

ABOUT THE AUTHOR

Ernest Crim III is an Emmy-nominated public school teacher, anti-racist educator, hate crime victim, husband, and father of four daughters, who uses (Black) historical narratives to empower and educate through a culturally equitable lens. Mr. Crim, a South Side Chicago native and University of Illinois Urbana-Champaign graduate, is a former high school history educator of twelve years who now also advocates for social justice issues and teaches Black history to the world through social media with a platform that reaches millions of people each month. As such, he has created content for companies such as HBO, Hulu, Disney, Paramount, and the History Channel. Additionally, he is the CEO of Crim's Cultural Consulting LLC; an international speaker who has spoken at Harvard University, University of Chicago, Microsoft, Colin Kaepernick's Know Your Rights Camp, and to audiences in the UK and Canada; an author of two books; and a passionate progressive education activist who has worked closely with organizations to advocate for educational and political equity, reparations, mental health awareness, and food justice. Mr. Crim has been featured on and collaborated with CNN, HBO, *The Washington Post*, ABC, WGN, PBS, CBS, NBC, *Newsweek*, and various other outlets.

WORKS CITED

13th. Dir. Ava DuVernay. 2016.

Adweek. Dylan Imus Calls Rutgers' Women's Basketball Team 'Nappy-Headed 'Hos'| MSNBC Distances Itself. 6 April 2007. adweek.com/digital/imus-calls-rutgers-womens-basketball-team-nappy-headed-hos-msnbc-distances-itself

Alkalimat, Abdul. Alkalimat.org. "Talks and Interviews." 2017.

All Time 10s. 10 World Leaders Assassinated By The US Government. 16 June 2017. youtube.com/@Alltimes-fx4dx

Asante, Dr. Molefi Kete. "Afrocentricity." 1 July 2004. ISBN: 9780913543795, 0913543799.

Bennett, Geoff. "For Light-Skinned Only?" NPR, 16 October 2007. npr.org/sections/newsandviews/2007/10/for_lightskinned_only.html

Berman, Mark. "Prosecutors won't seek third trial for former Ohio police officer who shot Samuel DuBose." *The Washington Post*. 18 July 2017. washingtonpost.com/news/post-nation/wp/2017/07/18/prosecutors-wont-seek-third-trial-for-former-ohio-police-officer-who-shot-samuel-dubose

Bernstein, David. Martin Luther King Chicago Freedom Movement. 25 July 2016. chicagomag.com/chicago-magazine/august-2016/martin-luther-king-chicago-freedom-movement

Works Cited

Blake, John. Malcolm and Martin, closer than we ever thought. 19 May 2010. ccsdli.org/assets/grade_12_modules/malcolm_and_martin_ closer_than_we_ever_thought_-_cnn_com.pdf

Bossip. Yung Berg Says His Anti-Dark Skinned Women Comments Are Immature. 13 October 2014. bossip.com/1046968/color-struck-yung-berg-says-he-regrets-anti-dark-skinned-women-slander-ive-had-dark-butts-on-my-face

Britannica. Chicago Race Riot of 1919. 2019. britannica.com/event/Chicago-Race-Riot-of-1919

Brook, Tom. The Birth of a Nation: The most racist movie ever made? 6 February 2015. bbc.com/culture/story/20150206-the-most-racist-movie-ever-made

Burke, Minyvonne. Georgia officer charged with beating woman with his baton. 31 May 2019. nbcnews.com/news/africa/georgia-officer-charged-beating-woman-his-baton-n1012416

California Newsreel. A Long History of Affirmative Action—For Whites. 2003. newsreel.org/guides/race/whiteadv.htm

Christian, Tanya. Waitress At Denny's Tries To Make Black Customers Pay Their Bill Before Being Served. 4 October 2017. essence.com/news/dennys-Black-customers-racism

Corley, Cheryl. The Driving Life And Death Of Philando Castile. 15 July 2016. npr.org/sections/thetwo-way/2016/07/15/485835272/the-driving-life-and-death-of-philando-castile

Delong, Katie. Homemade political sign mentioning Obama, featuring noose causing uproar. 6 October 2012. fox6now.com/2012/10/16/homemade-political-sign-mentioning-obama-featuring-noose-causing-uproar

Donovan, Lisa. Vandals Send Message of Hate. 16 July 1999. chicagotribune.com/1999/07/16/vandals-send-message-of-hate

Douglass, Frederick. 3 September 1894. Teaching American History. teachingamericanhistory.org/document/blessings-of-liberty-and-education

Dudek, Mitch. Holocaust-denier gets nearly 40 percent of vote in 2 Mount Greenwood precincts. 7 November 2018. chicago.suntimes.com/2018/11/7/18449701/holocaust-denier-gets-nearly-40-percent-of-vote-in-2-mount-greenwood-precincts

East of England Broadband Network. "James Ramsay (1733-1789): The Ship's Doctor & Preacher." 2009. theabolitionproject.web.archive.org/web/20200229042629/http://abolition.e2bn.org/people_28.html

Editors of Encyclopedia Britannica. Middle Passage. n.d. 1 January 2020. britannica.com/topic/Middle-Passage-slave-trade

Edwards, Breanna. Atlanta Cop Fired Following Video Of Him Tackling Black Woman To The Ground, Tasing Her. 23 May 2019. essence.com/news/maggie-thomas-james-hines-police-brutality

Edwards, Meridith. Ex-South Carolina cop Michael Slager gets 20 years for Walter Scott killing. 7 December 2017. cnn.com/2017/12/07/us/michael-slager-sentencing/index.html

EJI. Black Man Lynched in Alabama for Failing to Call a White Man "Mr.". n.d. calendar.eji.org/racial-injustice/jun/21

Works Cited

Ferak, John. Joliet Cop Adam Stapleton Assaulted Me, Konika Morrow Tells Patch. 12 July 2019. patch.com/illinois/joliet/joliet-cop-adam-stapleton-assaulted-me-konika-morrow-tells-patch

Foley, Marybeth. Boardwatch July 23, 2008: Mount Greenwood story is still one of racism. The more things change, the more they stay the same. 1 September 2008. substancenews.net/articles.php?page=576

Foster, Mary. 5 Years Later, Jena 6 Move On. 25 August 2011. nbcnews.com/id/wbna44275022#.W3zWK-hKg2w

Garennes, Christine Des. Two Greek Houses on UI Campus Face Sanctions. 29 November 2006. news-gazette.com/news/two-greek-houses-on-ui-campus-face-sanctions/article_a5e9aae9-147a-5b51-9eac-bfa6cd9f63b9.html

Ghana Cultural Etiquette. 2001. easytrackghana.com/cultural-overview-ghana-cultural-etiquette.php

Gonnerman, Jennifer. Kalief Browder Learned How to Commit Suicide on Rikers. 2 June 2016. newyorker.com/news/news-desk/kalief-browder-learned-how-to-commit-suicide-on-rikers

Gregory, Todd. REPORT: New York City Television Stations Give Lopsided Coverage To Black Crime. 22 August 2014. mediamatters.org/nbc/report-new-york-city-television-stations-give-lopsided-coverage-black-crime

Grio, The. Is BET in the business of silencing smart hip-hop? 21 July 2011. thegrio.com/2011/07/21/is-bet-in-the-business-of-silencing-smart-hip-hop

Gyekye, Kwame. African Cultural Values. Sankofa, 1996.

Hanna, Jason. No charges against officers in Alton Sterling death. 27 March 2018. cnn.com/2018/03/27/us/alton-sterling-investigation/index.html

Helsel, Phil. Ex-Minneapolis officer who killed Justine Damond sentenced to 12.5 years. 7 June 2019. nbcnews.com/news/us-news/ex-minneapolis-officer-who-killed-justine-damond-sentenced-12-5-n1013926

Huffington Post. UN Condemns U.S. Police Brutality, Calls For 'Stand Your Ground' Review. 30 August 2014. huffpost.com/entry/un-police-brutality-stand-your-ground_n_5740734

Jackson, Charreah. Kodak Black Is Standing By His Brash Comments About Dark-Skinned Black Women. 27 June 2017. essence.com/celebrity/kodak-Black-Black-women-comments

Kas, Ras. Nature of the Threat. 30 September 1996. genius.com/Ras-kass-nature-of-the-threat-lyrics

Keckley, Elizabeth. Behind the Scenes: Or, Thirty Years a Slave, and Four Years in the White House. Martino Fine Books, 2017.

Klass, Caila. Afflueza DUI Case: What happened night of the accident that left 4 people dead? 31 December 2015. abcnews.go.com/US/affluenza-dui-case-happened-night-accident-left-people/story?id=34481444

Lambert, Bruce. At 50, Levittown Contends With Its Legacy of Bias. 28 December 1997. nytimes.com/1997/12/28/nyregion/at-50-levittown-contends-with-its-legacy-of-bias.html

Leeds, Jeff. Denny's Restaurants Settle Bias Suits for $54 Million. 25 May 1994. latimes.com/archives/la-xpm-1994-05-25-mn-62027-story.html

Library of Congress. Born in Slavery: Slave Narratives from the Federal Writers' Project, 1936-1938. Asheville: Library of Congress, 1938.

Lopez, German. Debunking the most pervasive myth about Black fatherhood. 19 June 2019. vox.com/2015/6/21/8820537/black-fathers-day

Lussenhop, Jessica. Clinton crime bill: Why is it so controversial? 18 April 2016. bbc.com/news/world-us-canada-36020717

Magee, Ny. ESPN Anchor Under Fire For Comparing Cops To 'Slave Patrols'. 31 July 2017. blackamericaweb.com/2017/07/31/espn-anchor-under-fire-for-comparing-cops-to-slave-patrols

Malooley, Jake. Mount Greenwood is Chicago's Upside Down. 21 December 2017. chicagoreader.com/news/mount-greenwood-is-chicagos-upside-down

Massie, Victoria. Why asking Black people about "Black-on-Black crime" misses the point. 25 September 2016. vox.com/2016/4/28/11510274/black-on-black-crime-poverty

Matshego, Lebo. How Many Languages of Africa Are There? 2010. africa.com/many-african-languages

Mershon, Matthew. Brother of man who assaulted PCSO deputies says incident agitated man's mental condition. 21 December 2018. katv.com/news/local/brother-of-man-who-assaulted-pcso-deputies-says-incident-agitated-mans-mental-condition

Mises Institute. The Brutality of Slavery. 14 November 2018. Viewed 1 January 2020. mises.org/mises-daily/brutality-slavery

Moran, Tim. Housing Discrimination Found in Mt. Greenwood, Meeting Called. 29 April 2019. patch.com/illinois/beverly-mtgreenwood/housing-discrimination-found-mt-greenwood-meeting-called

Moshtaghian, Artemis. $1.5 million settlement for woman beaten by California patrol officer. 25 September 2014. cnn.com/2014/09/25/justice/california-police-videotape-beating/index.html

Moya-Smith, Simon. Ugly Precursor to Auschwitz: Hitler Said to Have Been Inspired by US Indian Reservation System. 27 August 2017, updated 13 September 2018. ictnews.org/archive/ugly-precursor-to-auschwitz-hitler-said-to-have-been-inspired-by-us-indian-reservation-system

Murphy, Bill. People Are Boycotting Waffle House After Its 4th Alleged Racial Incident in 12 Days. Here's Who's Leading It. 11 May 2018. inc.com/bill-murphy-jr/people-are-boycotting-waffle-house-after-its-4th-alleged-racial-incident-in-12-days-heres-whos-leading-it.html

NAACP. Criminal Justice Fact Sheet. n.d. 2 January 2020. naacp.org/criminal-justice-fact-sheet

NAACP. History of Lynching in America. naacp.org/find-resources/history-explained/history-lynching-america

New York Civil Liberties Union. Stop and Frisk Data. 2016. nyclu.org/data/stop-and-frisk-data

New York Civil Liberties Union. Stop and Frisk Facts. 23 May 2017. nyclu.org/en/stop-and-frisk-facts

New York: Miller, Orton & Mulligan, 1855. page 55.

Works Cited

NewsOne. Florida Denny's Turns Away Black Churchgoers And Forced To Apologize. 13 August 2018. newsone.com/3821715/dennys-floridia-black-church

Northup, Solomon. Twelve Years a Slave: Narrative of Solomon Northup.

Norwood, Morgan. Man accused of punching Trump protester apologizes in Fayetteville court. 14 December 2016. abc11.com/trump-protester-punched-rally-assault-fayetteville-john-mcgraw-rakeem-jones/1655658

Nsehe, Mfonobong. The Black Billionaires 2019. 5 March 2019. forbes.com/sites/mfonobongnsehe/2019/03/05/the-black-billionaires-2019

Official Black Wall Street Team. The Race Riot that Destroyed Black Wall Street. 22 July 2015. blackgwinnett.com/racism/black-wall-street-and-the-race-riot-that-destroyed-it

Oliver, Mark. The Racist Origins Of America's Suburbs And The Story Of The First Black Family To Move In. 19 November 2017. Updated 31 July 2024. allthatsinteresting.com/william-levitt

Oppman, Patrick. Fidel Castro survived 600 assassination attempts, officials say. 26 November 2016. cnn.com/2016/08/12/americas/cuba-fidel-castro-at-90-after-assassination-plots/index.html

Otieno, Mark Owuor. What Was Operation Cyclone? 9 March 2018. worldatlas.com/articles/what-was-operation-cyclone.html

Pabarah, Azi. Media Matters: New York TV news over-reports on crimes with Black suspects. 23 March 2015. politico.com/states/new-york/city-hall/story/2015/03/media-matters-new-york-tv-news-over-reports-on-crimes-with-black-suspects-020674

Prez, Dead. I'm a African. 8 February 2000. genius.com/Dead-prez-im-a-african-lyrics

Prez, Dead. They Schools. 8 February 2000. genius.com/Dead-prez-they-schools-lyrics

Pruitt, Sarah. 5 Myths About Slavery. 3 May 2016. Viewed 3 January 2020. history.com/news/5-myths-about-slavery

Randall, Vernellia R. The End of Reparations Talk: Reparations in an Obama World - IV. Reparations in an Obama World. 2019. researchgate. net/publication/228320460_The_End_of_Reparations_Talk_ Reparations_in_an_Obama_World

Reboot Illinois. A Minimum Wage History in Illinois. 9 July 2013. huffpost.com/entry/a-minimum-wage-history-in_b_3569831

Reneegede. Mychal Bell of 'Jena 6' Graduates from Southern University with Degree in Education. 17 December 2014. urbanintellectuals.com/ mychal-bell-of-jena-6-graduates-from-college

Riley, Ricky. 8 Inhumane and Barbaric Forms of Torture Used on Enslaved Black People. 4 November 2016. atlantablackstar. com/2016/11/04/8-inhumane-and-barbaric-forms-of-torture-used-on-enslaved-Black-people

Rock, Amy. Black Preschoolers 3.6 Times More Likely to Be Suspended Than White Students. 4 December 2017.Viewed 2 January 2020. campussafetymagazine.com/safety/Black-preschoolers-suspension

Roy, Avik. 5 Ways The Government Keeps Native Americans In Poverty. 13 March 2014. Viewed 2 January 2020. forbes.com/ sites/realspin/2014/03/13/5-ways-the-government-keeps-native-americans-in-poverty

Works Cited

Ruiz, Rebecca. Baltimore Officers Will Face No Federal Charges in Death of Freddie Gray. 12 September 2017. nytimes.com/2017/09/12/us/freddie-gray-baltimore-police-federal-charges.html

Saloy, Mona Lisa. African American Oral Traditions in Louisiana. 1990. louisianafolklife.org/LT/Articles_Essays/creole_art_african_am_oral.html

Say Her Name: The Life and Death of Sandra Bland. Dir. Kate Davis. 2018.

Sertima, Ivan Van. Golden Age of the Moor. United States of America: Journal of African Civilizations, 1992.

Sides, John. What data on 20 million traffic stops can tell us about 'driving while Black'. 17 July 2018. washingtonpost.com/news/monkey-cage/wp/2018/07/17/what-data-on-20-million-traffic-stops-can-tell-us-about-driving-while-black

Stuster, J. Dana. Mapped: The 7 Governments the U.S. Has Overthrown. 20 August 2013. foreignpolicy.com/2013/08/20/mapped-the-7-governments-the-u-s-has-overthrown

Sun, Elizabeth. The Dangerous Racialization of Crime in U.S. News Media. 29 August 2018. americanprogress.org/article/dangerous-racialization-crime-u-s-news-media

Sutter, Lexi. 'It's Hate, It's Ugly, It's Horrible': Residents Unite Against Hate After Racist Fliers Put on Cars in Mt. Greenwood. 10 July 2019. nbcchicago.com/news/local/its-hate-its-ugly-its-horrible-racist-signs-mount-greenwood-beverly/131065

The Bureau of Investigative Journalism. Drone Warfare. 2019. thebureauinvestigates.com/projects/drone-war

The Final Call. Willie Lynch Letter: The Making of a Slave. 22 May 2009. Viewed 1 January 2020. new.finalcall.com/2009/05/22/willie-lynch-letter-the-making-of-a-slave

The White House. Progress of the African-American Community During the Obama Administration. 14 October 2016. obamawhitehouse. archives.gov/the-press-office/2016/10/14/progress-african-american-community-during-obama-administration

Time: The Kalief Browder Story. Dir. Jennifer Furst. 2017.

TMZ. 'KRAMER'S' RACIST TIRADE. 20 November 2006. tmz. com/2006/11/20/kramers-racist-tirade-caught-on-tape

University of Illinois Urbana-Champaign. The University of Illinois in the Cold War Era 1945–1975: Project 500. Updated 2022. guides.library. illinois.edu/c.php?g=348250&p=2350891

US Department of Health and Human Services. Women's Health USA 2013. 30 April 2013. Viewed 1 January 2020. web.archive.org/web/20140123021228/https://mchb.hrsa.gov/whusa13/population-characteristics/p/us-female-population.html

Voice of America News. Nigeria's Population Projected to Double by 2050. 12 April 2019. web.archive.org/web/20191208064515/https://www. voanews.com/africa/nigerias-population-projected-double-2050

Wald, Elijah. Talking 'Bout Your Mama: The Dozens, Snaps, and the Deep Roots of Rap. Oxford University Press, 2012.

Washington, Jasmine. California Officer Under Investigation After Body Slamming Black Woman. 10 May 2019. ebony.com/california-officer-body-slamming-black-woman

Washington Post. "Full Text: Donald Trump Announces Presidential Bid." 16 June 2015. *The Washington Post*. washingtonpost.com/news/post-politics/wp/2015/06/16/full-text-donald-trump-announces-a-presidential-bid

Waxman, Olivia. Time Magazine. 18 May 2017. time.com/4779112/police-history-origins

Weiss, Rick. Scientists Find A DNA Change That Accounts For White Skin. 16 December 2005. washingtonpost.com/wp-dyn/content/article/2005/12/15/AR2005121501728.html

Wills, Amanda. All the countries that had a woman leader before the U.S. 28 January 2019. cnn.com/interactive/2016/06/politics/women-world-leaders

Wray, Christopher. Countering the Terrorist Threat Through Partnerships, Intelligence, and Innovation. 29 August 2018. fbi.gov/news/speeches/countering-the-terrorist-threat-through-partnerships-intelligence-and-innovation

X, Malcolm. Genius. 5 May 1962. genius.com/Malcolm-x-who-taught-you-to-hate-yourself-annotated

Mango Publishing, established in 2014, publishes an eclectic list of books by diverse authors—both new and established voices—on topics ranging from business, personal growth, women's empowerment, LGBTQ studies, health, and spirituality to history, popular culture, time management, decluttering, lifestyle, mental wellness, aging, and sustainable living. We were named 2019 and 2020's #1 fastest growing independent publisher by Publishers Weekly. Our success is driven by our main goal, which is to publish high-quality books that will entertain readers as well as make a positive difference in their lives.

Our readers are our most important resource; we value your input, suggestions, and ideas. We'd love to hear from you—after all, we are publishing books for you!

Please stay in touch with us and follow us at:

Facebook: Mango Publishing
Twitter: @MangoPublishing
Instagram: @MangoPublishing
LinkedIn: Mango Publishing
Pinterest: Mango Publishing
Newsletter: mangopublishinggroup.com/newsletter

Join us on Mango's journey to reinvent publishing, one book at a time.